TOOLS AND WEAPONS

Illustrated by the Egyptian Collection
in University College, London.

SIR W. M. FLINDERS PETRIE

OXBOW | books
Oxford & Philadelphia

This edition published in the United Kingdom in 2023 by
OXBOW BOOKS
The Old Music Hall, 106–108 Cowley Road, Oxford, OX4 1JE

and in the United States by
OXBOW BOOKS
1950 Lawrence Road, Havertown, PA 19083

Paperback Edition: ISBN 979-8-88857-014-2
Digital Edition: ISBN 979-8-88857-015-9 (epub)

First published by the British School of Archaeology in Egypt, 1917
Facsimile edition published in 1974 by Aris & Phillips Ltd

Oxbow Books is grateful to the Petrie Museum for their collaboration in bringing out these new editions

Printed in the United Kingdom by Short Run Press, Exeter

For a complete list of Oxbow titles, please contact:

UNITED KINGDOM
Oxbow Books
Telephone (0)1226 734350
Email: oxbow@oxbowbooks.com
www.oxbowbooks.com

UNITED STATES OF AMERICA
Oxbow Books
Telephone (610) 853-9131, Fax (610) 853-9146
Email: queries@casemateacademic.com
www.casemateacademic.com/oxbow

Oxbow Books is part of the Casemate Group

Front cover: Bronze barbed arrowhead. From Gurob, Egypt, Dynasty 18 (*c.* 1550–1069 BC). Petrie Museum UC7761.
Image courtesy of the Petrie Museum of Egyptian and Sudanese Archaeology, UCL.

CONTENTS

INTRODUCTION

SECT. PAGE

1. Limits of this work 1
2. System of this work 1
3. Detail of arrangement 2
   Abbreviations 3

CHAPTER I

THE PLAIN-BLADE AXE (A)

4. Difference of axe and adze 5
5. Cypriote imports to Egypt 5
6. Pillowy forms of axe 6
7. Methods of copper working 6
8. Flat cast axes 6
9. Wide copper axes. 6
10. Plain blade of bronze 7
11. Round axes 7
12. Axes with lugs 8
13. Battle axes 9
14. Scolloped axes 9
15. Flanged axes 10
16. Pole axes 10
17. Edged batons 10
18. Halberds 10

CHAPTER II

THE SOCKETTED AXE (O)

19. Bronze axes 11
20. Plain iron axes 11
21. Deep socket axes 11
22. Recurved blades 12
23. Circular sockets 12
24. Long-back sockets 12
25. Tubular sockets 12
26. Oriental axes 13
27. Double axes in use 13
28. „ „ ceremonial 13

SECT. PAGE

29. Local types 13
30. Made in different centres 14
31. Weights of double axes 14
32. Purpose of weights 14
33. Conclusions 15
34. Adze axes 15
35. Pick axes 15

CHAPTER III

THE ADZE (Z) AND HOE (J)

36. Early Egyptian adzes 16
37. Early European adzes 16
38. Round-topped adzes 16
39. Later adzes 17
40. The lug-adzes 17
41. The late lug-adze 17
42. Hafting of adzes 18
43. Eastern socket adze 18
44. The Egyptian hoe 18
45. Source of the hoe 19

CHAPTER IV

THE CHISEL (C)

46. The bare chisel, square 19
47. „ deep 20
48. „ wide 20
49. „ round. 20
50. The tang chisel, square 20
51. „ deep 21
52. „ wide and round 21
53. The socket chisel, square 21
54. „ deep 21
55. „ wide and round 22
56. The gouge 22

CHAPTER V

THE KNIFE (K)

SECT.		PAGE
57.	Classes of knives	22
58.	Flaying knife	22
59.	Straight-backed	23
60.	Straight-edged	23
61.	Hollow-backed	24
62.	Hollow-edged	24
63.	Recurved	25
64.	Crook-backed	25
65.	Khopesh	26
66.	Double convex (U)	26
67.	Double-edged	26
68.	The sword (E)	27
69.	The sabre	28

CHAPTER VI

THE DAGGER (D) AND SPEAR (H)

70.	Prehistoric Egyptian daggers	28
71.	xiith dynasty daggers	28
72.	xviith—xviiith dynasties	29
73.	Inlaid handles	29
74.	European dagger, rivetted	30
75.	„ tang daggers	30
76.	Spears of the copper age	30
77.	Evolution of the British spear	31
78.	Wide blade spears	31
79.	Ceremonial spears	31
80.	Forms of various regions	32
81.	Concave-edge spears	32
82.	The fin-blade	32
83.	Flat-blade spears	33
84.	Spear butts	33

CHAPTER VII

THE ARROW, THROWSTICK, HARPOON, &C.

SECT.		PAGE
85.	Forms and uses of the arrow (R)	33
86.	Manufacture of the arrow	34
87.	Flat arrow heads	34
88.	Ribbed arrow heads	34
89.	Triangular arrow heads	34
90.	Barbed arrow heads	35
91.	Rhombic arrow heads	35
92.	Peculiar types	35
93.	Wood and bone arrow heads	36
94.	Bows	36
95.	Throwsticks (V)	36
96.	Slings and bullets	36
97.	Harpoons	37
98.	Fish-hooks	37
99.	Scale armour	38
100.	Rasps and scrapers	38

CHAPTER VIII

ARTIZANS' TOOLS (M)

101.	The brace	38
102.	The pump-drill	39
103.	The bow-drill	39
104.	The rimer	39
105.	Bits	39
106.	The auger	39
107.	The drawing knife	39
108.	The plane	39
109.	The anvil	40
110.	Wooden mallets	40
111.	Hammers	40
112.	Tongs	41

CHAPTER IX

BUILDERS' TOOLS (B)

113.	The trowel and mortar rake	41
114.	Wedges and wooden chisels	41
115.	Moving of stones	41
116.	Dressing of stones	42
117.	Plastering and brick-making	42
118.	The plumb line and level	42
119.	The square	43

CHAPTER X

THE SAW, SICKLE, AND BILL-HOOK

120.	Egyptian copper saws (S)	43
121.	European bronze saws	43
122.	Iron and steel saws	43
123.	Framed saws	44
124.	The file and rasp	44
125.	Hard-stone sawing	44
126.	Tubular drilling	44
127.	Nature of cutting points	45
128.	Stone sawing at Tiryns	45
129.	Mauls for hammer-dressing	46
130.	Egyptian sickles (F)	46
131.	European sickles	46
132.	The southern bill-hook (P)	47
133.	The northern bill-hook	47

CHAPTER XI

SHEARS, CUTTERS, TOILET TOOLS, AND THREAD WORK

SECT.		PAGE
134.	Shears (Q)	48
135.	Scissors	48
136.	Hair curlers (X)	48
137.	The scraping razor	49
138.	The notched razor	49
139.	The rotating razor	50
140.	Leather cutters (L)	50
141.	Cutting-out knives	51
142.	Egyptian tweezers (Y)	51
143.	European tweezers	52
144.	Borers (N)	52
145.	Papyrus knives	52
146.	Pins	52
147.	Needles	53
148.	Reels and netters	53
149.	Spinning	53
150.	Shuttles and looms	53

CHAPTER XII

AGRICULTURE AND CATTLE (G)

151.	The wooden hoe	54
152.	Other wooden tools	54
153.	The Italian iron hoe	54
154.	The spade	55
155.	The plough	55
156.	Forks and rakes	55
157.	The snaffle horse-bit (W)	55
158.	The curb	56
159.	The spurs	56
160.	Brands	56

CHAPTER XIII

DOMESTIC

SECT.		PAGE
161.	Fire hooks	57
162.	Manacles	57
163.	Staff head	57
164.	Fish-spears	57
165.	Flesh-hooks	57
166.	Shovels	57
167.	Ladles	58
168.	Spoons	58
169.	Pounders and grinders	58
170.	Fire drills	58
171.	Strigils	59
172.	Benedictory crosses	59
173.	Bolts	59
174.	Tumbler locks	59
175.	Pin locks	59
176.	Fork keys	59
177.	Lifting keys	59
178.	Rotating keys	60
179.	Pulleys and toggles	60
180.	Compasses	60
181.	Chains	60
182.	Casting crucibles	60
183.	„ moulds	61
184.	„ *cire perdue*	61
185.	Detailed moulds	62

CHAPTER XIV

SOME HISTORICAL RESULTS

186.	The synopsis sheets	62
187.	Forms peculiar to Egypt	62
188.	Forms unknown in Egypt	63
189.	Forms widely spread	64
INDEX		

For list of plates, see SYNOPSIS SHEETS.

PREFACE TO THE 2023 EDITION

In the 1970s, a much-anticipated new series of publications illustrated objects and themes related to the excavations of the archaeologist William Matthew Flinders Petrie (1853–1942) in Egypt, and aspects of the collection of University College London's Petrie Museum of Egyptian and Sudanese Archaeology. A young couple setting up in business in the early 1970s, Aris and Phillips published these works, written by members of the UCL Egyptology Department, in their *Modern Egyptology* series. Building on Petrie's own observations, the authors of these volumes aimed to complete the great task of publishing the Petrie Museum of Egyptian and Sudanese Archaeology's vast collection, and to present some of the research that Petrie himself was not able to address in his own published works during his lifetime. As the current Curator of the Petrie Museum, it is a great privilege for me to support Oxbow Books in their mission to republish the series, which remains a key source of information for all those interested in object-based approaches to the study of the ancient world.

The Petrie Museum, part of University College London (UCL), is home to one of the largest and most significant collections of Egyptian and Sudanese archaeology in the world. Free to visit, this extraordinary collection tells stories about the lives of ordinary people who lived along the Nile Valley thousands of years ago. Originally set up as a teaching collection, the Petrie Museum comprises over 80,000 objects housed together with an internationally important archaeological archive. It is a collection of world firsts and 'oldests': the oldest woven garment; the oldest worked iron objects; the first known depiction of loom weaving; the oldest known written document about women's health; the earliest veterinary treatise; the oldest will on paper. The Museum has Designated Status from Arts Council England, meaning that it is considered to have outstanding resonance and national cultural significance. The collection has a substantial, visible international reputation for research, supporting hundreds of researchers every year, both remotely and in person.

The Petrie Museum is named after Flinders Petrie, who was appointed in 1892 as the first Professor of Egyptian Archaeology and Philology in the UK at UCL. Over three-quarters of the material in the Museum comes from excavations directed or funded by Petrie, or from purchases he made for university teaching. In 1880 at the age of 26, Petrie travelled to Egypt to survey the Great Pyramid. For the next five decades he was at the forefront of the development of archaeology in Egypt and later in Palestine, and his detailed methodological approach continues to shape the discipline today.

Petrie worked at more sites, with greater speed, than any modern archaeologist: seeing his life as a mission of rescue archaeology, Petrie aimed to retrieve as much information as possible from sites that were shrinking dramatically in size as Egypt modernised during the late 19th and early 20th centuries. He published a large part, but not all, of the finds from his excavations in his illustrated typological volumes, arranged according to object types and themes. Today, much of the Petrie Museum's collection is displayed and stored in a way which reflects these publications: for example, several storage cupboards are dedicated to the material illustrated in the 'Objects of Daily Use' volume, and objects in the drawers are arranged according to the order of the published plates. This offers a unique opportunity for researchers to engage with Petrie's typological and methodical approach to archaeology, as well as with the history of museum collections.

The first catalogue to be published in the *Modern Egyptology* series was *Amarna: City of Akhenaten and Nefertiti* in 1972 by Julia Samson, Petrie Museum Honorary Research Assistant. As official publishers to the UCL Egyptology Department the series went on to produce facsimile reprints of eight of Flinders Petrie's most important site reports and many of his object catalogues, originally published through the British School of Archaeology in Egypt. The substantial annual royalties from these reprints were paid into the 'Petrie Fund' at the time, which provided special grants to students in financial need.

In many ways, the new reprints of this classic series can be seen as the latest layer in a vast 'publication stratigraphy' of the thousands of finds from Flinders Petrie's excavations, which now live in museum collections around the world. On reading these volumes, I hope that readers will also be inspired to learn more about the Petrie Museum collection and its fascinating history.

Dr Anna Garnett
Petrie Museum of Egyptian and Sudanese Archaeology,
University College London
January 2023

PUBLISHER'S PREFACE

Oxbow Books is pleased to present this title in our *Classics in Egyptology* series. This series of facsimile re-issues is comprised of two sub-series. The first consists of 16 typological catalogues produced by W.M. Flinders Petrie based on his massive collection of Egyptian artefacts. Mostly excavated by Petrie during many seasons of campaign in the last years of the 19th and early decades of the 20th century, they now reside in the Petrie Museum at University College London. Published between 1898 and 1937 and long out of print, the catalogues were re-issued in facsimile by publishers Aris and Phillips in the 1970s. These were followed in the next 15 years or so by publication of a number of newly commissioned titles, based on more recent examination of elements of the Petrie Collection by contemporary experts, under the name *Modern Egyptology*. A selection of these additional titles forms the second component of our own series.

The archaeology of Egypt continues to fascinate. Multi-disciplinary investigation and research continues unabated, encompassing methodologies, scientific and data processing techniques, theoretical approaches, and even whole paradigms that were unheard of in the 1970s and undreamt of when Petrie was working in Egypt. Yet all the titles included in this series continue to be invaluable sources of basic data, providing an unparalleled resource that can easily be cross-referenced with the actual materials they describe and discuss. They remain within the Petrie Collection where they may be accessed and re-examined as new research flourishes. As historic documents, the Petrie catalogues stand as exemplars of the craft of typological classification, the backbone of modern archaeology – much of which, though refined by absolute dating and another 100 years of research, still stands the test of time.

A note on presentation

The facsimile titles of Petrie's catalogues re-issued in the 1970s were produced from scans of the original publications. Scanning technology at that time was not of the standard or resolution of today. The scans are no longer available, nor has it been possible to obtain, and in doing so destroy, original copies of the Petrie catalogues. These titles have therefore, of necessity, been rescanned from the 1970s re-issues. Where necessary the pages have been digitally enhanced for clarity of reading and to ensure the good quality of the plates, though inevitably a few are not of the standard we might wish, because of the quality of the previous scan, and occasional blocks of text are not precisely 'straight' or evenly situated on the page. However, some pages in the 1970s re-issues had been inserted in the wrong order and this has been corrected. The originals were produced at a folio size. The pages have been reduced slightly to standard A4 for ease of shelving and because this has the effect of slightly improving the scanned images. In some cases, illustrations were presented to scale and the original scale is given on the plate. There were also no digital files available for titles included in the *Modern Egyptology* series, so these too have been scanned from printed copies.

TOOLS AND WEAPONS

INTRODUCTION

1. IN touching such an immense subject as the history of tools and weapons, it is needful to accept various limitations to the scope of the enquiry, as otherwise it would be unmanageable. In the first place this account refers to Egypt, and only to other countries as illustrating that. The Egyptian material is given as completely as may be, regarding types and dates, and photographs of the specimens at University College, of which this is a catalogue; duplicates in other collections are not noticed, but only such specimens as amplify the subject. From other countries comparisons are merely an index of outlines, to show varieties of types and their geographical range, but without any attempt to give all the minor variations of form or place. The sources and dating of each form have been the main object in view.

Other countries being only taken here in relation to Egypt, it was not within the scope to notice types which were unknown in Egypt. Thus the great series of the flanged and socketted axes, the very varied forms of sword, the pointed halberds, the British looped spear heads, are all unnoticed. These have been so well and fully studied in special papers and books already, that there is the less need to say more about them.

Stone implements are not touched on here, as the abundance of such from Egypt would require a volume to themselves. No doubt they are the parents of many of the metal forms; but the complex question of the reflex influence of metal forms upon the later stone working, makes it desirable to treat the metal quite apart, and then to apply the results to the study of the stone implements.

The main object being the relations of Egypt, most attention has been given to Mediterranean forms, rather than to the northern material which is less significant. This being only a secondary publication as regards materials outside of Egypt, it has not been thought needful to copy details of ornament, or damages, which do not affect the comparison with Egypt; nor have precise details of localities always been given, as the district or country is all that is required here. As every outline has the reference to the original source placed below it, there will be no difficulty in turning to the primary publication for further information.

Such are the limits which it has seemed necessary to place upon this attempt to unify the early history of most of the tools and weapons of the last few thousand years. The enormous mass of material renders selection needful, unless a lifetime could be given to the subject. All previous publications have looked only to one country or one civilisation, or else handled only one type. There has been no *corpus* for reference to comparative types of various lands and their transmission, or of various ages and their history of change. In default of such a *corpus* this volume may serve for general reference, though I am well aware that it can only be called materials for a history of tools. Much here has been gleaned directly from the museums, particularly in Greece and Italy, which I have not found hitherto published; about a quarter of the outlines are directly from cases in museums.

2. Hitherto tools have been much neglected. Weapons have been ardently collected, but the historical evolution of tools has scarcely been touched. Even when the best samples of Greek tools have been presented to a national museum, they have been thrown away by the head of the Department, who remarked that they were ugly, and he did not care for them. We read of ninety camel loads of excellent steel picks being discovered at Khorsabad, but how they have vanished is unrecorded.

The aim here has been to regard the purpose of each form, the mode of its use, the reasons for its changes, the connections of its variations with differences of climate and conditions. It is only by looking at tools and weapons from the point of view of the actual user, that we can understand them, and put them in their place as forming an important support to the general history of civilisation.

At first the distinctions of tools and weapons hardly existed. The same form might serve many purposes, with more or less success; much as we may still see penknives ruined by levering corks out of bottles. Civilisation is marked by the specialising of men and materials; and after the adoption of specific forms for different uses, it is needful to distinguish them in the terms we employ. Even in standard works we may find no discrimination is made between the sword for slashing and the rapier for thrusting, or between the knife and dagger, or the axe and adze.

In classifying the material here, the genetic connection of changes has been followed, where it was distinct; but, in confused instances, simple differences which can be quickly seen may make more practicable lines of division. Thus the spear forms are best arranged by the broad spear used for slashing, the straight cut-or-thrust spear, and the narrow pike only for thrusting. To some extent these belong to differences of clothing and of climate, but they are not necessarily lines of descent. Where there is a great variety of forms from one place and age, only the limits of the variation are given here, as limiting types.

3. As regards the detail of the materials, the scale of reduction of the figures has been unified. Of all classes of objects which are not too large, the photographs are on a scale of one half, and the outlines (being only secondary publication) on a scale of one quarter. Where forms are taken from small figures, ancient or modern, they are generally one-twentieth of the full natural size, as it would be inexact to expand a rather vague figure to the size of the accurate outlines. Such smaller figures are obvious among those of the uniform larger scale. Where no scale is known, the letters N.S. are appended. For unilateral forms such as axes and knives, it is desirable to place them all in one direction, preferably that in which they would naturally be used by the right hand. So far as possible the axis of the handle has been placed upright, so as to display the direction of the cutting edge clearly. It would be well if all publications would keep to these points, which are necessary in any comparative study;—uniform scale, uniform direction, vertical handles. In a group of axe-heads recently set out in a museum for exhibition, they are mounted without any uniformity, and it is difficult to realise how far they resemble one another, or anything elsewhere.

In the order of the outlines the different metals have been followed, so far as types would permit. There is always a presumption that the copper, bronze, iron, and brass tools succeeded in that order, unless there is some individual evidence of dating to the contrary. The objects of each metal have therefore been placed together, and marked thus as a class; while exceptions brought in, by dating or by type, are separately marked with the name of the metal.

The place names are stated in a form for easy recognition of their meaning. Where a site is well known, it is stated; if the site is obscure, the district or region is stated. The purpose is to enable any reader to see at once from the plates the range of distribution. Further detail is often given in the text, or can always be found by looking out the reference. The list of abbreviations used for reference is given on the next page. Where more than one reference is stated to an outline, the first is the direct source, and the other references are to examples that are merely similar. The dates of Egyptian objects are given in dynasties, in order to avoid the confusion caused by various arbitrary reductions of the Egyptian dates in years. "Egypt" only is stated, as the place-names may not be familiar to all readers; the exact place is given by the title of the book quoted, or in the text. For facility of reference the page is stated rather than the plate number; and in series, the year rather than the volume number. In the Mykenæan objects at Athens, the Roman numerals are those of the circle graves of Schliemann. Many of these objects are unpublished.

Having to refer both to photographs and to outlines there is unavoidably some irregularity in the numbering. Whether the plate numbers or the text number should be continuous, has been decided by the convenience of reference in each case. In many cases the outline pages have cross references to the photographs or scattered figures. Usually the photographs and the outlines of the same series are placed facing; even if other plates intervene, such can always be held upright, so as to get a view of plates which should be compared together. A main consideration has been the possibility of seeing in one view all material for comparison. Hence many plates are crowded in order to include the whole of one type. A few figures have been passed on to an end plate to avoid breaking up the subjects by mixing them on plates.

The subject of the dates of the introduction and use of different metals has not been followed here. What is known from Egypt is stated in *Ancient Egypt*, 1915, p. 12.

No attempt has been made to follow the movements of types as indicating the movements of races. There is not enough yet known, to come to any safe conclusions from such arguments. Sometimes the distribution of a type may be referred to historically known movements of peoples at the same period, which is a legitimate use of history; but at present in our great ignorance of distribution of types, of the dating of objects, of the extent and direction of trade, it is premature to deduce history from types of tools. All that can be said is that strong negative evidence may be drawn from proved dissimilarities, which contradict supposed lines of connection.

ABBREVIATIONS EMPLOYED

		FIGURES
A.	Archaeologia (Society of Antiquaries, London), 1860— . . .	100
A.A.	The American Antiquarian . .	12
A.A.iii.	Ayrton (E. R.), Abydos iii. 1914 .	1
A.C.	Athens, Central Museum . .	38
AL.	Pro Alesia	1
AN.	L'Anthropologie, Paris . . .	21
A.P.	Athens, Polytechnic Museum . .	28
A.R.	Anger, Graberfeld zu Rondsen .	1
A.S.	Aspelin (J. R.), Antiquités Nord Finno-Ougrien, 1877–84, i–v .	13
A.V.	Cabinet of Antiquities, Vienna .	1
A.W.	Mitt. Anthrop. Gesell. Wien . .	28
B.	Bologna Museum	37
B.A.	Bissing (F. W. von), Ein Thebanischer Grabfund, 1905 . .	1
B.B.	Bertholon, Berberie Orientale .	1
BERL.	Berlin Museum	3
B.F.	Bologna Fonderia (great group of fragments found together) . .	50
B.L.	Bathurst (W. H.), Roman Antiquities at Lydney Park, Gloucestershire, 1879	2
B.M.	British Museum	123
B.P.	Bullettino di Paletnologia Italiana .	60
B.R.	Abh. K. Bayern Rom. Alterthum, 1840	1
B.T.	Bayeux Tapestry, ed. F. R. Fowke, 1875, 1898	7
C.A.	Caillaud (F.), Recherches sur les Arts et Métiers, 1837 . . .	7
C.C.	Chantre (E.), Recherches dans le Caucase, 1885	21
C.D.	Carapanos (C.), Dodone, 1878 . .	18
C.M.	Cairo Museum	11
C.N.	Curle (J.), A Roman frontier post, the fort of Newstead, 1911 . .	21
C.S.	Cartailhac (E.), Âges préhistoriques de l'Espagne, 1886 . . .	4
D.A.	Delgado (Rada y), Museo Español de Antiguedades, 1872–80.	
D.C.	Dussaud (R.), Les Civilisations Préhelléniques dans le Bassin de la Mer Égée. 2nd edit. 1914 . .	11
D.G.	Davies (N. de G.), Rock Tombs of Deir el Gebrawi, i . . .	2
D.L.	Dechelette (J.), La Collection Millon, 1913	8
D.M.	Dechelette (J.), Manuel d'Archéologie, 1908—	19
D.W.	Demmin (A.), Weapons of War, 1870	2
E.B.	Evans (J.), Ancient Bronze Implements of Great Britain, 1881 .	9
E.D.	Engelhardt (C.), Denmark in the Early Iron Age, 1866 . . .	16
F.	Florence, Archaeological Museum .	18
F.M.	Foote (R. B.), Madras Museum, Catalogue of the Prehistoric Antiquities, 1901	20
F.T.	Feldhaus (F. M.), Technik der Vorzeit, 1914	4
G.A.	Garstang (J.), El Arabah, 1901 .	8
G.C.	Gozzadini (G.), Mors de Cheval, 1875	11
G.M.	Garstang (J.), Mahasna, 1902 .	18
G.N.	Gargiulo (R.), Musée National de Naples, 1870	1
G.P.	Gross (V.), Les Protohelvètes, 1883	9
G.R.	Papa Giulio Museum, Rome . .	3
G.T.	Gross (V.), La Tène, 1883 . .	33
G.W.	Gardner Wilkinson (J.), Manners and Customs of the Ancient Egyptians, ed. 1878	4
H.M.	Hoernes (M.), Natur- und Urgeschichte des Menschen, 1909 .	1

		FIGURES
H.U.	Hempel (J.), Alterthümer . . . in Ungarn, 1905	26
I.S.	Bryan Fausset and Roach Smith, Inventorium Sepulchrale, 1856 .	13
K.U.	Körte (G.) and Brunn (E.), vol. i, Rilievi delle Urne Etrusche, 1870, 1890, 1896	6
L.A.	Lissauer (A.), Alterthümer der Bronzezeit in der Provinz Westpreussen, 1891— . . .	1
L.B.	Layard (A. H.), Discoveries in the ruins of Nineveh and Babylon, 1853	3
L.D.	Lepsius (R.), Denkmäler . .	47
L.I.	Lee (J. E.), Isca Silurum, 1862 .	1
L.N.	Layard (A. H.), Monuments of Nineveh, 1849	4
L.N.R.	Layard (A. H.), Nineveh and its Remains, 1849	1
M.	Die Alterthümer unserer heidnischen Vorzeit . . . Römische-Germanische Central Museum in Mainz, L. Lindenschmidt, 1858–1911	97
M.A.	Monumenti Antichi, 1889–1914 .	72
M.A.F.	Mission Archéologique Française.	
M.B.	Randall-Maciver (D.), and Woolley (C. L.), Buhan, 1901 . . .	8
M.C.	Rosellini, Monumenti Civile . .	6
M.D.	Morgan (J. de), Fouilles à Dahchour, i 1895, ii 1903	3
M.E.	Martha (J.), L'Art Étrusque, 1889 .	3
M.I.C.	Montelius (O.), Italie Centrale .	10
M.I.S.	Montelius (O.), Italie Septentrionale	14
M.J.	Müller, Juellinge Fundet . .	7
M.K.	Montelius (O.), Alteren Kulturperioden.	
M.K.A.	Much (M.), Kunsthistorischer Atlas, 1889—	13
M.KG.	Woolley (C. L.), and D. Randall-Maciver, Karanog, 1900 . .	6
M.L.	Munro (R.), The Lake Dwellings of Europe, 1890	48
M.M.	Martin (F. R.), L'Âge de Bronze au Musée de Minoussinsk, 1893 .	26
M.P.	Morgan (J. de), L'Âge de la Pierre et les Métaux, 1896 . . .	5
M.R.	Randall-Maciver (D.), El Amrah, 1902	2
M.R.R.	Rosellini, Monumenti Religiose .	5
M.S.	Délégation en Perse, Mémoires (de Morgan, Susa, etc.) . . .	30
M.V.	See M., vth volume.	
N.	Naples Museum, and number . .	139
N B.	Newberry (P. E.), Benihasan, i–iv, 1893–1900	12
N.O.	Naue (J.), Die Bronzezeit in Oberbayern, 1894	10
N.S.	Notizie degli Scavi . . .	6
N.V.	Naue (J.), Vorrömischen Schwerter, 1903	11
Perugia.	Museum	10
P.	Perugia, Guardobassi Cabinet .	4
P.A.	Petrie (W. M. F.), Abydos, 1902–3 .	12
P.D.	,, Diospolis, 1901 . . .	18
P.Ds.	,, Deshasheh, 1898 . .	4
P.E.	,, Ehnasya, 1905 . . .	4
Peet.	Peet (T. E.), Stone and Bronze Ages in Italy, 1909	10
P.F.	Petrie, Defenneh (in Tanis II), 1888	39
P.G.	,, Gizeh and Rifeh, 1907 .	9
P.H.	,, Hyksos and Israelite Cities, 1906	4
P.Hw.	,, Hawara, 1889 . . .	6
P.I.	,, Illahun, 1891 . . .	11
P.K.	,, Kahun, 1890 . . .	9
P.L.	Labyrinth and Gerzeh, 1912 . .	1
P.M.	Parma Museum	3
P.Md.	Petrie, Medum, 1892 . . .	4
P.Mp.	,, Memphis, 1909–15 . .	1
P.N.	,, Naukratis, 1886 . . .	11
P.Nb.	,, Nebesheh (in Tanis II.), 1888	10
P.Q.	,, Naqadeh, 1896 . . .	3
P.R.	,, Royal Tombs, 1900–1 . .	12
P.S.	,, Researches in Sinai, 1906 .	2
P.S.A.	Proceedings of the Society of Antiquaries, 1860	16
P.S.T.	Petrie, Six Temples at Thebes, 1897.	
P.T.	,, Tarkhan, 1912, 1914 . .	10
P.W.	Mitt. Prehist. Commission, Wien .	21
Py.T.	Pumpelly (R.), Explorations in Turkestan, 1908 . . .	4
Q.H.	Quibell (J. E.), Tomb of Hesy, 1914	4
R.	Rygh (O.), Norske Oldsager, 1885 .	52
R.A.	Revue Archéologique, 1904— .	1
R.C.	Pitt-Rivers (L. F.), Cranbourne Chase	1
R.K.	Rome, Kircherian Museum . .	27
R.M.C.	Rosellini, Monumenti Civile . .	1
R.N.C.	Rome, New Capitoline Museum .	4

		FIGURES
S.A.	Schäfer (H.), PriesterGräber(Abusir), 1908	5
S.A.N.	Mémoires de la Soc. Roy. des Antiquaires du Nord . . .	1
S.D.	de Sarzec (E.), Découvertes en Chaldée, 1889—	2
S.F.	Bulletin Soc. Préhistorique de France	19
S.H.	von Sacken (E. F.), Graberfeld von Hallstatt, 1868	11
S.M.	Seager (R. B.), Explorations in the Island of Mochlos, 1912 . .	3
S.P.	Siret (L.), Premiers âges du métal en Espagne, 1887	18
S.S.	Schuchhardt (C.), Schliemann's Excavations, 1891 . . .	1
S.V.	Schlemm (J.), Wörterbuch zur Vorgeschichte, 1908	
V.	Virchow (R.), Graberfeld von Koban, 1883	1
V.A.	Verhandlungen der Berliner Ges. für Anthopologie, etc. . .	5
V.M.	Viollet-le-Duc, Dictionnaire du Mobilier Français, 1858–75 .	41
W.M.	Wells Museum	7
W.P.R.	Pitt-Rivers (L. F.), Excavations in Cranbourne Chase, vol. i, Woodcuts, 1887	1
Z.A.	Zeitschrift für Aegyptische Sprache	3
Z.B.	Zannoni (A.), La Fonderia di Bologna, 1888	3
Z.E.	Zeitschrift für Ethnologie, Berlin .	19
	Photographs	7
	Miscellaneous	31
1694.	Luiken (J. and C.), Het Menselyk Bedryf, Amsterdam, 1694 . .	32

CHAPTER I

THE PLAIN BLADE AXE: (A) PLS. I TO VIII

4. THE natural divisions of the great variety of axes are (1) those with no form of attachment, (2) with projections for a handle, (3) with a hole to haft a handle. In general, the first division is confused with forms of adze, under the common modern term of celt; as that word is only a cloak for confusion, it is better to keep to the real definitions of axe and adze. The axe has the edge parallel to the handle; the adze has it across the handle. The axe is mounted into a handle, or a handle into it; the adze is bound on to a handle, in general (pl. xviii). The axe is equal faced and edged; the adze has one face longer or flatter, and is usually ground on one side. The axe is to drive into wood to split it; the adze is to take a thin slip off a larger mass. The axe usually has a short body, and means of pulling it back or twisting it loose from the grip of the cloven wood; the adze has a long body, and (in ancient times) only a weak attachment to the handle, as it was never struck in deeply. The axe is thick in order to bear shock and carry weight; the adze is thinner, strength not being required. Those various differences were not all developed fully at first. In the stone ages a single tool seems to have served for many uses; root-grubbing, breaking branches or skulls, and throwing at animals, were probably all done with one handy weapon. The growth of civilisation is marked by increasing specialisation of men and of means, until we now have dozens of varied forms of hammer or of chisel. In the classification of the present material, as the axe is the earlier type, it has been credited with any forms that are not distinctive, and the adze is only accredited with forms unsuited for axes.

5. In Egypt, the adze long preceded the axe; metal was scarce, and to squander a pound of it for a single tool would have been extravagant. It is only at the close of the prehistoric age, after the incoming of the dynastic people, and within a generation of Mena and the 1st dynasty, that copper began to be freely used (A 7, 8, pl. i). Now, simultaneously with this, we find the adze greatly increased in size (Z xv, xvi, 8, 66, 67, contrast with the early forms 60–65); and the larger adze was of a new form, widely splaying. This form resembles that found in Cyprus (Z 7) more closely than any other. As it would be absurd to suppose copperless Egypt exporting tools to Cyprus, the copper land, it seems that these larger heavy adzes came from Cyprus; and arrived in the same generation in which the heavy copper axes appear, at the epoch of final conquest by the dynastic people; the evidence so far is that the dynastic people brought the free use of Cypriote copper into Egypt. This does not prove that they came from Syria, but only that they were in trade intercourse with Syria. It may be noted in passing that the name *cuprum* was derived from that of Cyprus (and not *vice versa*), as the Greeks long knew of Cyprus

without using that name for the metal, and before it superseded the earlier word *aes* in Italy; indeed Pliny writes of *aes Cyprium.* If the most recent view should be proved—that the earliest Cypriote copper came from the mainland—then Cyprus and Egypt in the 1st dynasty both drew from that unknown source.

6. In accordance with copper being scarcer in early Egypt than in other lands, we find that the forms of axe in Cyprus, Italy, Spain, Sweden, and America (A 1–5) imitate the pillowy rounded outlines of stone axes, while the Egyptian tools were economically made with straight sides. In short, copper was not freely used in Egypt until man had already mastered the right form for metal tools. This does not imply that the pillowy forms elsewhere are actually older than the straight forms of Egypt, but that they were relatively older in the development of each country. At the same time, the straight-sided Cypriote great adze (Z 7), apparently contemporary with the 1st-dynasty adze in Egypt, is clearly long after the passing away of pillow forms (as A 1–5); and, so far, we may probably date these earlier forms in Cyprus as older than the 1st dynasty in Egypt.

7. We should consider now the method of manufacture. In casting, it is easier to make a flat form, as an open mould can be used for it: but hammering is easier along the edges where the metal can spread. Hence the pillowy form is natural to hammered work, and it is also a direct imitation of the form needed for a stone axe, to preclude snapping across the middle. Thus on adopting the unbreakable metal the same form continues, as it is that which is most readily shaped by hammering. In North America it appears that all work in copper was done entirely by hammering native copper. Nadaillac states that all copper objects were made by hammering unheated (*Prehist. Am.* 179); and the making of beads by rolling up strips of sheet copper, shows how far the American was from casting the metal. May it be supposed that the pillowy forms in the Old World were likewise due to hammering native copper? The pure metal is found in many places in Cornwall (a mass of as much as three tons), also in Anglesey, Antrim, Chessy in France, in South Hungary at Moldava on the Danube, and in Russia. The resemblance of form between the certainly hammered axe of Wisconsin (A 1), and the axes of Cyprus, Italy, South Spain, and Sweden, suggests that they also were likewise beaten from native copper, and not cast. To cast a mass curved on both sides would require a closed mould, fitting so well as not to allow of leakage. Certainly it is the more likely that man began by using the native metal in each country; and when the art was discovered of reducing copper from ores, and casting it, the old method of shaping by the hammer would continue until the economy of labour by casting would be devised.

8. The earliest castings may be presumed to be in thick sheets in open moulds, a mere directing of the outline of the most primitive pouring out of the metal, to avoid the inconvenience of working up a lump left at the bottom of the furnace or crucible. Accordingly all the earliest straight-sided adzes and axes are flat and almost equally thick, except at the edge, where the hammering both shaped and hardened the metal. From Egypt there are the dated examples from sequence date 77 or 78, the age of the earliest kings of Abydos (*Tarkhan*, i, 3), to 81, the middle of the first dynasty (see A 6 to 9). The examples in the collection, A 101–104, are not dated by the finding; but 103 is of about the middle of the first dynasty, by the resemblance of the name on it, Kash, to the names of that age painted on the tombs (*Royal Tombs*, i, lxiii). With this was found the adze Z 71, xvi, which has the same name on one side, and on the other the name Să. neit, which agrees to the same period. The sign on A 104 occurs with similarly rounded ends on an early slate palette of S.D. 33–41 (*Diospolis*, v, and xii 43), and recurs on pottery marks in the latter part of the first dynasty (*Royal Tombs*, ii, lv, D, 464, 485). It had therefore a long usage, and was well established as a mark, unchanged during a long period; its history afterwards was unbroken, through the Greek three-stroke s, down to the modern s. The slight splay of A 104 indicates a later date than the parallel axes; this is seen also in the axe A 9, dated to the middle of the first dynasty, and in A 105. After this the parallel-sided axe is not recorded from Egypt; it seems to have given place to the round axe, and, later, to the axe with lugs.

9. The later development of the axe in the copper age is seen in the forms A 10–30, arranged in the order of the widening of the cutting edge. The first step is that of the earliest Persian type from the tombs at Susa (A 11, 12), where the sides remain parallel, but the edge is widened outward

in the beating. This was combined with increasing splay of the sides in the examples from Portugal, Spain, Italy, Switzerland, Poland, and Hungary. The blade made long, narrow, and very thick, with a wide edge (A 24), seems in each of these features to be adapted for splitting wood; when driven into a log it could be struck on the side in order to force the crack wider. The shorter axes (26–30) from Italy and India agree in having a deep, circular edge; this was not suited for cleaving nor for light wood-cutting, but rather suggests a fighting axe; the shortness of the blade would agree with this, as the axe would not be held by a wound it inflicted, and so a strong attachment to the handle was not needed. Two examples that look like copper are outside of the regular Egyptian types, vii, 142 and viii, 194. They probably belong to some barbarous invaders.

10. The next stage was the discovery of bronze. In the earlier copper age, the metal was hardened by arsenic, by oxide of copper left in metallic solution, and, rarely, by bismuth or by tin. Probably, in all these cases, the alloy was due to using impure ores of copper, which were found to give a superior result for use. The regular use of tin ore smelted with the copper, and, later, of metallic tin added to the copper, cannot be traced farther back than the Hyksos period in Egypt, or about 2,000 B.C. in Europe. The advantage was not so much in hardness—for copper with arsenic, well hammered, is even harder than bronze—but rather in the greater fusibility and freedom for casting. The forms of bronze axes were continued from the earlier copper age. The parallel-sided axe with expanded edge lasted on in Italy (31), in Sardinia (32), and is usual in Hungary (33, 34); while its appearance on the Rhine and in Ireland may be due to importation. The Chinese example (33) is placed with these, as it is of the same family, though socketted, and does not agree with any of the other socketted axes. The splay form was, however, the more usual development, as the bronze did not favour the expanding of the edge by hammering. It is around the Mediterranean, and in the west, that the splay form in bronze mainly spread, though it is known in Hungary and Central Asia (Minussinsk). It was usual in England (50–52); and, strangely, continued till the Roman time in Italy, made of iron (54).

None of these axes show any hammering on the top edge, and they must have been permanently hafted. The narrow top would seem unsuited to resistance in a handle; it shows that the blow was given by the weight of the blade itself, and not by any weight in the handle behind it. A heavy handle would have split itself on the back of such an axe as 39, 41, or 50, almost as readily as the axe cut into the wood in front of it. The handle must have been light, and the blade probably secured by some slightly yielding material; the blow must have depended on the weight of the blade, and not on any push given to the handle. An actual hafting is of deer horn as a socket, set upon a wooden handle like the head of a mallet (Peet, *S.B.A.I.*, 253). The developments of a stop ridge on the side of the axe, and of the winged sides, ending in the complete socket, are outside the present scope, for they are never found in Egypt; as they have been well traced in previous works, there is the less need to deal with them here.

11. A type of axe which is peculiar to Egypt is the round form, A 55–70, 106–121. This originated at least as early as the ist dynasty, as it appears as a hieroglyph in the reigns of Den and Qa (*Royal Tombs*, i, xv, 16; ii, xii, 6). The transition stage from the square axe is A 105, which is almost the same as A 9, of the middle of the ist dynasty. The next stage, A 108, is exactly like the axes of Khosekhemui, and doubtless came from his tomb, belonging to the close of the iind dynasty. The hole for tying it on to the handle was later modified as one, two, or three smaller holes; see A 62 left side pl. lxxiii with original handle (and a duplicate), and A 112 and 115. The large number of holes A 109, 111, 113, 114 have been drilled in modern times by natives, hoping to improve specimens. On 108 is the numeral 43, probably the number of it in a series for the tomb. After this rudely rounded form of the iind dynasty, more regular forms arose in the iiird dynasty; see A 55, 56, from the tombs of Hen-nekht and Neter-khet. The figures in the tomb of Hesy, also of the early iiird dynasty, 57, show how the axe was bound in. A shallower form, 60, is figured in the vth dynasty, in the fighting scene at Deshasheh; this serves to date the similar specimen A 114 (from Dishneh?). The fully deep axe with lugs arises in the vith dynasty, A 58, 59, 63. To this date may probably be assigned the specimens A 106, 107, 110, and the form with the lugs turned down to hold the lashing, A 112, 114, 115. The type with a single projecting lug, as A 111 (Selamiyeh), 113, is probably later.

Some similar examples have been ruined by natives cutting away the blade to form a second lug; the two blades here are original. There is contradictory evidence as to the mounting of the skew blade A 113. The model from the tomb of Mena at Dendereh, 121, of the vith dynasty, shows the wider part at the end, which would be the suitable way to use it; but the drawing of Rosellini, A 64, of about the ixth or xth dynasty, strangely puts the wider part toward the handle. This may perhaps be an error in the drawing.

Reaching the xiith dynasty, two models (A 69, 153, the latter from the tomb of Emshat, Asyut) show how the blade-seat was recessed in the handle, so that the binding should be protected by the wood at each end. The figures 64 used by carpenters, 67 used by a boat builder, and 68 by a carpenter, show that these were artisan tools, as also 57; but A 60, the shallower form, is a battleaxe. The figure 68 serves to date the specimen A 117 to the xiith dynasty. The perforated axe 118 is of the type on pl. vi; but differs from that in having a base and lugs, like the other round axes. It is doubtless of the xiith dynasty, as also is the beautifully made small axe with the lotus flowers, A 119; this latter retains the original high polish of the metal where protected by the handle. Round axes with lugs lasted into the xviiith dynasty, at least for ceremonial use, as in the specimen of Amenhetep III, A 120. On the whole it is seen that the main use of these round axes is from the ist to the xiith dynasty, and the heavier axes with lugs A 72, 73, 122–133, are from the xiith to the xxvith dynasty. It seems, then, that the round axe may have rapidly changed in the xiith dynasty from the thinner round form 116, 117, to the heavier straight-sided form A 122 and onwards. The ferrules which were often used to hold the lugs of the round axes were at last united to them, as in A 70, which has two tubes at the ends to retain the handle, while yet keeping the tying holes.

Before leaving the round axe, we should observe some ceremonial models A 191–193 of the vith dynasty, and ceremonial copies in stone, A 195–197. These latter could never be used, as they have no edge, but are about equally thick all round. A 195 is inscribed for the *uab* priest Sekhenu, with the determinative of a pillar. This does not seem at all early, and is more likely an archaistic form of the xixth dynasty.

12. Another type peculiar to Egypt was that with broad lugs by which to secure the blade to the handle, and a widening of the back to prevent the handle being split on the blade. The stages of this form are shown in the collection, A 122–130 of copper and bronze, 131–133 of iron, in the drawings 72, 73 of iron, and probably the same form shown mounted in 75 to 80. Strange to say, this method of handling is totally absent from the rest of the Mediterranean lands, North Europe, and Asia. It seems almost incredible that a type characteristic of Egypt for thousands of years could never be established elsewhere. The two examples at Gezer, on the frontier, were doubtless imported to Palestine. It shows that however advanced Egypt was, it was surrounded by civilisations sufficiently developed to hold their own course completely. Yet this type recurs as the regular form in Peru and Central America (A 74). The entire absence of it in many intermediate lands, must preclude our supposing a case of borrowing. It is one of the strong examples of an independent invention. The cause is not far to seek. In the endeavours to give a better attachment to the blade, the European peoples were working in bronze, more fusible, and better for casting, than copper. Hence they could proceed on the socket system, pl. ix. The Egyptian, like the Peruvian, was inventing his form in the copper stage, when hammering was the process rather than casting; hence both went on the natural lines of lengthening the blade along the handle, to give a larger bearing and a means of firm lashing.

The history of the type in Egypt is not traced before the xiith dynasty, A 122, when it is found with slightly made lugs. Those with rather larger lugs, 123, and 124 front and back, may be a little later. The incised designs of the flower and the wheel-pattern (flower?) are unusual. The longer lugs appear in the xviiith dynasty; at the beginning of pl. lxxiv is the top of an axe, A 71, dated to Amenhetep II, showing that A 125 is of about the middle of the xviiith dynasty. The design of fish and lotus on A 127 rather suggests the age of Amenhetep III; this is much the most carefully made of these axes, the ends of the lugs turning down to hold in the lashing, and the edge much hammered out. From this hammering, and the softness and clean state of the red metal, it appears to be copper rather than bronze. The latest bronze axe of the type is A 130, which is of about the xxiind dynasty, from Gerzeh. Next comes the transfer of this type to iron in which A 132 is one of the finest examples of early iron work; the ends of the lugs are rolled over to hold the lashing in place. On A 133 the leather lashing remains entire, although the wood has been eaten out by termites. This was found in the store chambers of the Ramesseum; and, as nothing there appeared later than about 800 B.C., this is probably one of the earliest iron axes. The blade splays like the previous bronze axe from Gerzeh, whereas the other iron axes, 72, 73, 131, 132 are square in form. All of the above axes were evidently for carpentry and heavy work.

13. The battleaxe was a lighter variety of the same type. The earlier stages appear with very slight lugs, as A 134, 135, probably in the xth and xith dynasties. Certainly by the time of Senusert I the lugs were fully squared out, as in the beautifully made example with his name, A 137. The fine work of the engraving makes it less likely to belong to one of the later Senuserts. A 138, 139 and a duplicate, are of the same age. The type continued in the xivth dynasty, A 82, 83, but began to show the unsymmetrical sloping form, which later developed so much, as in A 88, 89. These seem to have been merely fashionable sports, as it is impossible to suppose that so long a form could be handled with the precision of a shorter axe. This fanciful form is not dated later than the beginning of the xviiith dynasty, A 90. Soon after, under Hotshepsut, 92, and Tahutmes III, 93, a broader type came into use, as in A 144, 151, 152. This continued to be the ceremonial form to the close of the xviiith dynasty, as it appears in A 146 of Amenhetep III, but there is no later example of it. Outside of Egypt it appears in a changed form with a midrib, from Central Syria, pl. lxxiv, A 95. The total absence of this type in Europe in its earlier well-marked stages, makes the more remarkable a small example of a late stage, A 96, found at Fifehead in Wiltshire. It seems to come in the series at about the close of the xviith dynasty, see A 84, 85. Apparently it must be an importation of about 1600 B.C., traded over to Britain. The presence of apparently Egyptian beads in England about four centuries later, leads us to believe that there was widespread commercial intercourse in these times. An exceptional form from Transcaucasia (A 97) differs so widely from the Egyptian, by having a square tang for hafting, that the resemblance in outline is probably fortuitous. A similar square tang occurs on two late Egyptian iron axes (A 98–9) from the eastern frontier at Defenneh. These tanged axes may be all three Asiatic, from one source; such a fastening is unknown in Europe or Egypt otherwise. The socketted axe (A 100) is a rare form; by its curve it is quite distinct from the hoes on pl. xix.

14. The next type, that of the scolloped axe, pl. vi, is of much interest as a foreign importation into Egypt. In contrast to the axe with lugs, and the round axe, both of which are unknown in Europe and Asia, and were never diffused from Egypt, the scolloped axe is widely spread in Carthage, Greece, Syria, and Georgia. The modifications of it in Syria show that it had a long history there, and it may probably be accepted as Syrian in origin. The simplest form, and therefore probably the earliest, is the plain sheet of metal scolloped out, which is preserved in Egypt, while only the later development with a socket has yet been found in Syria. A significant point is that, in a painting of the xiith dynasty, where the Egyptians carry the axe 165, let into the handle, the Syrian in the same scene carries the axe 173, which is distinctly socketted, with three eyes around the handle. This shows that the Syrian had developed socketting as early as the xiith dynasty, and was thus much ahead of the Egyptian.

It should be observed that the earliest Egyptian example (A 160) is figured in a tomb of the vth dynasty at Deshasheh, as being made by an artisan in Egypt. This proves that the type was already known in the Old Kingdom: yet no actual examples, or figures of it in use, appear until the xiith dynasty. Then we have the figures of the deep form 161, 162, and the actual example 164. This form continued long in the west, being known in Carthage in Greek times, A 163. In the xiith dynasty it became much shallower in Egypt, as 157–159, 165–167, influenced apparently by a different weapon, the edge on a stick 178–180, which will be dealt with below. But this shallow form was only Egyptian, and did not influence the main line of descent in Asia. The deep circular form with three bands, around the handle, 173, was used by Syrians in the xiith dynasty, and brought into Egypt in the xxth dynasty, 174. The next stage of development was the linking of the socket bands together by a cross bar, as in the Vapheio example, 175, which shows the extension of the type to the Peloponnesos about the xviiith dynasty. Next, in Syria the three loops became merged into a single long socket, 168, a usual form, of which there are four examples in the British Museum from Beyrut. This was further modified by lengthening the blade and shortening the socket, as in 169 from the Orontes, and 170 at the bottom of pl. lxxiv from Central Syria. The open spaces in A 169 have been dwarfed, until they are almost closed. The same type is given from Beyrut in xi, O 142, to show its relation to Central Asian (143) and Chinese forms (144, 145).

Another line of development was apparently contemporary, as it is found together with the last form in the group of four axes, in precisely similar condition, from Central Syria, pl. lxxiv, 171. In this the back was lengthened to gain a hold on the handle, and the two end eyes were only carried half round. A simpler form of this is from Georgia (Transcaucasus), A 172, vi, where the socket is wider, but without any extension down the back, and the ends merely hitch into the stick. Without having any dates or connecting examples it cannot be said which is the earlier of these forms. Certainly the Georgian is furthest from the earliest dated type in Syria, A 173. It is curious to see how closely the Egyptian scolloped axe was re-invented in France, A 176, 177, with almost exactly the same curves; as the Egyptian type vanished over two thousand years before the French examples, this is a certain case of recurrence of a form.

15. The flanged edges of the Egyptian forms, A 158, 159, 164, 166, 167, should be noticed. Hammering on the edge of a tool, so as to raise a rib or flange on the margin of the face, greatly stiffens the blade. This was the usual mode which began in the early bronze age in Central Europe, while it was not used in the Mediterranean or in the early Italian lake dwellings (Peet, 255). It appears to have been a northern invention arising after the close of the copper age, and developing during the bronze age until it reached the form of the winged, and lastly the socketted, axe. The whole of that development is excluded from this volume, as it did not touch Egypt. Yet in the examples above quoted the slight beginning of flanging is seen around the scollops in the back of the blade. This indicates the northern or Asiatic origin of the scolloped axe. The use of raised ribs on tools is specially Asiatic, as will be seen on the Oriental axes, lower part of pl. xi. The taste for such treatment is like that for the flanged edges, and these start from Hungary, which was always an open field for Oriental types. Broadly, then, flanged edges seem to be an Asiatic invention, passing with an Asiatic type of axe into Egypt, without spreading there; also passing into Hungary after the copper age, and thence developing in northern bronze forms without being accepted on the eastern, western, or southern Mediterranean (Peet, 397).

16. A very unusual type of fighting weapon (A 181–3) is called by Wilkinson the pole-axe. This name refers to the fighting pole-axe of Germany, but it is not easy to understand the real nature of it. The colouring of 181 may help us. The blade is blue, the oval upon the blade is brown, the handle is yellow. It was used for swinging overhead blows. The most probable interpretation of it is that the blade was iron, but so valuable that it was stiffened by a large bronze oval on each side of it, which attached it to the handle of wood. This use of iron for the edge, supplemented by cheaper bronze, is seen in the knife of iron with a bronze handle cast upon it (see K. 246 across pl. xxix). The reign of Rameses II, to which the pole-axes belong, is exactly the time when iron was first being used as a rarity; this would agree to the interpretation just given.

The Frankish axe 184 seems to be a re-invention of the axe with holes, by which to bind it on to the handle.

17. The edged fighting baton was a peculiarly Egyptian weapon, not found elsewhere. It would be quite useless upon clothing, and only effective on bare flesh; hence it could only be a hot-country weapon. The simplest forms are A 154–6, where the edge was simply backed into the baton, and secured by ties through four or five holes. The next stage was to make a lug at each end (A 178) to hold it in by ferrules round the stick, as well as ties. Another form was carried out over the end of the stick as a point, A 179. The scolloped axe affected it, and produced the type which is only fixed in the baton at three points, A 157, 180. All of these seem to belong to the xith and xiith dynasties.

18. The halberd is intermediate between the edged baton and the axe. It is so obvious a form that it arose independently in America, as seen by the two from Wisconsin, A 185, 186. The latter is curiously like the Coptic form, viii, 189, in its attachment. The earliest example is the iron halberd, vi, 187, which is dated to the xxth dynasty by being found in a thick sand bed of the temple

of Rameses III at Abydos. The iron halberd, viii, 190, may be of some later date, before the fine Coptic example 189, which is engraved with zigzag lines, a cross, fishes, and vine pattern. A form similar to these halberds is used as a hoe in South Africa, see Z.E. 1882, p. 541.

At the end is placed a very uncertain object, 188, which suggests some ceremonial weapon; it was found at Gaualgesheim in Germany, and it has been interpreted as the crest of a helmet. A crest of such a form would, however, be Greek rather than Roman.

CHAPTER II

THE SOCKETTED AXE (O) PLS. IX, X, XI, XIII

19. THE second great class of axes is that of the socketted axes, marked here by the letter O. The use of a socket was very slowly adopted by the Egyptians; they never employed it for bronze or for hammers, and only a few socketted iron axes have been found, which are probably Greek or Roman importations. Egypt therefore gives no light on the history of socketting elsewhere. We have seen how the socket appears to have been used in Syria as early as the xiith dynasty (A 173), and in Greece in the xviiith dynasty (A 175). The evidence of material certainly places socketting before the introduction of bronze. Socketted axes of copper are known from Monte Rovello (Rome) O 1, in Sicily (Siculan II), Kalenburg O 2, and Hungary O 134–136, and socketted copper adze-axes from Serbia, T 49–51, xiv. Nevertheless, socketting does not seem to have been very prevalent in the bronze age, as we have only twelve of bronze out of more than a hundred axes, and many more iron axes might have been copied here, but not more of bronze. It is curious how slowly the most effective kind of handle came into use.

Among the bronze axes, note the broken-off casting duct on the heel of O 4, as in the Sicilian (Peet, 466). This gives a clue to the origin of the projections on the back of O 9, 10. It seems to have been found advisable to make a clear projection on the back to serve as a hammer, O 9 to 14; if a mere socket was hammered, the expansion of the metal would deform the socket, hence the need of a projection. The bronze model axe, pl. xiii, O 116, is of an early form, used for an amulet as in Sicily (Peet, 465). The Italian and Greek forms are almost straight and symmetrical, O 1, 3 to 14. But in Germany the curved axe O 2 seems to have been copied from a still more curved form in Hungary (see M. 2.3.2). Hungarian types are usually connected with Oriental types, and the curved axe probably came in from the East. A widely splaying axe appears on the Nineveh sculptures (O 15, 16); whether of iron or bronze is not known.

20. The iron axes began by copying the bronze forms, as O 19 (like the modern Canada axe), 20, 21, 24, 25. The Hungarian axe O 23 retains the curved form noticed above. Soon the true iron forms develop, with a wide splay and thin blade, O 26–36. In these, no special attention is given to the socket; no great strain was to be put upon it, and the purpose was probably for fighting, or at Pompeii for butchers' work. The Pompeian forms are very common, some forty of them being at Naples, varying between the limits O 29 and 30. These forms occur in Egypt, O 31, 32 doubtless of Roman age; and also the iron axe amulet O 117. The purpose of the extreme type, 34, 35, must have been to make a very wide cut quickly, keeping the axe as light as possible for the sake of rapid handling. Next there appear various developments of the socket. The curved form O 37, 109–112 (lxxix) is the *francisca*, or throwing axe of the Franks; 109 is like the axe found in the tomb of Childeric I (481 A.D.) now in the Louvre. Other axes show a lengthening of the back as a hammer, usually with an enlargement of the socket beyond the sides of the blade. This must have been done in order to use a weaker wood for the handle; and it would seem that all these (O 40 to 44) are of northern source. The hardest wood now used for handles is the Syrian *shūm*, largely exported to Egypt for adzes and other tools. This is far harder than the ash wood usually employed for handles in the north, or even than oak. Hence it may be taken that the northern peoples required larger hafts for axes, in order to use the softer woods without bruising and spoiling them by the strains on the axe.

21. The deep socket is another stage of development. Slight deepening is seen in O 45, 46, of the first iron age and La Tène (second iron age). The Carniola axe, 47, is of the curved Hungarian type. Other slight deepening appears in Germany, O 48 to 51, with a great expansion of the blade. This runs to an excess in the early mediaeval age O 52,

53, like the modern cooper's axe; but these may be for fighting. A similar form is seen in a bronze amulet axe of Roman age, O 54 on pl. xiii.

A lengthening of the socket to correspond with the blade, is required for the violent shocks of a woodman's axe, such as O 17, 18. From this is derived the drooping blade, which is found beginning as early as the xiith dynasty for the woodman's axe O 55. Much the same was used in mediaeval France, 56, and in modern Brazil. It was developed much further for carpenters' and butchers' axes O 57 to 60, and the modern joiner's axe, which type arose at least as early as Merovingian times (D.W. 155, 39). Other mediaeval axes greatly widened the blade, as used for decapitation, O 61 to 64. A still longer blade, 65, almost became a halberd; yet it was used as an axe for stripping the bark off branches, the blade being slipped in between the wood and the bark, as shown in the Bayeux tapestry. The axe with a spike at the back is Italic, being figured on Etruscan sculpture, O 66. Much the same form was used for a fighting axe in Germany in the xivth century; and was the Dutch butcher's axe (67) for killing cattle in 1694. See also O 124, pl. lxxix.

22. Another stage is the recurving of the ends of the blade. This began as early as the Ist century A.D. in Germany, O 69, 70, as shown on a silver *signum* of a cohort, found at the camp of Niederbiber by Neuweid. This was a Danish type (72) and was brought by the Northmen into France. From it was derived the typical Norman axe (71), which continued to the xiiith century (73). A somewhat similar form was used in Roman Britain, with a very deep socket (68). The great size of this, and of G 18, causes some doubt as to the scale stated for them.

23. A different style of socket came into use in the North, to allow of a sideways wrench of the handle, for loosening the axe when it was struck home. The socket was deepened at the sides into a circular form. Excepting one axe found at Perugia, all of these are cold-country weapons, adapted to the softer woods used for handles in the North, like the pattern of the Scotch axe. The great length of the edge in some of these, as 83 to 88, also required a greater depth of socket to be proportionate to the strains in use.

Another form of this deeper side to the socket was developed mainly in the North, not as a circle, but extending to a point above and below, as in O 94 to 101. In modern axes the point below is in the Newcastle and Yorkshire axe, and the point both ways in the Kent and Irish axe. This form also gives a hold on the side of the handle, but not so effectually as the circular box socket, because the point would soon crush into the grain of the wood. The form is mainly Swedish.

24. A different use of the axe belonged to Germany. The previous sockets were to meet a side wrench, probably in fighting; the next type was to meet a lift of the handle, probably to loosen it out of the grip of cloven wood. The socket is deepened, mainly downward, so as not to crush the handle when strained to lift. In some the socket swells out to the back (O 103–108, and the *francisca* 109 to 112, lxxix); in others, it is ostentatiously projected along the back, separate from the sides (O 113 to 115).

25. Another family of socketted axes is distinguished by the tubular socket, O 118 to 129, which in various shapes joins with what we may call the Oriental axe, O 132 to 145. The characteristic of the Oriental axe is the ornament which is in raised ribs on the surface. This was seldom, or never, made in the West. The characteristic of the West is incised line and shading ornament (as on the razors pl. lx, 61, 94), which is seldom, or never, found in the East. These two opposite families of decoration seem sharply to mark the sources in opposite regions. There is perhaps a structural cause for this difference. To produce the raised relief around a socket, the casting must be done in a closed mould, and little is left to hammer work; the incised ornament is natural on the flat surfaces resulting from open moulds and beating out the form.

Even on the simplest example of this family, the socket is strengthened by raised ribs, O 118; these are further advanced on 119, pl. lxxiv, from Central Syria. In the latter, the casting duct is in the middle of the back, joined with a deep flange to stiffen the back of the socket. This family of tubular sockets is remarkable for the narrowness and length of the blade (O 123, 126 to 129); also for the knob more or less ornamented, which is placed on the back (O 125-6-7, 129). The purpose of these forms is not obvious. The narrow blade suggests a fighting axe used on clothed enemies, and hence beginning in Hungary rather than in Syria. The Danish example, 129, is covered with fine spiral pattern, dating it to the best period of the bronze age. Other variants of this type are like 127, but with a plain disc and spike, from Hungary (M. 2.3.2) and from Bavaria (M. 1.4.2); also, without a spike, from Hungary (M. 2.3.2). The strangest of all is the Bohemian O 128; which end was used is hard to say. An almost exactly similar form is said to come from Hungary, and to be in the Zurich Museum (M. 2.3.2); perhaps the attribution is wrong, and they are two versions of the same specimen.

26. The more distinctly Oriental axe has flamboyant curves, merging into figure reliefs in the truly eastern examples, as O 140, and the Hamdan axe in the British Museum. Polished stone axes with such curves come from Troy, O 130, and as far west as South Jutland. Noting the absence of such work in the western metal axes, it seems as if the western stone axes must be due to importation, or to an invasion from the east of a small group whose ideals of art soon perished. The flamboyant type of axe comes from Perm, Western Persia, the Caucasus, and the Caspian region. Thence it spread into the west of the Black Sea, in Hungary (134–136), where its finest examples appear in the nine gold axes of Czofalva in Transylvania (O 139). The Persian development, O 141, is evidently later, as the socket has been turned almost to right angles, the blade is turned down toward the hand, and the former back of the axe is developed as the working edge. The Syrian axe from Beyrut, O 142, is the later form of the scolloped axe, A 168, with the holes further reduced. This underwent a curious change on passing into Central Asia; the Minussinsk axe, O 143, has the two oval holes shifted from the front to the back of the haft, and thus reduced to a mere ornament. This, in its turn, seems to be a probable source for the Chinese forms O 144, 145.

THE DOUBLE AXE: (T) PL. XII

27. In the series of the Double Axe, the considerations of its actual use, and origin, are complicated by its having undoubtedly been also a ceremonial object, and perhaps a standard of exchange of a fixed weight. The ceremonial aspect of it has overshadowed all else in recent years, in the study of the Cretan symbols. It is therefore needful to begin by seeing the utilitarian purpose of the form, before considering the purposes of symbol or exchanges to which it was applied.

That the double axe was employed for ordinary tree-felling in Nineveh is proved from the sculptures, where the form T 21 is used. It appears as an ordinary fighting axe in Etruria, T 18, 19, 20, 22, 23, 24, and on a cist, T 25. It is found made of iron with a full-sized haft hole, and modified for various uses, at Ephesos (35) and Pompeii (40, 44), and in Egypt (T 41, xiii), in which conditions it is unlikely to have been ceremonial. It is still a tool used by bricklayers. The great elongation of it in Sardinia, T 10, 11, 14, does not seem as if a sacred type were being maintained, but rather that it was modified for use, perhaps for hewing rock. In general, it seems reasonable—after seeing these working examples—to suppose that all the axes with full-sized hafting holes were for actual use.

28. On the other hand, a large proportion of double axes have a hole too small or irregular for a haft, or no hole at all. Such must have been for purposes of either ceremonial or exchange. That a type of weapon which was continually in practical use might also have a ceremonial significance, is shown by the great spear heads here figured, and many other examples, see sect. 79.

29. Apparently the earliest form—most nearly copied from stone axes—is that of T 1, 2. The Hungarian example has a flamboyant touch at the ends; but this may be only local style, and not show an Oriental origin of the weapon. From these it may be concluded that the curved ends as on T 3, 7, 8, 9, 13, 15 (early Minoan II), 16, 21, are earlier than the square ends, as 5, 6. The use of the square-ended type with a slight splay, is dated to the 1st century B.C. by its occurrence on the coins struck at Corcyra by the Proculeia gens (12). It should be observed that the axes with curved ends, 13, 15, have oval holes; those with flat ends, 4, 5, 10, have round holes. The earliest dated example, however, from Mochlos, 15, has a round hole and curved ends.

The local distribution of types explains much of the history of the double axes. First, we see that the axes intended for use, having effective hafting holes, belong almost entirely to the Aegean and Crete, also to Caria as shown by coin types, and one distant branch in Sardinia. They are thus limited to the Mediterranean. On the other hand, the axes with ineffective hafting, and therefore ceremonial, are not found in the Mediterranean (except some in Crete) but belong to the north. Sixteen are from Germany, six are Serbian, two Swiss, and two French.

Not only are the effective and ceremonial types thus separated, but the ceremonial types vary in their form with locality. On Lissauer's map in his important article (Z.E. 1905, 519) the sources are seen to be grouped in the Elbe Valley, the Rhine valley, and some scattered in France and Switzerland. On reviewing the varieties, it is seen that each of these centres has its peculiar form. A short form with narrow waist, and a mid ridge (as 31) belongs to the Elbe basin, a long, narrow form (as 33) to the Rhine basin, and a large bell-shaped form (as 30, 32) to Switzerland and France. It appears, then, that there are at least five different forms belonging to different localities—the three just named, the Aegean forms of Crete, Naxos, and Mykenae (as 5, varying to 15), and the long Sardinian form (14).

30. The theory which has been put forward that all these axes were made in Cyprus, and distributed thence, is thus strongly contradicted by the facts. Not only is the type rare—or absent—in Cyprus itself, but the entire separation between the effective forms in the south, and the ceremonial in the north, and the localisation of form in at least five separate regions, could not occur by chance trading. Moreover the Rhine form is decorated with rows of punch cuts, which is a style of western rather than of Mediterranean ornament. It would seem absurd to suppose all these peculiarities to be made in Cyprus, or any other centre, and sorted out by trade in five distinct regions.

31. Another consideration that has been put forward is that these double axes are made of definite weights. This view starts from the statement in a gloss on Hesychios that the Greeks made bars of 10 minae in weight in the form of the *bipennis* or double axe. None of these double axes are as much as 10 minae in weight, so the connection is not certain; and it would seem that ingots of as much as 10 minae might be cast somewhat like the larger trade ingots known to us, and be termed *bipennis* as the best word for the form, without implying the finished shape of a weapon, like these axes. However that may be, the idea has been followed up by showing that three of these axes agree with the Aeginetan mina. The weights of eleven axes are published, and we can proceed to classify them all, as follows, in grammes.

Pyrmont . . .	910	1½ of	607
Locras . . .	3040	5 ,,	608
Börssum . . .			616
Flonheim . . .	1240	2 of	620
Mainz . . .	935	1½ ,,	623
Serbia . . .	628		628
		Average	617
Petersberg . . .	1000	2 of	500
Rheinhessen . .	1049	2	524
Calbe, Saxony (two) .	540		540
		Average	521
Friedelsheim . .	1445	2 of	722
Weinsheim . .	730		730
		Average	726

Now these three averages are all well-known ancient standards. 617 grm. is the Aeginetan, corresponding to a drachm of 95 grains with variation 94 to 97. 521 grm. is the *necef* of Syria, corresponding to a drachm of 160·8 grains, varying from 154 to 166 as is usual. 726 grm. is the Phoenician, corresponding to a drachm of 56 grains, or shekel of 224. All of these are closely the recognised mean values of the ancient standards. The distribution of the standards is not separated by the regions; Aeginetan and 80-grain are in both the Elbe and Rhine basins, but the two of the Phoenician unit are both on the Rhine. It may be remembered that the great octopus weight of Knossos is on the Aeginetan standard, and both this and the Phoenician are much older than the importance of Aegina or Phoenicia.

32. What may have been the purpose of the axes conforming to different standards of weight? It was not as mere rough ingots; they are too well finished for that. It could hardly be for the sake of exact sale values, as they belong to an age when such precise trading is scarcely to be expected. Rather should we connect these with the standard weights kept in religious centres for public reference. From the temple of Byblos come the large marble standards with double breasts in relief; from the temple of Set at Nubt comes the haematite head of a hippopotamus, marked with its numeral value as a weight; in the temple of the Capitol at Rome were kept the standards of the

Republic; in the Serapeum of Alexandria were the standards of Roman Egypt. It would be then in accord with ancient usages if the weights kept for reference in different centres had a religious connection as ceremonial forms. The existence of three different trade standards in a single region is to be expected, seeing that half a dozen different standards were used in each of the great commercial countries.

One further matter must be noted, that—so far as examined—these double axes are all of copper, or the Serbian of silver, without any bronze appearing. Possibly this was due to a religious archaism, like the use of flint rather than metal in ceremonies, or the dislike of iron as a new metal. Yet at least it would show that bronze was not in universal use, and the copper age forgotten. The period of these standards of weight is then of the copper age, or early part of the bronze age.

33. The conclusions are, therefore,—

1, that varieties are strictly localised, and made locally;

2, that while the southern examples were for use, the northern were ceremonial or sacred;

3, that they agree to three of the common weight standards;

4, that they may be the religious standard weights of the Germanic and Gaulish trade, the form being adopted, from the veneration shown to it by the traders, as a religious emblem.

5, that they belong to 1500 B.C. or earlier.

A different type of double axe is found in Sardinia, T 36, 37, which is linked to those having tubular socketting. Much the same is found in Central Asia (38), though the form of the ends as a pick, axe, or adze, is not clear from the photographs. As the tubular axe, which is probably Asiatic, reaches as far as Epirus (O 125) and Denmark (O 129), it is quite possible for it to have been carried to Sardinia. The Norman boatbuilder's axe, T 34, was probably descended from the forms in Roman use T 35, 40. The fine iron double axe from Egypt, pl. xiii, T 41, is doubtless also of the Roman family, being closely like T 40.

ADZE-AXES AND PICKS: (T) PL. XIV

34. From the double axe, a further step is to make the two ends different in function. The earliest change was to combine the axe and adze together. This type began in the earlier part of the bronze age, as in the beautifully made tools from Sparta and Crete, T 45, 46, and the simpler —perhaps earlier—form from Kythnos, 47. A longer form appears in Sardinia, 48, similar to the lengthening of the Sardinian double axe T 14, 36, 37. The tubular haft of the latter two is repeated in the adze-axe. A distinct family appears in the graceful long tools from the second city of Troy, and from the Serbian mining region. T 49 was found by the mine of Brestovac, and T 50 at Kanitz, near the gold mine of Slatina. An example similar to T 51 is said to come from Hungary (M. 2.3.2); perhaps this may be only a wrong source for the previous example. These Serbian adze-axes are all in copper, pointing to a very early date, before those from Greece; yet the fine form and tubular haft indicate a later age. Perhaps the supply of Serbian copper tended to continue the copper age longer there than in Hungary or Greece.

After these tools of the full bronze age, or before, there is a break, until the type recurs in iron, beginning with the Nimrud pickaxe, 52, but mainly of Roman age. The small example, T 53, from Boscoreale (Pompeii) is most like the earlier Greek of Kythnos; and is a continuance of an early type there, like the plain blade axe, A 54, of Boscoreale. The class of large adze-axes T 54 to 60, resembles the modern mattock. The reason for this may be that they were for working in woodland, where a main need was the cutting of roots, so that an adze edge was required. Our modern pointed pick-axe is for earth work, in cleared land where only the breaking up of the soil is required. The form 61 is stated to be the *francisca* or throwing axe; but O 37, 109–112 (lxxix) are also claimed as the *francisca*, and with much better reason, as the pointed end to the edge would be more effective. 62 is a very heavy tool probably for smith's work. The straight adze-axes 63, 64, are not for earth work, but probably for wood splitting and trimming. T. 65 is a leaden model of the same form (pl. xiii). T 66, 67 being much narrower may be for stone working.

35. T 52 and 68 are the only true pick-axes. The Central European type 70 has apparently a blunt pick end, as also the Egyptian form 69 found at Defenneh. These are so much alike that it looks as if the Defenneh example had been brought there by a Greek from Europe. T 71, 72 are stone-breakers' or quarrymen's picks, like the modern stone-pick. T 73 appears to be an adze-hammer;

from the angle of it, perhaps it is a cooper's hammer, or a caulking tool. T 74 is a miner's pick-axe, with a point to split stone, and an axe for trimming. T 75 to 77 are miners' pick-hammers from the Spanish mines. The typical miner's pick has varied very little in the form and angle in the course of ages. The Pompeian shapes, T 78, 79, are much like the mediaeval, 80, and the later Dutch, 81. The Norman pioneer's pick in the Bayeux tapestry, 82, is more square on the handle, but with the same angle of point as the others.

CHAPTER III

THE ADZE AND HOE

THE ADZE: (Z) PLS. XV, XVI, XVII

36. THE adze is only second to the axe in importance as a primitive tool; the distinctions between the two forms have been already noticed. The earliest adzes known are the small thin blades found in the prehistoric age of Egypt, such as Z 60, 61. The edge view of many of the adzes is here shown at the side of the front view. Later on in the prehistoric (60? S.D.) a larger size appears, as 62 from grave 702 Naqadeh, 63, 64 from unknown sites, and 65 from Ballas. Another (68), probably later by its thickness, may come from the beginning of the 1st dynasty.

Just before the 1st dynasty, or perhaps in the reign of Mena, a sudden start was made, with a much larger blade, considerably splayed, Z 8, 66, 67. This—as we noted before—is closely of the Cypriote form of copper axe; and it is probable that the new type in Egypt was an importation from Cyprus, or from the same source as the Cypriote form.

37. Turning next to the European types of the flat-topped adzes, the earliest seem to be the copper adzes of pillowy forms from Sicily, Z 1, 2. The unsymmetrical form of these, much more curved on one side than on the other, shows that they were attached on the flatter side, and not used as axes. The same is true of the flat form from France, Z 3. The following figures are here arranged in the order of increasing splay. This is not always the order of development; the forms 14, 15 are from early Susa, vaguely described by de Morgan as of the "age of Naram-sin and Khammurabi," over a thousand years apart; but the form 29 is said to be the earliest from Susa, and is much more splayed. The best line of study is to note close resemblances of form, within a likely range of trade. Thus the long narrow Egyptian adze of the prehistoric age Z 23 is very close to the Kythnos form Z 19, 20. The tapering to the top in the Knossos adze Z 21 is like the Mykenaean forms 17, 18, 22. The Cypriote form Z 7 may well be the source of the Central Italian 10 and North Italian 9. With more hammering of the edge it might result in the Kythnos form 24, 25. The latest form, 6, reverts nearly to the most primitive, and the Madras iron, 5, has the same simplicity.

38. The round-topped adze began in Egypt with the dynastic people, starting along with the large splayed adze. Two new types arriving in the same generation, are probably from the same source. As the later bronze adzes, from Cyprus, have the rounded top (Z 55, 56) it is the more likely that the round-topped adzes of Egypt also came from there, with the great adze. The form of the long parallel-sided adze is a natural type in hammered work, as shown by the Wisconsin form, Z 30. In Italy it is found curved (31), but this is very unusual. The parallel-sided adze is the earliest form, in the generation before Mena (Z 32, 69, 73, Tarkhan tomb 412); it became slightly concave in the sides during the 1st dynasty (Z 33 to 36, 70 to 72, the latter of Zet at Gizeh). Similar forms are found in Spain and Italy (Z 37, 38), perhaps also derived from a Cypriote type. Next a rounded head began to develop from the side contraction, at the close of the iind dynasty (Khosekhemui, Z 74), and early iiird (Z 41, 42). This became a definite head in the iiird dynasty, Z 45. It next had a ridge below the domed head, at the close of the iiird dynasty, as in Z 76 dated to Sneferu; see also *Medum*, xxix, 11. The forms 77 to 81 are immediate descendants of this form, probably in the ivth and vth dynasties. (Duplicates of 78, 79, 80, 81.) The dated examples in the vth and vith dynasties have a rounded head, Z 46 to 49. A slight ridge below the head is seen in the xith dynasty, Z 50, and this may well be the date of the similar example in Cairo, Z 51. In the xiith dynasty, the round-headed adze appears in a drawing, 52; but in general the forms of the xiith dynasty show a degradation of the head, as in 83, 84, from Kahun. Yet the idea lasted on to the xviiith dynasty, as in the two models of Tehutmes III from Nubt (87), and Quft (88), of Amenhetep II from Thebes (89), and lastly of Saptah in the xixth dynasty (90, from his temple).

A corrupt form is seen on an adze from Gurob (91) of the xviiith or xixth dynasty. This series of forms traceable over nineteen dynasties (4,000 years according to the Egyptians)—and dated to within a generation in much of the course of it—is the most complete history known of any type of tool.

39. In some adzes of the xviiith dynasty, the head entirely disappears, as Z 85 from Gurob. This is so closely like the Italian form Z 44, that they may well be contemporary. A roughly pointed head appears in the xxvith dynasty (57). The round or polygonal head occasionally appears in Persia (Z 43), Greece (54), and Cyprus (55, 56). The irregular form 58 is not an axe, as it is quite thin; this and 59 are very rough, and show that the type was not important in Central Italy, though it was well made at Lago Maggiore (Z 44). The example Z 75 from Egypt is without date or locality; it is very rude and not connected with any form known there, yet it is too large to be of the earliest period. Probably it is due to a barbaric invasion.

At the close of this series there are the signs of a new type approaching. Z 92 has shoulders at the sides, and bears an incised figure of a branch. When bought, it was stated to be from Gebeleyn. Z 93 from Gerzeh, about the xxiind dynasty, 900 B.C., has more distinct projections, and marks the beginning of the following type. A similar form occurs at Gezer.

THE LUG ADZE: (Z) PL. XVIII

40. This type has been but little noticed hitherto, yet it is very widely spread, and has passed through several stages. The first suggestion of it may be in the Cretan form, Z 94, where projections begin from the side. The use of such projections cannot be like that of the stop-ridge across an axe—to prevent the handle working down on it. These being on the edge do not concern the handle; but, on looking at the actual adzes on handles, as 133, 138, it is evident that the binding might work down the adze, and come loose. These side lugs are therefore intended to bear against the lower turns of the binding. The swell on the Cretan form, 94, would wedge up the binding; and as the lugs develop wider, up to 122, the binding would be the better secured. The early stages had a firm footing in Sardinia, 95 to 97. Another early stage is in Hungary, 98, and we have seen it similarly in Egypt, 93. It is of no use to regard the late stages, 107 and onward, in looking for the source of this type, as they must have arisen later than the slighter forms; and this order of growth is confirmed by the far advanced forms in iron, Z 116, 122. The simplest beginnings are in Egypt 92–3, and in Crete 94. A further point is that the start must have been near Sicily, as the type reached Sicily (101, 104) and South Italy (103) during the copper age; everywhere else it appears to be of bronze or iron. The source therefore seems to have been in, or near, Crete. Its spread to Hungary and Western Persia need not have been contemporary, but may have been moving eastward, while later forms were developing in the Mediterranean. In any case it points to the importance of western forms having travelled eastward. That Crete should influence Spain, in Z 99, is quite likely; this Spanish form turns the lug upward to retain the binding more securely. A curious variation in Spain is the adapting of lugs to a socket adze, Z 106. In the simpler form, the adzes with lugs passed to Sicily, Italy, Spain, and Ireland, on the west; to Egypt, Hungary, and Persia, on the east.

41. The later development was that of lugs sharply square with the blade. This proceeded in Epirus (109), Italy (107, 108, 112), Sicily (114), and the British Isles (117–120). Eastward it reached Syria (111). In the northern route, it followed the earlier type to Austria (115) and the Crimea (110). This was, however, late in its course, as most of the northern forms are of iron, in which metal it spread to Hallstatt, Saxony, Bosnia, Silesia, Styria, and Poland (113, 116), and in its most marked form to Poland and Hanover (121, 122). As regards the date of it, the beginning must be while Sicily and Italy still used copper, that is, before the close of the First Siculan period. This is connected at Cannatello with a form of bowl with drop handle which is characteristic of the xviiith dynasty and onward (Peet 450, 453); and as the close of the copper age in Egypt is just before the xviiith dynasty, it may well be contemporary with the same stage further west. This type, then, could hardly have started later than 1600 B.C. in Crete. It had not advanced far by 1000 B.C. in Egypt (the earliest date for Z 93). Yet on its translation to iron at 800 B.C. it was fully developed (113). The further change of adding a projection

at the top, to hold the binding, is the work of the iron age. As no trace of this type is found with Roman remains, it probably died out about 400 B.C. killed by the advance of socketting.

42. The hafting of adzes is figured in early examples from Egypt, 123, 124, used by ship-builders. The handle was about five feet long, and the blade about a foot long, evidently the great adze blade, Z 8, 66. The shorter form is figured in the xiith dynasty, 125. From the xviiith dynasty is the model of the adze, 128, at the top of pl. lv. The latest example of Egyptian hafting is the pair of zes said to be from Abydos, 132. In these, the blade, the wedge, and the band are of iron; the old system of binding has given place to a massive iron band and wedges; yet no haft hole seems to have been adopted. Probably these are ceremonial implements of Ptolemaic times. A wooden ceremonial model of an adze is in pl. xvi, 131. Some modern examples of stone adzes are given, to show modes of lashing on the handle, 133, 134, and the transition to an iron blade inserted into a wooden handle, 135. The adze with a socket hole finally superseded all the methods of binding. It was probably a variation of the socketted axe in its origin, and does not seem to have been adapted from any of the unsocketted adzes. It probably arose independently, in the west under Rome, and in Persia. Z 136 is the Roman adze-hammer; and 137 the double adze. Another form of attachment to the handle was by adapting the adze with a band, as 132, to a long, straight handle as in 140. In this the old form of the adze handle (as in 132, 133) is continued, and the band which held on the upper end of the blade; but, to retain the blade better, two strips of iron pass along the sides of the handle. This method of fastening became usual in mediaeval and modern hammers. In this form, Z 140, the blade is bent in order to bring it at right angles to the hand holding a straight handle; the older adze kept the blade straight, and bent the handle to bring the hand at right angles to the cutting movement. The blade here is reduced to a rod at the upper end, ending in a ball. The tool thus produced resulted in an adze-hammer, bent as before, but with a tubular hafting for the handle, as 138. This was a very common form in Roman times, there being eleven at Naples, and others at Mainz. A somewhat similarly bent form, but with a plain haft hole, was found at Silchester, Z 145 on pl. lxxviii. A short adze-shaped tool, perhaps a rivetting hammer, is shown in 141. 142 is a link between the adze and the tubular axe haft, such as O 42, 123. It was found in the beginning of the late Celtic level, in Wookey Hole, belonging to perhaps about 50 B.C.; it seems to be another of the changes of the axe types to the adze form of cutting.

43. An entirely different family is the eastern adze, adapted from the eastern axe. The original figure of 143 is vague, and not certainly axe or adze; but the angle of it is that of the adze 144, and is much better suited for adze than for axe. 144 from Mesopotamia has the Oriental relief bands to strengthen the socket. The western socketted adze is not common. One of iron from Egypt, is probably Roman, pl. xiii, Z 146; a sketch of a similar one at Florence is 148, no date or scale. The same form adapted to a gouging adze is found at Silchester, 147 on pl. lxxviii. A figure on an Etruscan sculpture shows apparently an adze-hammer, Z 149; and an adze with a tubular haft was used in mediaeval times, Z 144. In the East, the socketted adze, rather like Z 146, is universally a carpenter's tool, for trimming wood and hammering, used throughout Russia, Turkey, and Egypt. Thus the adze, though secondary to the axe throughout historic times, still retains a large amount of use in the world.

THE HOE: (J) PLS. XIX, XX

44. The use of metal hoes has not been hitherto recognised, but these forms have been classed along with axes and adzes all together under the vague term of celt. From the unsymmetrical profile in all cases (as J 19), it is clear that the hoe cannot possibly have been used as an axe, but must have been used parallel with the adze. The very weak socket, generally not even closed round, proves that it was not used on any material which had elasticity or strength to hold it. The bluntness of the edge which is found in many cases shows that the material wrought on was rough and loose, as earth. The very wide thin blade, as J 33, 50, 51, could not have been used on anything firmer than light soil, without bending or breaking. We are justified therefore in taking most of these blades as garden hoes, while leaving the question of the cast sockets (J 34 to 38, 53 to 55) to be considered later.

The forms J 1, 2, show the early Egyptian hoe

without a cross tie, which was intended for a garden tool. For agriculture the heavy hoe with a cross tie was used, see sect. 151. The double-pointed hoe seems to have been intended for light soil, rather than for clod breaking. The forms 1 and 2 have evidently a blade bound on to a wooden arm; such blades originally were of flint, and may have continued so down to the xiith dynasty.

The first dated example of the metal hoe is the largest, J 39, found with a group dated by a spear-head with the name of Rameses II. This is somewhat narrow. Two models of Saptah, 47, 48, are rather wider; and two in a group of about the xxiind dynasty from Gerzeh (41, 42) are shorter and wider. The splay seems to increase as time went on; and therefore the narrowest forms from Cyprus, 4 and 5, are probably the earliest (see also those from Enkomi, D.C. 250). The whole of the other examples of moderate width 7 to 25 are of iron, and therefore later. Among the Egyptian bronze hoes, 45 is from Memphis and 50, 51 from Bubastis. J 56, of iron, was found with an iron chisel, C 110, pl. xiii, in the ruins of the temple of Amenhetep II at Thebes. J 57 and 58 are from the Ramesseum, and therefore probably not later than 700 B.C. J 59 is of Roman age from the Fayum; it is shown on a lesser scale with its handle, on right side pl. lxxiii.

45. The source of this type might well have been Egypt. In no country are these hoes so usual in the bronze age, and the few bronze hoes from Cyprus might have been made for Egyptian use. If they were made in Cyprus, about 1300 B.C., they would travel by trade to the other countries. It is strange that there are none from Greece, Italy, or Spain, except the large Roman 31, and Perugian 15. After these the most southern is La Tène, 10, 29, 30. Then on the west, Chalon (21), Dorset (17), Sussex (18), and Sweden (23, 24). On the east Carniola (7, 9, 11, 19, 22), Styria (12, 13, 14, 25), Böleske in Hungary (8), and Kiev (6). It would be very unlikely that a northern form in iron, presumably not before 800 B.C., or 1200 B.C. at the earliest, could originate bronze forms in Egypt of 1200 B.C.; nor is it likely that Egypt would introduce forms to the north. Cyprus is more likely therefore to have been the distributing centre, though the main use and invention was probably Egyptian.

The cast socket hoes have usually been classed as axes. When symmetrical, the form is ambiguous; but those from Egypt, 53, 54, have never been sharpened, and were left with the rough-cast rounded edge; further, 55 is askew and therefore not an axe. It seems as if they were hoes. Similar forms are from Hungary in copper (37), and from Central Asia (36) and British Isles (34, 35) in bronze. An iron tool like these (38) is stated to have been found on a handle, mounted as an axe. It would be needful to make sure that such is the original mounting, and that it had not been turned, since it was used. Altogether it seems doubtful how these cast sockets were used. They might be spuds, instead of hoes or axes. The large iron hoes, 58, 59, are probably the parents of the modern hoes of Egypt.

CHAPTER IV

THE CHISEL: (C) PLS. XXI, XXII, XXIII

46. For classifying the great variety of chisels, the method of holding them is the main distinction to be followed. The divisions are

A—D . . .	Bare metal.
E—G . . .	Tang in handle.
J—M . . .	Handle in socket.

Each of these divisions may be alike divided into four classes, lettered separately—A square bar, B deep bar and narrow edge, C thin and wide edges, and D circular bar; in the other divisions marked E to G and J to M. Thus there are twelve classes of chisels, and the gouges which follow are arranged similarly. In the photographs and drawings there are often two views of the same tool.

A, the bare metal chisel, without any wooden handle, is the earliest type. It is found even in the first period of prehistoric Egypt on a very small scale, as a kind of hand graver; it is sometimes sharpened at each end, C 44, 45, 46, pl. xxii, proving that it was held entirely by the middle. These three are from graves 807 (S.D. 49), 63 and 297 (S.D. 38), Naqadeh. (Also duplicate of 45, 45 with one end pointed, 45 one end square.) Later, the use of end pressure became usual, and a mere pad of wood was put on the end, which was accordingly made flat, as in the first-dynasty chisels C 1, 2, 3. The prehistoric chisels slope on both sides, but in the first dynasty the single slope—or true chisel edge—was preferred. At Susa, the earliest chisels

(4) are very similar, with a double slope. A little hand-graver with an edge and a point, comes from the Heathery Burn cave, C 5. The small square bar continued long in use in Egypt, shown here at the end of the iind dynasty (Khosekhemui, C 47), at the beginning of the iiird dynasty (C 6), at the end of the iiird (C 53, Nefermaot, Meydum), in the xviiith dynasty (C 57 Amenhetep II; C 60, 61, 62 El Amarna), in the xixth dynasty (C 63, 64, Saptah; C 66 Ramesseum and duplicates), beside others of unknown date, C 59, 65, 67, and smaller duplicates of 67 from Amarna and Gurob. The square chisel was also used in Europe, such as the beautiful square bronze forms from North Italy (C 7, 8), and the later iron chisels from Idria in Carniola, and from Greece (9, 10).

47. B. The chisel was not only used for cutting, but for levering out the pieces cut; this was especially needed in the large amount of mortise cutting, done for the joining of planks edgeways. The weakness of the square bar soon led to deepening it, to gain strength for levering out the chips from the narrow slits of the mortise holes. This form began with the first dynasty (C 12 to 15), was shaped with a chisel end in the iind dynasty (C 48), and with the double slope (C 69, both Khosekhemui). In the iiird dynasty the mortise chisel is usual (C 15, 17, Hen-nekht; C 18, 19, 20, Neterhen). A large and very deep chisel is of the vith dynasty, C 23 and probably of the same age may be C 71. Of the vith and xith dynasties are models of this form, C 21, 22, and 70 from the tomb of Emsaht, Siut (and duplicate). Large deep chisels belong to the xviiith dynasty, as C 82, with edge view of tip at the side, and C 58, 83, 84 from Gurob. C 56 is of Tehutmes III from Nubt. Sometimes handles remain, as C 73 from Gurob, and C 86 of Amenhetep III from Kahun, with C 85 showing the side view of an exact duplicate of 86. The broken tip, 89, from Quft is probably of the same date, and so may be 87 from Gurob and 88 from Quft. The type is last seen in the models from Saptah's temple (xix) of which 74 and 75 show the two views. 72 is undated, as also a smaller one from Quft. This deep chisel with double slope is one of the tools peculiar to Egypt, and not recorded from any other country.

48. C. The wide chisels are seldom found in Egypt, and are more usual elsewhere. They occur as early as the first dynasty, C 24, 25; and larger in the iind dynasty, under Khosekhemui, C 49, 50. After that there is no wide chisel, except the massive tool (which may be ceremonial) with the name of Aohmes I, C 68. This weighs 21,003 grains, just three pounds. From Ireland comes a beautiful little graving chisel (27), with a wide and a narrow edge, and a cross bar to grip it by in the middle; this is part of the goldsmith's group in the British Museum (note that being bronze tools, they could not be used to cut equally hard bronze). The flat iron chisels were known at La Tène C 28, but are mostly Roman (29 from Athens, 30 Rhine, 31 Pompeii). As this is the modern caulking iron or chisel, they were probably ship-builders' tools. The Dutch mason's chisel is C 32.

49. D. The round bar chisel is that generally used by stonecutters; the stout body of it withstands heavy blows without bending or shortening. The early round chisels are slight, and were perhaps used in sculpture, as C 51 from Gizeh, iiird dynasty; and in the xviiith dynasty C 55 of Tehutmes III from Nubt. The regular stonemason's chisel is the stout form, as C 33, 76, 77. The latter has been cast in a V groove, and then roughly hammered round. A better formed example of the xixth dynasty is from Sinai, C 34. C 78, 79 are masons' chisels of the xiith dynasty from Kahun; the latter was found with the largest copper mirror. C 80 is the only chisel with the owner's name; the first sign is indistinct, it has been read *mer* "Overseer" or *neterkherti* "Miner," next is "the elder Ambu." It is probably of the xiith dynasty. A similar chisel of the xixth dynasty was found at Serabit in Sinai, C 35. C 81 from Memphis is dated to Rameses II, by being found in his foundations (*Memphis* I, 12). Two small round chisels of iron are in pl. xiii; C 36 was found in the ruins of the temple of Amenhetep II with C 110, probably dating before the xxvith dynasty. C 37 is from Gurob, probably Roman. Passing from Egypt, we find that the round bar chisel occurs at La Tène, C 38, 39, at Pompeii C 40, 41, 42, and at Silchester, 43 (lxxviii), but it is perhaps the least usual form of chisel.

50. E. The Tang chisel, to fit into a handle, is scarcely found in Egypt before Roman times. As a formal matter we are bound to class the chisels with a handle, C 90 to 95, with tang chisels; but it is most probable that all of these were of the forms 12 to 23 which were used either with or without handles. The distinction of two forms of handle should be noted; for striking, the handles

were centred, as 90 to 94, but for graving by pressure, the handle was fitted on the side of the blade, which was retained by a side-loop of the handle as 95. This form of handle seems to have been suggested by the adze-blade fastened on sideways to its handle; the use of it may have been in order to detach the blade easily by pushing the butt of it, so as to use it in a different manner.

The first period in which true tangs and flanges were adopted is the grand development of tools of the bronze age, best fixed by the immense *fonderia* deposit of Bologna. This hoard of thousands of damaged bronze objects, anciently collected to be melted up, gives a group closely of a single age, perhaps 900 B.C. The square bar form is seen in C 101 and 104, which has been bent, and the little chisel from Gorzano, west of Bologna (C 116). C 108 is so like a modern brick-dresser that it is probably a mason's tool. The square bar chisel is varied by the truncation of the edges, forming an octagonal bar, as in the large and beautifully formed chisel 115, from the *fonderia*. Later are the iron chisels, with a stop ridge on each side. This type is widely spread, C 110, pl. xiii, from Egypt (in the ruins of the temple of Amenhetep II), C 111 from Nubia, 112, 113 from the Assyrian group at Thebes, and C 114 from Westbury on Trym. The latter would point to this type being of Roman age, but it is not found in the Italian or Germanic Roman work.

51. F. The deep-bar, or mortising chisel, is a usual form at Bologna, as C 96 to 103. The points of 97, 98 have been sharpened irregularly, probably as hand gravers; though broken off, 96 to 101 appear to belong to the tang chisels. The regular Roman mortise chisel is C 118, and a slender form, perhaps derived from it, is the Madras chisel 120. A fine example of the tang mortise chisel, with handle and ferrule complete, is C 119, pl. xiii, from Wushym in the Fayum, of Roman age.

52. G. The broad tanged chisel may perhaps be credited to the xviiith dynasty, from the figure in C 109; but the first well-formed example belongs to the fine bronze age of Italy, evidently of the same family as the *fonderia* group, though now at Florence, C 121. This has a very thin blade, apparently for surface shaving. Another bronze one is from Como, C 122. Others are of iron, in the north Italian 105, the Greek chisel from Naukratis, C 106, and the broad chisel probably from Assyria, though found at Thebes, C 107. The iron shaving chisels of Roman age are from Pompeii, C 108, 123, and from the Fayum, C 124 (xiii). The same form is found in Sweden C 126, and is shown in the Dutch example C 125.

H. Only one example has been noticed of the round tang chisel; among the varied forms of the *fonderia* group is the specimen C 127 from Bologna.

53. J. The socketted chisel was invented about the same time as the tang chisel, both first appearing together in the *fonderia* group. The socket was square in most of the earlier examples, though usually round in later times. The specimen C 128 has unfortunately lost the end, so it is not certain in form; it is finely made with bold ribbing round the top to strengthen the socket. The socketted chisel was also developed in Peru, and commonly made by hammer-work and lapping.

54. K. The deep-bar mortise chisel C 129 has a wide end to clear a cut, evidently for deep mortising; it is from Castel Porpetto near Palma, now in Udine Museum. A similar chisel, with a fluted square socket, source unknown, is in Stettin Museum, C 130. A much narrower socket appears in C 131, source unknown, in Munich Antiquarium. Almost the same type as these is found in Styria, 133, and in Central Asia, C 132. (A similar one in Wiesbaden Museum, M. 1.5.3, is of unknown source.) This suggests that a large number of examples must be missing, in the transit over so long a course; and it should be remembered that most of the weapons which we know, have come from graves, while there was no inducement to bury tools in the same way. But for the *fonderia* discovery we should know very little of the great age of Italian tools; and no such groups, or ancient towns, have been cleared in the long spaces of Eastern Europe and Asia. Hence our knowledge of the distribution of tools must be much more imperfect than what we know about weapons. A model from Naukratis (135) shows the same form to have been used in Ptolemaic times. All the preceding are of bronze, but the type lasted into the iron age, as at Idria, Carniola, C 134. The Norfolk specimen, 136, is most like that from Palma, as the blade does not swell out wider than the socket. The French form, 137, seems more akin to the Greek and Roman. So far we have dealt with double-slope chisels.

The single-slope chisel begins also with the *fonderia* as C 138; but in general this was a later type than the previous, as the other examples are of iron. A very slender chisel comes from Dodona, 144. The stout one from Pompeii, 142, is much like three Roman chisels from Silchester, 139 to 141, pl. lxxviii. The socket chisels from La Tène, 145 to 147, do not seem to be very deep, nor is the model from Naukratis, 149. The French form 148 is fairly deep. The Yorkshire specimen from Heathery Burn cave, 150, does not seem descended from any of the previous, but rather as if the maker knew of the idea, and carried it out with as little metal as possible. The modern Dutch form 161 does not look very deep, but yet it was used for mortising.

55. L. The flat socketted chisel seems to have begun in Italy, as in the Chiusi example, C 151, which by its thinness was hardly made for an axe. The type passed northward, to Styria, 152; and east to the Greeks, who carried it on to Naukratis, 154. The Norwich example, 153, looks like independent work, without a model to copy, as was the Yorkshire, 150. In Italy the form continued common in Roman times, 155, 156. It passed into France in the bronze age, 157, if this should be classed here, and not as a derivative of 128–133.

M. The round-bar socket chisel seems to be entirely Italian. A slender one, 158, comes from grave xv at Bologna, of bronze, though dated as *umbri ultimo*, or late La Tène period. A short and wide one was in the *fonderia*, 160. The small one, 159, seems derived from the Italian type, and it may have been brought from Italy though now in the museum at Stettin.

56. The gouge is much less common than the chisel. This is strange, as it is very useful in hollowing out wood, owing to its cutting all the grain, and not needing to break the grain through at the sides of the cut. It is almost entirely a northern tool, there being only three (Bologna, Vetulonia, Athens) from all the Mediterranean area. The reason probably is that the southern woods are harder and break away short, while the northern woods are more open and stringy, and the grain requires cutting through. There are hardly enough examples to trace the course of varieties. The fluted socket, 165, seems to be copied from North Italian bronze, and the tool might have been imported to La Tène. More than half the examples are from the British Isles and Siberia, the northern range of tools; in view of this it is curious that there are none from Scandinavia.

CHAPTER V

THE KNIFE: (K) PLS. XXIII—XXIX, (U) XXX, XXXI

57. The various types of cutting and slashing tools and weapons may be sorted in eleven classes, according to their forms. No distinction can be made between tools and weapons; not only are we often ignorant as to the actual use, but also the same knife might be used for any purpose that was required. The classes are numbered as follows:

58. Flaying knife, sharp around, weak handle, 1–15, xxiii.
59. Straight backed, 16–56, xxiv.
60. Straight edged, 57–75, xxv; 216–226, xxviii.
61. Hollow backed, 76–99, xxv.
62. Hollow edged, 100–111, xxv; 214–234, xxviii.
63. Recurved, 112–167, xxvi.
64. Crook-backed, 168–189, xxvii.
65. Khopesh, 190–202, xxvii.

The Symmetric Knife (U).

66. Double convex, 1–23, xxx.
67. Double edged, 24–69, xxx, xxxi.
68. Sword (E), 1–39, xxxii.

The broad difference in size between the knife or dagger, and the sword or rapier, is—that the knife or dagger is used at close quarters on an enemy held, or within reach—the sword or rapier is used to prevent an enemy coming to close quarters.

58 (pls. xxiii, xxxi). *The flaying knife* is a well-marked form from the prehistoric age of Egypt, K 1 being of S.D. 49; K 4 (xxxi) from Tarkhan (grave 22) is of early 1st dynasty (also a duplicate), and evidently 2 and 3 (and two duplicates) are of nearly the same age. These knives are sharp all round, slightly dished so as to fit over the curves of an animal's body, and have a weak handle unfit for much pressure. These details all agree to the use for flaying; and the safe removal of skins from animals, for water skins or dress, must have been an industry which was all the more important before weaving became common.

K 5 is sharp all round, and is perhaps a dynastic flaying knife.

K 6 is only sharpened on one edge; it may therefore be a side-razor, rather than a flaying knife. K 7, 8 (xxiii) are later flayers (and duplicate of 7), more roughly made. K 9 is a flayer from Asia Minor. K 10 is called a spud or chisel, and from the photograph it is not clear which edge is sharp. From the small size, and weak handle in proportion to the blade, it seems like a flayer or razor. There is a puzzling class of Italian tools K 11 to 15, and other decorated forms in B.P. 1902, 120–4; 1903, 28. The most decorated seem to agree with the description as "sacral palettes," though how used is not clear; other simple forms as K 11, 12, seem more like razors or flayers. The use of these various forms cannot be settled without examining the edges to see if they were sharpened for cutting, and what part might be so used.

59. *Straight-backed Knives.*—The flint knives K 16, 17, 18, represented in paintings of the xiith dynasty, seem to be the earlier forms, from which the metal type was derived. The same form is shown in the ivth and vth dynasties, K 19, 20. An actual knife of copper of the same form, K 22, is dated to the vith dynasty, and probably 23 is of the same age. This form was nearly arrived at in the independent copper work of America, 24; and another American form, 28, is near that of the Egyptian copper knives, 26 and 27. These resemblances naturally arise from similar needs and materials. Other examples of these Egyptian knives of copper are K 227 (at top), 239, 240, pl. xxix. The last one has a house sign cut upon it. All of these are self-handled knives, having handles made in one with the knife.

Another class are the tang knives, made for wooden handles. K 21 is a model of the xiith dynasty, corresponding to the vith-dynasty blades. K 29 is probably of the xviiith dynasty, agreeing with the blade of Tehutmes III from Koptos K 235, and that of Amenhetep II from his foundation deposit, 236. From a Nubian tomb at Buhen, of the age of Tehutmes III, is a knife with handle in one, K 30. The knife from Troy, 31, had probably a single curve, like 32, before it was reduced by sharpening. K 32 is an Italian form. Some straight backs have an almost parallel edge, such as K 228 from the tomb of Khosekhemui iind dynasty; K 33 from Rhodes was probably similar to this before it was reduced by sharpening. K 233 (and a duplicate), perhaps the latest of the bronze straight backs, has an elegant curved handle ending in a duck's head, apparently late in the xviiith dynasty or early in the xixth.

The iron straight-backs are not early, as none of the Hallstatt period occur. The largest development was in southern Germany, K 34 from Traubingen, and similar from Franconia. The butt is evidently a degraded animal head, see K 92, 93, a fashion of that region. Such a large size was probably for hunting. The long and almost straight knife, 35, from La Tène is like the Egyptian forms, 210, 211. 210 from Oxyrhynkhos is said to be Arabic. Other long forms of straight-back occur in Egypt, K 255, 256, from Tehneh, probably pre-Roman. Knives with a loop or turn at the end of the handle, were doubtless to be hung at the girdle. Such is a fairly early type, occurring at the Ramesseum, K 253, probably of 700 B.C. or earlier, also at Gurob, perhaps Roman. This is the usual form at La Tène, K 37 to 40. A similar form of blade from Stillfried (41) is of bronze, which implies a fairly early date for the preceding examples. Of Roman age is the pointed straight-back, K 42, from near Mainz, K 259 from Hawara in the Fayum, with a wooden handle, and probably also K 258 from Egypt. K 207 was probably the same form originally: it is from Gurob. These take with them K 43 to the Roman age; part of the handle (of wood?) has decayed but the pommel of ivory still remains. The wide and clumsy forms from Bologna, K 44, 45, are of the latest Umbrian, just before the Gallic invasion, 600 B.C.?; they resemble a coarse blade, U 70, from Hawara, and the late Livonian, 46. A rather earlier blade of the same family is K 47, of the *Umbri posteriore*. Probably K 203 was of the same form before it was worn; it is from Oxyrhynkhos.

Roman blades have the round socket for a handle, K 48, 49. Perhaps the blades in pl. lviii, Q 27, 28, 29, may also be knives, though they seem like parts of shears. K 50 is probably pre-Roman, by the resemblance of the bone handle to that of the bronze knives 165 to 167. The sharp turn of the end of the handle in 51 to 54 looks as if it were derived from the handles just named. The little broad knife in a bronze handle, 55, is a common form among surgeons' instruments at Pompeii. The mediaeval mason's pick, and chopper for trimming the soft limestones, are seldom represented, so a dated instance of 1362 at Bologna is valuable, K 56. It is closely like the modern Scotch butcher's cleaver. With this must be classed the same form K 260 (xxxi), stamped with the hieroglyphs *Ra-ne-măot*, belonging therefore to the funerary service of Amenemhot III in the late period, and found by the ruin of the Labyrinth at Hawara.

60. *Straight-edged Knives.*—The first group of these, K 57 to 64, are girdle knives, with a loop for hanging. They link K 57 (duplicated as U 16)

with U 17, 18, 19; and K 60 with K 124 to 129. The forms K 57 to 64 show a similarity in very different regions. The Sicilian (58), Spanish (60), and French (64), may well be of one family; and, if we include the British from Tring (62), the Danish (61) may also be accepted. A difficulty about the British knife being native, is caused by the animal head on the handle. This is like the Bavarian and Oriental animal heads; but the knife handle, 63, from Gloucestershire points to this type being also British. This type of knife then seems to hold together over western Europe; and what then of the Chinese 57 being similar? In pl. xxx there is a strong connection in the form, and angle of the blade with the handle, between the La Tène U 17, the Siberian U 18, and the Chinese U 19. It seems as if there had been some relationship between the west European and the Eastern Asiatic groups. Another blade of much the same form though tanged for a handle, is from Como K 65.

The short knife, K 66, is entirely of bronze, both blade and handle, and therefore probably early. The same form of blade is of iron at La Tène, 67. Similar knives from Egypt are K 216–219, the latter from Oxyrhynkhos, also a duplicate of 218. The steeper ended blades are usual from the Rhine, 68 (like the modern shoe-maker's knife), Italy 71, and Egypt, 69, 70. The Egyptian knives are not dated; two are of bronze, 220 is of iron from Oxyrhynkhos, and the last, 226, is a model of wood.

The handle of 72 is intended to protect the hand, like the handle of E 40, and of the swords, E 32, 35, 36. This shows that it was for rough work, probably a hunting knife. K 73 is a magnificent specimen, with steel blade inlaid with designs of bronze, and with a bronze handle made to fit the fingers. It is the only instance of a combined blade of two different forms; the straight part gives an exact cut, as in cutting up an animal, the hollow part gives a strong cut, as in trimming a branch. The same curved back is seen in the surgeon's knife, K 74, and the curious knife, 75, which is of bronze entirely cast in one piece. 252 has a bronze handle to the iron blade.

61. *Hollow-backed Knives.*—These are intended for sweeping cuts, especially required in hunting knives for cutting up game. They are of large size, extending up to the dimensions of the smaller swords. The type begins with the flint knives, usual from the first dynasty in Egypt. The same continued in use till the xiith dynasty, as in K 76, 77. The copper knife of the same form, in the Old Kingdom, is K 78. In the xiith dynasty the same appears at Kahun, K 243; and in the xviiith dynasty there is the fine form 232, with the gazelle-leg handle. Just the same outline of blade is contemporary with this at Knossos, K 79, and also a blade much wider at the end, 80. Pointed crescent blades belong to the late Umbrian age in North Italy, 81, 83, and to France, 84. Another similar form in Egypt, 82, may be contemporary with these, as another like it, 87, is of the xxvith dynasty. This is perhaps descended from a form which is probably of the xiith dynasty, 241: another Egyptian knife, much the same, is 245. A similar curve was used at Mykenae, 85; this has the original end, square and unbroken. Much straighter forms occur in Egypt, as 86, 88. Sweden has a small curved knife of the hunting type, 89, with the hollow handle, which is generally eastern in origin.

The great hunting knife was of the largest size in Egypt, 90, with a handle formed by plates rivetted on either side of the sheet of the blade. These handle plates were probably of horn. Unfortunately neither date nor locality of this example is known, and there may be a doubt as to its antiquity, see D 27, 28. A similar form, 91, comes from the Marne. A broader form occurs in Bavaria, 92, which is dated to the first La Tène period, 93 is undated. The handles are more or less modified from birds' heads. An independent derivation of the curved-back knife is from Wisconsin, 94; this is very much like the Egyptian form, 242. The curious little knives, 98, 99, are stated to have been toilet instruments.

62. *Hollow-edged Knives.*—These are mainly for cutting material which is held in the left hand, such as food, or grass in India. This type is unknown in Egypt until introduced by the Romans. The earliest example is from the great tombs at Mykenae, K 100, like one from Cyprus, 101, and another, 102, with continuous handle, from Colophon. The Syracusan 105 is probably of a different family, varied from the form of 58. The fewness of these examples in bronze is evidence that this was an unusual type in early times. In iron it is much commoner. From Egypt there is the bronze knife 234 (and duplicate) with a duck-head handle; and also pieces of such knives in iron, K 214, 215, and others which vary the form to a cut off at the end, K 221, 222, 223 (214, 222, 223, are from Oxyrhynkhos.) The Italian form 104 is dated to the Gallic

period; and very likely of the same age are 106 to 109. It is remarkable how closely the form from Idria in Carniola, resembles the grass-cutter's knife or sickle from Madras, 110. Much the same curve was evolved for fighting purposes in mediaeval France, 111.

63. *Recurved Knives.*—This is the best and most varied type of the knives. The motive of it is to combine two forms, the convex edge for a wiping cut, and the hollow edge for a heavy cut. There are several divisions of type. 112 to 120 are but little developed from the preceding plain forms; all the examples are from the Central Mediterranean, except the probably independent form 115, in the South Caucasus and Armenia. 121 to 129, with the back curving round from the handle, are all northern forms, from Hallstatt out to Siberia; the one from Ancona was probably an importation down the Adriatic. 130 to 140, 231, is a Sicilian and Egyptian group, with a branch to Troy and the Euxine. In Egypt it only appears after the Mediterranean wars of the xixth and xxth dynasty; it is coloured blue for iron, which was then a foreign material for Egyptian weapons (135 and 136 are two versions of the same original). It seems therefore to belong to the Shakalsha-Siculi, who were raiding about by sea, and may have passed up to Troy. 231 is of bronze, apparently made in Egypt, with a gazelle-leg handle. Such a handle is reported to occur in the xiith dynasty (Reisner, in *Boston Museum Bulletin*, xiii, 79), but we await further details of that dating, and the present example being from Gurob is of the xviiith dynasty. The group 141 to 147 extending over Troy, Mykenae, Crete, and Egypt, seems to have originated the striking development in Italy 149 to 167. Along with 141 from Troy, compare 244 from Egypt (Gurob, xviiith dynasty). With the similar form, 146, from Troy, compare 229 from Thebes. 230, which is plainer than most of these, is a Hyksos knife from Tell el Yehudiyeh; this may be one of the prototypes.

The flamboyant Italian knife, 149 to 167, is never found in Egypt, nor anywhere in the Mediterranean outside of Italy. In its southern earlier forms the handle is in one line with the back, as from the *fonderia*, 161. La Tène northern forms of it always have the handle central, and the back projecting, as 156 socketted, 162 tanged. An approach to this latter form is in the Hallstatt example 151. This later age of a different form in the north points to the type originating in Italy. Starting there about 900 B.C. (K 161) it went north at about 700 to 600 B.C. It died out about 300 B.C. (K 153 with iron blade), but not later, as it was never made entirely of iron, except in Franconia (K 149), which is probably the furthest and latest stage of it. The openwork handles of 153, 154, are of well-known Italian work (see pl. lxx), and the Hallstatt handle (151) was copied from these. The ring and open-work handles were largely adopted in Germany, see many from Mecklenburg M. 1.8.4; but as such work is well fixed in Italy and Sicily (K 58), it probably originated in the south, and thence was carried north. This flamboyant knife is remarkable for having four entirely different forms of handle. The socket is the earliest (161); next is the openwork handle in bronze at Hallstatt and La Tène; the enclosed handle (165–7), being all bronze in one casting, may be the third; the tang (162–4) is entirely northern, and probably the latest. The form of 161 is widely spread, in Italy, Switzerland, France (middle and west), mid-Germany, Tyrol and Hungary (see S.V.).

64. *Crook-backed Knives.*—If we accept the guidance of the metal, there can be no question that this form started in Italy in the latter part of the bronze age. The two splendid examples in bronze from Pesaro (184) and Cuma (187), overlap the beginning of iron, as the Pesaro blade is duplicated in iron, from the same place (185). Other bronze knives are from Spain (183), and La Tène (173), which place was always linked with Italy. This was then another product of that mechanic fertility of North Italy, which gave the world the chisel forms and the flamboyant knife in such perfection. The motive for this form, in the early large stage, was to cut through the hide of animals, by turning the back concavity toward the body, and ripping through the skin, edge outward. This use (I am informed) survives on the Continent in cutting hard skin on cooked meat; the form is still very commonly made.

The next stage is of much interest. In the ruins of the store-rooms of the Ramesseum some tools lay scattered, and nothing there was as late as 700 B.C., so that any iron discovered was of an early date for Egypt. Probably 800 to 900 B.C. would be the period. The iron knives 246, 247, 249, 250, 251, 253, were all from that site. 246 is important, as the handle is of bronze, cast upon the iron blade. This implies that iron was still more valuable than bronze, and was only used for its superior quality. 246 is slightly crook-backed ; 247, which is clearly of the same family, has a marked hollow in the back. 250 appears to have had the same originally. These are perhaps the earliest iron knives of the type. On the Italian side the Pesaro and Ancona iron blades (185 186) copy the bronze type; and this is found up the Adriatic in Carniola (188), doubtless all belonging to Noricum. We have no links between these and Western Persia where it recurs (172) ; but so peculiar a type is more likely to have travelled over this gap than to have been re-invented. The type was commonly adopted by the Romans, and hence may have come the Pyrenean 177, the French 174, the Rhine forms 179, 189, the Crimean 168, 169, the Oxyrhynkhos examples 204, 208, 209, and the Anglo-Saxon 170, 175-6, 180-1. The mediaeval form 182 may perhaps be derived from the sabre type, as E 32, 33, xxxii.

65. *The Khopesh.*—This name is adopted from the Egyptian, as there does not seem to be a consistent name for the type in modern times. The peculiarity of the type is the deep hollowing of the back, and the projecting of the edge far in advance of the handle. By its great curvature it was intended for a wiping cut; and the retreat of the handle behind the edge was to protect the hand from the subject, and to gain a few inches of distance. The earliest dated example of the form is a small knife with the name of Tehutmes III, 190. But the type seems more Oriental than Egyptian, it only appears in Egypt after Oriental fashions had spread there, it occurs in Mesopotamia (191) and Assyria in 1300 B.C. (201), and it passed to Bavaria (192) more probably through the Oriental connections of Hungary than across from Egypt. The treatment of the form varies considerably in Egypt. It is interesting that in 198 and 199 the handle and back rib are yellow (bronze), while the blades are blue, apparently of iron. These small copies of sculptures, by the proportion of the figures, show that the weapons were in all cases larger than these two actual weapons that we have, 201, 202. These both had handles inlaid, probably with plates of horn or ivory.

THE SYMMETRIC KNIFE : (U) PLS. XXX, XXXI

66. *Double convex Knives.*—These have the back and edge both convex, and almost equal. The type was unknown in Egypt till Roman times. It seems to have originated in early Greece, where it is in Crete U 1-3, 11, Sparta 4, 5, Mykenae 6, 7, 8, Nauplia 12, and in Sicily at Pantalica 9, and Taranto 10. These include nearly all the bronze examples, and stamp the type as of southern Greece, passing on to Sicily and South Italy. The early iron blade from the Ramesseum, K 249, xxix, is not unlike the later forms of bronze blades. With the large square Italian handle, the type appears in iron in North Italy (13), and passed out north to Bavaria (15). The resemblance of the skew handle of La Tène (17) to that of Central Asia (18) and China (19), is remarkable. The utility of it for giving a dragging cut, rather than a pushing cut, seems unlikely to have caused so nearly the same angle to be adopted. The Minussinsk example being of bronze, while the La Tène knife is of iron, indicates that the form travelled from Asia to Europe, if there be a connection.

This blade was adopted in Epirus, 20 ; and the later forms were wider, as in the iron blades of Syracuse, U 21, and Egypt U 65 (Medinet Habu), 65 and 67. The Krems knife, 22, is probably of Roman origin ; and 23 is Italian, like the small knife with long handle from Oxyrhynkhos, K 205. A very clumsy iron knife from Egypt, 214 (xxviii), has no European parallel.

67. *Double-edged Knives.*—This is one of the types almost peculiar to Egypt, two-thirds of the examples coming from there, against one-third from all the other countries. The type starts with the great expansion of copper tools at the rise of the dynastic people. The great knives then made, U 24, were never exceeded in size. The tang was retained till the iiird dynasty (25 to 27) ; later it became only a continuation of the blade in the vith and xiith dynasties (28, 29), The tanged knife U 63 is probably of the Old Kingdom by the form. In the xiith dynasty the change took place of making the handle all in one with the knife, as in U 49 and 59 from Kahun (also two duplicates of 59). Similar knives continued to be made in the xviiith dynasty, as U 61 from Gurob (and duplicates from Gurob and Amarna)—worn down by sharpening, and U 62 (duplicate from Gurob, and duplicate with curled-over handle, from Kahun). The beautiful leaf-shaped knife, 58, belongs to the latter part of the xviiith dynasty, dated by U 55, 57 from Amarna, with which go 52, 53 from Gurob, 54 (duplicate from Amarna), 58 (and duplicate) and the slender 56 (with duplicate from Gurob). A wider,

clumsy form came with the xixth dynasty, dated by 50 from Saptah's deposit (and two with coiled handle, Gurob); this fixes also the knives 48 (Gurob) and 51, also two from Gurob, and another between 48 and 51, and two smaller from Gurob. The larger dagger-knife 60 is like one in the British Museum, 30, of xviiith or xixth dynasty. The long leaf blade (and duplicate of half size) of bronze recurs in Roman times, as 64 from Oxyrhynkhos. A very wide blade of iron, with iron handle covered with wood, belongs to the xxvith dynasty, U 31 from Defenneh, and K 254. Also a long straight knife is from Defenneh, U 32.

Turning to the few European examples of double-edged knives, there are three long straight blades from Mykenae, U 33, 34, 35; 34 is unusual as having the handle in one with the blade (compare E 1). The Spanish form, 37, is evidently of the same type, and probably the Sicilian 38. This is then a Western Mediterranean family, quite different from the Egyptian. The Spartan form 36 stands quite alone. The knife-dagger, and socketted knife from Heathery Burn, 39, 40, are also independent forms. The blade K 248 of iron must be early, from its relation to the bronze leaf swords, see E 2. The figures 41, 42 from Peschiera are called knives, but look more like small daggers, see D 111, as also does the Swedish 43. The Anglo-Saxon 44 is a pocket-knife, and 45 is stated to be of the scramasax type. Examples from Mainz, M. 1.7.6, 3.2.5, termed scramasax, are likewise equal-curved; but the name is also applied to the crook-backed knife, K 175. The Indian forms, 46, 47, suggest daggers or spear heads, rather than knives. Thus the double-edged knife was but rarely made outside of Egypt, and there is no family of them except the British examples, and the few straight blades of the Western Mediterranean.

THE SWORD: (E) PL. XXXII

68. The varied forms of the sword—blade, pommel, and chape—have been so fully discussed by Naue and others, that there is no need to deal with them here, especially as the weapon is foreign to Egypt, and very rarely was imported. A few forms are given on pl. xxxii, and examples of two families which are scarcely connected with Egypt, but are of interest. These are all to a scale of 1 : 10.

Of swords properly so called, there is only one from Egypt, pl. li, E 41, right side; this is of iron with fragments of the bone handle. The seller stated that it came from Defenneh, and the blade and handle are closely like the sword from the xxvith dynasty palace at Memphis (*Memphis* iii, xxxviii). Both are probably Persian swords.

Of rapiers, or thrusting swords, there are three from Egypt, pl. xxxiv, in the series of daggers. D 39 is rather unusual in the depth of the hilt without any tang. It differs in this from the Italian forms, and I have not exactly met with it elsewhere; one from Cyprus (N.V. vi, 4) is so near an approach that it would be futile to look further. D 40 is dated to Rameses II, and is closely like the broad rapier, D 18, carried by the Shardana auxiliaries; this is placed in D as it compares with other Egyptian daggers. D 41 is a typical Cypriote rapier, and may have been imported to Egypt in modern times or anciently.

The bronze sword of Vapheio, E 1, which (though only single edged) is a larger version of the Mykenaean double-edged knife, U 34; shows how little the typical sword blade of later times was then in view. E 2, 3, 4 are of bronze, and carry back the iron double-edged knife, K 248, to the beginning of the iron age, by the close similarity of form. This type seems to have started in North Italy or South Tyrol, and to have been brought to Egypt by the northern invaders, both in bronze, 4, found at El Qantara on the Suez Canal, and in iron, K 248. The long bronze rapier typical of Hallstatt, 8, was brought into Egypt, as 5, 6, and 7; the latter is dated by the names of Sety II, about 1205 B.C. The hilt is seen developing in 9, 10, and 11. The narrow tapering form of rapier appears early in Spain, 12, probably connected with the Shardana blade, D 18, 19, 40. That type goes under in later times, until it reappears in Anglo-Saxon burials, 13. The swords 14, 15, 16 belong to the early iron age in Sweden, and 17 to 20 to the later iron age. These Swedish weapons are nearly all swords, sharp on one edge, and not rapiers sharp on both edges. The strange form from Perugia (Frontone) was probably attached to a wooden staff to give it strength.

In Egypt there is the sickle-like weapon, E 23, which seems without parallel elsewhere. The falx 24 from Etruria was curiously paralleled in the Burgundian *glaive*, E 25. This shape may throw light on a strange form in the foundation deposit of Saptah, K 237.

The flamboyant sword from Cassibile, E 26, in

bronze, perhaps about 700 B.C., is strangely like an iron sword, 27, from St. Michael, Adelsberg in Carniola, but connection seems unlikely.

A curious type, E 28 to 31, must apparently be of Dacian origin. It figures as a national weapon of the north on the silver *signum* of Niederbiber (31), and is found in Carniola (29, 30). Compare with these, K 183–189. The example from Pesaro must have descended the Adriatic. It is the ancestor of a weird form of knife, U 71, which I bought in Egypt; from its condition the latter might have come in the last few centuries from Slavonia.

69. Perhaps the most picturesque form of weapon is the sabre, E 32–39. It is well described by Achilles Tatius in his romance; he says that in a picture of Perseus the hero was "armed with a weapon between a straight sword and a scimetar; from the hilt to the middle it is a sword, it then partakes of both, remaining sharp so as to inflict a wound, and becoming curved in order to follow it up and improve the stroke" (Book viii). The Gurkha *kukri* is the same type of weapon only shorter, and thus broader in proportion. Probably it was a legacy of the Bactrian Greek kingdom.

The form of 32 seems strange for action, with two separate curves in the edge; yet the position of the guard leaves no question as to how it was held. The variations of this type in Italy and Spain, and on Greek vase paintings, are clearly of the same family, and all appear to fall between 400 and 100 B.C. The source is probably Italian, adopted in Magna Graecia, and spread to Spain. E 40 at the end is of the hunting knife type (K 92, 93); but the bronze handle suggests defence so much, that it may well have been used in warfare.

The fragment of a sword and handle E 42, li, from Egypt, is probably of Crusading age; the large circular pommel belongs to the xth to xivth centuries (see D. W. 165, 167, 180, 182, 185, 374, 375).

CHAPTER VI

THE DAGGER: (D) PLS. XXXIII TO XXXVI

70. As the Egyptian daggers are so numerous, they give the best dated series for comparison; they are therefore taken as a whole, first of all, before noticing the daggers of other countries. Apart from the Egyptian daggers, the main division is by the method of attaching the handle. The earlier portion of the European forms are rivetted on to a handle, the later have a tang, which may even become a handle. Those which have both tang and rivet, are in form like the tang-, and unlike the rivet-, daggers. They are therefore classed with the tang daggers. It must be remembered that the dagger passes indistinctly into the knife on one hand, or into the spear head on the other hand. In view of that it is placed here between those two weapons.

The Egyptian dagger is unmistakeable, from the earliest to the latest. The handle, generally surviving in the dry climate, fixes its purpose as in no other country. The earliest example is, happily, quite complete, although broken (D 1, xxxiii): it is dated about Sequence Date 50, or the earlier part of the second prehistoric age. The blade is a plane sheet of copper. The handle of ivory is curiously formed; it is scolloped out so as to leave two horns overlapping the blade. This appears to be the prototype of the later handles, with side horns running along the blade. There is one small rivet. The second dagger has lost the handle; but as it is from the same cemetery, and as the previous handle would be quite applicable to it, there is little doubt that both were mounted alike. This second blade, D 2, has a slight thickening to the middle.

An entirely different type is D 3, of S.D. 60, with a sharp mid-ridge and hollowed faces. It is the perfection of stiffness for its amount of metal, in contrast to the weak, flat blades just noticed. This is of the same form as the Cypriote rapiers (see D 41); and, when contrasted with the other daggers, it suggests that the Cypriote type was already established, and that this was imported into Egypt. Apparently derived from this is the wooden funerary model dagger, of painted wood, the handle blue, the blade white, D 36. It was found at Lahun, 1888, probably of the xiith dynasty. A long handle is also shown by the wooden models 179, 180, 181, pl. li; 179 is from Tarkhan of S.D. 78.

71. Unfortunately no daggers remain to us from the Old Kingdom, nor do I remember seeing any represented on sculptures, except in the hand of a Syrian or Edomite child in the siege scene *Deshasheh*, pl. iv. Contrasted with the next age, it looks as if the dynastic race did not use the weapon. The xiith dynasty, on the contrary, abounds with daggers. There is the plain blade

with a crescent butt, and a good grip to hold (D 4); there is also the discoid butt, which must have been held with the fingers on either side of the handle, as in D 6 which is dated to Senusert III. The latter handle was the regular type of the xiith to xviiith dynasties. Probably of the xiith dynasty, or perhaps the xith, are the beautifully made blades D 37, 38, 42, 43. These have parallel lines of ribbing in relief running down the mid-line of the blade, of exquisite regularity. This decoration is peculiarly Egyptian, for I have not met with a single example of it from other lands; everywhere else the decoration is parallel to the edges, as in D 95. From the form of the handle of D 46 it is of the same date as D 5. The form of the xivth dynasty is given by D 7, 8, 9, which have flattish blades with a slight wide band down the middle; the form is poor and weak, a great contrast to the exquisite shapes of the earlier daggers. The Hyksos dagger, D 10, has been narrowed by sharpening, but originally it was like 8 and 9. D 44, though clumsy, is not as bad as those of the xivth dynasty, and it has ribbing on the mid-line; probably it is about the xiiith. D 45 has a faint flat ridge of the Hyksos type, but it is probably of the xiith. The clumsy shape of D 47 might raise doubts of its antiquity; but the rusting of the rivets to red oxide of copper is certainly ancient. The lines impressed on the blade are unlike any Egyptian design, and it is probably a foreign blade, handled in Egypt in the Hyksos age. Naue (N.V.) does not give any example of pattern lines concave toward the handle. The blades 48, 50, 51, are probably of the xiith or xiiith dynasty, as also the set of funereal models 53 to 58. These last were not models for currency values, as the original amounts are quite irregular, 43 to 106 grains.

72. The xviith dynasty is well represented by the Aoh-hetep daggers and others. D 11, 12, 13, show that the general type of the xiith dynasty was modified by a narrower blade, more length of the side clutches, and a shorter space between the circular handle and the heel of the blade. The exaggerated handle and slender waist of 14 mark it as an ornamental weapon, much like a dagger in the Berlin Museum (G.W. 40). It lately appears that this was a Nubian form of the xiith dynasty, and therefore imported into Egypt (see Reisner, *Boston Mus. Bull.* xiii, 80). D 15 may be of the xviiith dynasty, by its resemblance to the knives U 60, 61; and with it may go D 49. The dagger with a falcon-head handle, 16, is probably invisible in its sheath, as it is worn in the belt. D 18, 19, are evidently the same, only one plain, the other decorated. There is no question about the source of 18 as it is carried by the Shardana auxiliaries. These large rapier-daggers clearly show that the source of D 40 was from the Shardana; it was found at Gerzeh dated to Rameses II. Curiously like this type is the much smaller D 17 from the Caucasus. The small daggers, 20, 21, with mid-rib, differ from any that we have from Egypt, by the leaf form and handle. They rather suggest that they are an importation from the *terramara* people, such as the blades D 112, 117.

The famous dagger of Aoh-hetep, D 23, is unique in having the heads on the gold handle. It should be noted how the openings under the crescent handle in 5 and 6, change in 12, and become dwarfed in 14; thence we see the origin of the two semicircular openings at the top of the blade in 23. The other dagger of Aoh-hetep, 24, is purer in the curves, and in the grace of the form. Evidently of the same family is the dagger 25, with a band of spiral pattern round the handle. The round butt recalls closely the earliest handle, D 1. A dagger, 26, of evidently the same type, with spirals, is from Cyprus.

The two large blades, 27, 28, are of the same family with D 59, and D 27 was apparently bought with K 90. I was offered D 27, 28, or some like them, in Egypt, but did not feel satisfied about their age. They have never been sharpened, as 28 and 59 have the original casting duct left at the tip. The crude work of them is not like ancient style; and the enormous handle two inches thick on 27 and 28 would be almost impossible to grasp, far exceeding any dagger handle known. The widest handle here otherwise is only 1¼ inches, D 169. In no case are they Egyptian work of any ancient period.

73. The inlaid handles are an interesting class, D 22, 29 to 35, 52. They seem of one family, but widely spread. All are of bronze. Four are Italian, two Greek, three Egyptian, one Ninevite, two from the Caspian. Other weapons with such handles are K 201, 202; one Assyrian and the other an oriental form in Egypt. Thus there is a balance on either side of Egypt, as regards numbers. Such an idea seems far from being Egyptian; and as a question of personal impression I should certainly put the source in the east rather than the

west, though I do not see any proof as yet in the internal evidence. The little model bronze dagger with a hawk's head, D 60, is Hungarian or oriental in motive, but it might be a Roman copy of an eastern original.

74. We turn now to the comparative series. Pl. xxxv is arranged with the rivetted blades on the left, and the tanged blades on the right. Pl. xxxvi is of tanged and handled blades. The Spanish blades, D 61, 62, 65, are put here with the dagger series, by their form; but they are only found in the graves of women, and never with men; the men have other weapons. This seems conclusive that they are knives for domestic use, and not daggers. The obvious wear that they have suffered, agrees to their being knives. Weapons are seldom used, and scarcely ever worn away; if there has been much wear it shows that the blade has been in daily use. Knives such as K 33, 146, 253 show heavy wear; and so do some dagger forms, as D 68, 96, 101, 102, 122, 134. These early forms, 62, 65, are also found in copper from the Italian lake dwellings, 63, 64. Looking at the large number recorded as being of copper (61–65, 74, 76, 81, 87, 99, 101, 108–110, 113, 122) it seems probable that most of the simple forms are really of copper, which has not been distinguished from bronze in the description. For instance, 113 is of copper; 112, like it, is recorded as bronze found with flint implements, and so in the eneolithic period, therefore probably of copper. Moreover the other implements from St. Blaize, 81, 101, are of copper. Hence it seems that two-thirds or more of pl. xxxv should be credited to the copper age. Some simple forms however are of bronze, as 68 from the Bologna *fonderia*. The prehistoric Egyptian D 1, 2, agree most nearly with the forms 70, 71, 74, 75, from La Tène, Mochlos, and Tiflis; this is to say, they belong to a type so widely spread that no conclusion can be drawn as to its source.

A distinction in general style may be seen, as the rhomboidal outlines, 72, 77, 78, 79, are of North Italy, while the longer blades with hollowed edges are from the south, Spain (87), Sicily (84, 102, 107), Crete (82, 83), and Egypt (85, 37, 38, 42, 43). Another characteristic is the C-shaped rivetted plate, 91 to 95. This is only found in the north and west, not on the Mediterranean; the places, in order, are England (91, 94), France (95), Po valley (95 at Polada by L. di Garda, at Castione by Parma, and at Verona), Switzerland (95 Wallis), Oberbayern (92), Bohemia (93), Halle (95), Denmark (92). Thus there are none south of the Po valley, nor on the Mediterranean coasts. The decoration with sloping lines like 94,95, is also found in North Italy, Parma, and West Prussia.

75. Among the tang daggers the large knife-like blade, 108, 109, 110, 139, 140 (N.V. xiii), is Egyptian and Asiatic, and never found in Europe. The date in Egypt being Hyksos, its origin is probably entirely Asiatic, and imported into Egypt. The hafting by a notched end, 111 to 114, 119, is peculiar; it seems copied from a stone type, and occurs along with flint implements; the sources are North Italian and Swiss, but one from Cyprus, 119, suggests that as a source. The blades of the same form, with rivets, are likewise all north Italian.

Pl. xxxvi gives the high-shouldered blades. These from 130 to 147 are all northern or Asiatic; a few in the Po valley, and one in Crete, are the most southern examples. The resemblance of detail in 136 and 138 suggests that the Wiltshire dagger may have been a Cypriote importation. The Cypriote 140 shows the source of the Tyrian 139, and both may be as well classed as knives, with the Egyptian, U 24. In the Spanish daggers the straight base to the hilt, 148, 149, 164, may well be due to the Keltic invaders. The self-handled daggers with pommels, 152 to 157, are peculiar to Sicily. The system of hammering up the edges of the handle to round it for the hand is Italian, but widespread, see 152, 168 from the *terremare* of North Italy, U 10 in the south, U 9 Sicily, U 11 Knossos.

Winged flanks to the blade are remarkable and rare, but very scattered. In the east in Palestine, 162, in the west in Spain, 163, and northward in Epirus, 161. A variant may be the rapier, 170, from the Caspian. Leaf-shaped blades are also widely spread, from Spain (164), North Italy (165, 167, 168), Crete (169), and the Caucasus (166). The long straight blades are northern, 174 to 177, but appear also in India (178). Until there are many more examples of these various forms, with some approximate dating to each, it is useless to guess what were their original sources.

THE SPEAR HEAD: (H) PLS. XXXVII TO XL

76. The classification of spear heads here follows the form of the outline. The convex outlines come first, in order of width; then the straight-edged

forms, the concave-edged, the scolloped, the barbed, the very narrow spears or pikes, the fin-blades, the flat unribbed heads, lastly the butts of the spear shaft. With the spears are also included all sizes of lances, as it is impossible to find any dividing line. The spear itself was often thrown, even of full size. Only the arrow heads are here separated, as being so small that they require the velocity of mechanical impulse to drive them to a distance. The spear heads that we have are nearly all of the bronze and iron ages. The only examples apparently of copper are four early ones from Egypt, 165–167, 170; the great spear from Telloh, 137; and the Wisconsin spears, as 140. Representations however show that the spear was common in the copper age; the row of warriors on the battle relief of Eannatum (S.D. 3″) carry large spears, of the same form as 137, but ten inches long, and four examples are given here (15, 29, 65, 89) of Egyptian figures of spears. These show that we have, so far, missed nearly all the early history of the spear. That lies probably in Syria and the East, which have been so little examined; it would be impossible to suppose that it was used in the western copper age of Italy, when we have so full a variety of weapons from that period without any trace of it.

Some of the spears of the bronze age may nevertheless be of copper. A suggestion of this is given by the instances of a hammered instead of a cast socket. That is the regular feature of iron spear heads (155–164), because the iron could only be wrought, not cast. In examples of the bronze age, as 128–9–130, 139, 143, 165 to 171, the hammer work is obvious, and some of these may be of copper, or only slightly alloyed. The regular type, before the iron age, is the cast bronze socket. This casting was carried out by *cire perdue*, and so skilfully that, in some instances, the metal was no thicker than cardboard.

77. The great article on the development of the British spear head by Canon Greenwell (*Archaeologia*, lxi, 439) gives good grounds for the tracing of the dagger into the tanged dagger, the use of that as a spear head, the addition of a ferrule to prevent the splitting of the wood, the union of ferrule and blade, the omission of the tang, and the ferrule-socket being extended into the blade as a mid-rib; then the omission of the rivet, as a source of weakness, the addition of loops to tie on the head, and the shifting of these loops up into the blade. Now we have seen before, instances of apparently original design in the remote region of Britain, following some known idea of type, but not making a direct copy; such are the dagger-knives U 39, 40, and the socket chisels C 150, 153. Hence it would not be at all unparalleled for the spear head to have had an independent history in Britain. That such a history was apart from its course elsewhere, is shown by the absence of loops outside of Britain, as noticed by the Canon; and also by the long course of lapped hammered sockets before cast bronze, and the many examples in the East long before there was any bronze for casting. Hence we need not take this theory of British development into our consideration of other sources. Only one instance of the looped spear head is given here, 83, merely as being one of the great ceremonial spear heads.

78. The spear was apparently used in various different ways. The broad blade is found scolloped out irregularly, 90 to 95. This could not add to its attacking powers, and it seems to have been a swaggering imitation of damages received in hard fight. Apparently the broad blade was used as a kind of long sword for slashing; and this would explain the great width of the blade, in order to inflict a deep wound before being stopped by the shaft and midrib. The thrusting spear was necessarily of different shape according to whether the enemy was bare or wore skins, or any kind of armour. The Egyptian, the Mykenaean, and the Briton fought bare, the Greek and the Roman armoured, the Gaul with basketwork shields, as shown by statues in Marseille Museum. On the bare body a wide spear head would be most effective; and the more the defence, the narrower must be the spear to penetrate it.

79. The spear has been in various countries an object of ceremonial dedication, if not of actual worship. The great specimens are evidence of this, being far too large, and with too slight a socket, to have been actually used in fight. See the Chinese ceremonial spear head of 761 A.D. (79), that from Sweden (80), from Chiusi (82), Croydon (83), Italy (84, found with three others alike), also (85) of iron. Above all, see the immense blade from Telloh, with dedicatory inscription (137). The Sacred Spear (λόγχη, Joh. xix, 34) seems to have been sanctified as St. Longinus of Christian legend. Livy mentions as an omen that "the spear at Lanuvium had shaken itself"

(xxi, 62), and that one of the divination tablets was inscribed "Mars shakes his spear" (xxii, 1). Another omen was "the spear of Mars at Praeneste moved forward of its own accord" (xxiv, 10). Spears were also kept in the temple of Moneta (xxxiii, 26). Later there was reported by the priests an omen that "the spears moved" (xl, 19). Thus the spear was a sacred emblem in the temples, and regarded as a source of divination.

Other weapons have in different countries been looked on as sacred, or as emblems of the gods. Herodotos (iv, 62) describes the Scythian altar of Ares, "On this heap an old iron scimetar is placed by each tribe, and this is the image of Ares, and to this scimetar they bring yearly sacrifices of cattle and horses." Ammianus (XVII, xii, 21) says of the Quadi, "drawing their swords, which they worship as deities, they swore to remain faithful." The sword was the sacred emblem for making an oath binding. Jordanes (*Hist. Goth.* xi) says of Attila that his self-confidence was increased by the discovery of the sword of Mars; this was found by a shepherd, who presented it to Attila. Thor was represented with the hammer in his hand (Heimskringla, *Olaf the Holy*, cxviii). The sacred Ancile was guarded by the Salii. In Rome the public health was believed to depend upon the ceremonial driving of a nail by the dictator. "There was an ancient law written in antique letters and words, that whoever is supreme officer should drive a nail on the ides of September. It was driven into the right side of the temple of Jupiter . . . there were seen at Volsinii also nails fixed in the temple of Nortia, a Tuscan goddess, as indices of the number of years" (Livy, vii, 3).

80. Regarding the form of the blade, some preference may be seen. The angular outline, 16 to 23, is Germanic in half the examples, and the rest are of North Italy, except a Mykenaean and a Georgian. The rounded outline 1 to 15 is Germanic in only two examples, and extends south to Spain, Egypt, and South Syria. Considering the mixture from flux of population, it is not too much to call the rounded the southern, and the angular the northern type. The long leaf blades seem to have been used equally north and south. The beautifully fluted stems, 31, 32, are on a scale of 1/4, to show the detail. The earlier Egyptian forms fall into the convex class. 165 is of the beginning of the 1st dynasty from Tarkhan, 168 is of the xixth dynasty from Gerzeh, 170 is from Thebes. All of these have hammered and lapped sockets. They are most nearly comparable with the Cumean spear 30, in outline and form of rib. The iron spear 175 was found with a sling at Lahun, probably about 800 B.C.; it most resembles the Spanish iron spear, 37.

A form with a full base to the blade is of the Western Mediterranean, 46 to 52, Spain, Sardinia, Cuma, and Otranto. The celebrated spear head of Kames, 57, stands by itself as regards the two ferrule rings, but is most like the Mochlos and Mykenaean 56, and the Riqqeh head (178), of the reign of Rameses II. There do not seem to be local classes among the few scattered spear heads with straight edges, 52 to 66.

81. The next division is of the concave edges 69 to 85. The Egyptian head 167, from Retabeh in the Wady Tumilat, is partly broken; it may have been a wider form of 174. The long, almost parallel, sides of 166 is most like the Caspian example, 62; it might have been an Asiatic importation.

The concave edges are mostly North Italian, twelve out of eighteen, the rest are scattered north and south. The resemblance of the Italian forms 86, 87, and the Anglo-Saxon 88, to the Syrian 89, is probably accidental, as they are of very different dates. The scolloped blades, 90 to 95, are very usual in the north, especially in the Slesvig deposits of Roman age. The scolloping was done in the making; and, as it would be of no use for fighting, it seems as if it were made in imitation of blades that had suffered in the fight. The barbed heads, 96 to 100, are probably for lances, to be thrown and to hold on the enemy, so as to incommode him.

The Madras form 101 looks more like a dagger, by the tang; but the little triangular knob at the base of the blade is like that on a family of arrow heads from Egypt and Dodona, R 126, 129. The very narrow blades, 102 and onward, lead into the pikes, 108 to 121. They are on the whole northern rather than southern; the two southern regions being those which were overrun by the northern Keltae, Dodona, and Spain.

82. The fin-blade is a curious type, of which an explanation is given in the British Museum by the Vancouver example, with a piece of shell fixed in a divided stick, 124. This material alone would not explain the form, but it was probably a fish spear originally, with barbs to hold the fish. No. 125 from Knossos is probably of this type, looking at

the straight sides of the blade swelling out toward the tip. No other form of spear has this character except 127, 128, 131, 132, here. Beside the Knossos example all the others, 126 to 133, are from Egypt or from England. Beside these, 173, 174 (and two duplicates) are also from Egypt. It seems too improbable that a type should be transmitted between two countries so far apart, without leaving a trace in the well-known forms of Greece, Italy, or France. The conclusion seems to be that here is another instance of re-invention in separate centres. This type seems to have passed into a shortened form as 134, 172 in Egypt, and 135, 136 in England. Of the last extraordinary form in bronzes, there are several examples. It is perhaps almost more than a coincidence that the fin-blade should have been similarly shortened in each of the countries which used it. Yet can we suppose our knowledge so imperfect that all trace of it has been lost between Egypt and England? Possibly the necessities of fishing modified it in both countries.

83. Lastly there remains the class of spears without any mid-rib—merely flat blades. The grand example of this is the great ceremonial spear of copper, 137, found by de Sarzec at Telloh. This is of so long a time before the others here, that it is useless to look for any evidence of connection. How such a form may be re-invented is seen in the entirely detached type of the Wisconsin spears, 140. This is less astonishing when we see that nearly all—perhaps all—of these flat blades are of copper or iron, that is to say, they are hammered and not cast. To hammer out a form with a mid-rib would be troublesome, to cast it in bronze is easy.

The narrower blade belongs to early Greece, in Sparta and at Mykenae, 138, 139, 142, 143. The latter three are obviously hammered. The similar blade was used a little later for a socketted spear head of iron, 141. One of the strangest specimens is the broad leaf-shaped iron blade, 144, from Nubia, unquestionably of the xiith dynasty. It lay with a burial in an inner part of a rock chamber, with undisturbed burials of the xiith dynasty in front of it. No such form in iron is known nor any iron weapons till long after this. The outline is, however, like that of the Syrian spear of that date, as in 15. The other iron spears are mainly northern; excepting one from Terni, they are from Dodona, La Tène, Spain (Keltic), the Rhine, Sweden, and Anglo-Saxon England. As we saw that the angular outlines 16 to 23 were Germanic, so again the same appear in the northern forms 161 to 164.

84. The spear butts have hardly received due attention. Their proportion to the head may be seen in H 28. At Bologna the *fonderia* contained examples varying from the tube to the ferrule, 192–4; 28 and 190 are also Italian. Very varying sizes occur in Egypt, 179 to 181. The plain butt also occurs in Cyprus, Spain, La Tène, Britain, 195 to 201 (next to 200 read 199, for 190, a lithographer's error). The forked butts are only known from Egypt, where they have been found with the spear heads 128–130, in graves with Cypriote pottery, probably therefore of northern mercenaries. They are described as "Religious and sacrificial instruments" in the British Museum; but the graves in which they are found seem good evidence of their purpose. The use of a forked end might be either to rest on the toe, or in a loop, when riding, or to hold to a cord in lancing the spear. The design of the *onkh* between two *uas* signs on 186, marks it as having been made in Egypt. 182 is one of the earliest of these, being made by hammering; it was closed up by lapping, and nailing with minute nails on to the wooden staff. The other specimens are all cast. There are three other examples of 189 in this collection.

CHAPTER VII

THE ARROW, THROW-STICK, HARPOON, ETC.

THE ARROW HEAD: (R) PLS. XLI, XLII

85. THE main divisions under which the arrow heads are here classed are Flat bladed (1–23), Ribbed bladed (24–53), Triangular bladed (54–72), Triangular solid (73–84), Flat barbed (85–111), Wide barbed (112–120), Rhombic (121–132), Spur (133–150), Lances (151–55), Square heads (156–8), Cones (159–61), Single barbs (162–4), and Splayed (165–9). The mode of attaching the head to the shaft varies with the material. Reed is the earliest kind of shaft, naturally straight, stiff, and light. The heads are necessarily fastened by a tang, the reed being bound with thread to prevent splitting. The tang needs to be very long, in proportion to the head (see R 1, 29, 97, 154), so that a side pressure does not exert too much leverage to split the reed. On the other hand, when wood is used for shafts, a tang is

impossible, as a slender shaft cannot be bored; a socket head is therefore necessary. The two classes of tang or socket, therefore, show the use of reed or wood shafts.

The different forms of head were adopted for different purposes. For attacking bare flesh the wider forms with sharp blades were made, as 15–18, 41–7, and wide barbs, as 112–120. The narrower forms were for penetrating clothing; and for piercing armour, heavy and small heads were necessary, as 74–76, 126–130, 156–161. The Nubian single barbs, 162–4, were for using with bows that were too weak to drive in a wide double barb; the barb brought nearer to the point, 164, must have been a very facile weapon. The forked forms are for cutting the legs of animals or necks of birds.

86. The manufacture of the flat forms, without rib, was by hammer work. The rib was also made by the hammer in iron, as 233–5. The ribbed head of bronze was generally cast, and the socket head was always cast. The mould was of two or three pieces according to the number of blades, and the casting duct was at the point, shown by the run of metal left on 241. As the point in any case would need to be sharpened by grinding, the removal of the duct and the sharpening were both done together. The solid triangular heads were cast rather hollow on the faces; thus both they, and the triangular bladed heads, were sharpened by rubbing down on a stone. The rhombic heads 123–32 were cast in a double mould, and then sharpened by grinding across the faces.

87. The earliest metal arrow head dated in Egypt is R 1, found in the sandbed of the temple of Sonkhkara, xith dynasty. Of exactly the same form are 170 to 176, a group brought together with eight others, duplicate. These, and the similar heads from Spain, 2 to 4, are doubtless all of hammered copper. The iron blades of the north have the same form from hammering, 5–8; but, owing to the lack of reeds, sockets were made to hold the shaft of wood. Longer blades were made in the bronze age of Greece (9–13), some socketted, some tanged. The iron blades were made very wide in the north; influenced in the case of R 18 by the very broad spear-head type, H 135, which preceded R 18 in the same region. Plain leaf-blades were used very widely (19–23). The lances from Susa (30, 31 before 2000 B.C.) are almost flat, and belong to the family of the spear, rather than the arrow-head.

88. Ribbed blades are not of early date. The oldest here is that from Mykenae, 38 (1100 B.C. ?), which differs but little from the previous flat blades. The Cumean blades may be the next, 24, 39 (800 B.C.?) and perhaps as early is that from Nineveh, 32. Wide, round-ended blades, 25, 26, come from Persia and Egypt; the form is so unusual that probably the Egyptian example from Defenneh was brought by a Persian soldier. The wide, leaf-shaped type, 41, 42 does not appear till the xxvith dynasty at Defenneh, and then it is of bronze. This shows that it only comes after the great Scythian invasion, and therefore it may probably be derived from the Asiatic type which is found at Minussinsk, 46, 47. One of the same (237) is from the fosse of the palace at Memphis, also of the Persian age.

89. The triangular heads have been studied by Dr. Hubert Schmidt in Pumpelly (R), *Explorations in Turkestan*, 1904, Washington, 1908, pp. 183–6. In this he gives references to about twenty publications; his results may be summarised as follows. The triangular arrow head was Graeco-Scythian, originating in S.E. Europe. Thence it spread west to Central Europe (54, 55), east to Central Asia (82), north and north-east to Siberia (60–76). The principal localities are the Euxine coasts and South Russia. They are usual in Scythian *kurgans*; many are in the Kertch and Odessa museums from Panticapaeum and Olbia. The three-edged heads in the Caucasus region are later than the post-Mykenaean burials. In Central Asia they are found in Persia and Bohkara. In Greece, at Kalymnos, Olympia, Attica, and Megalopolis. In Central Europe at Hallstatt (63), in Carniola (59), Carinthia, and Galicia. The most westerly is from Châlons-sur-Saône. As regards date, they are never found in Mykenaean sites, but in the Iliad "three-tongued" arrows are mentioned. The Hallstatt finds would put them about 800-900 B.C. The *kurgans* extend them down to 4th cent. B.C.

Now the Egyptian evidence is that this type is never found till after the great Scythian invasion of Syria, 624–596 B.C. The Scythian source of the Egyptian examples is therefore quite probable. The examples given here, show that triangular forms which differ considerably, are found alike in the north and in Egypt, 59, 60, 61; 74, 75 and 76. This points to direct contact of the users with Egypt, rather than to transmission by distant trading.

Elaborate three-bladed heads of iron come from Central Asia (Minussinsk, B.M.).

The sources of examples in pl. xlii are 177 Gurob, 178 Kahun, 179–185 Gurob, 187 Amarna, duplicate from Koptos, and another. 226–7 Defenneh, 236–247 Memphis palace fosse, Persian age; 248–252 Defenneh; 253–6 Memphis fosse. Duplicates are of 188, 5 as 189 smaller; 192 Gurob and another, also with blade half length, and long stem; 2 as 198, as 200 uninscribed, 209, 210 from Memphis and another, 2 as 213, 6 as 215, 4 as 216–7, 7 as 217, 3 as 218–9 smaller, 18 as 220, 11 as 223, 225; 28 as 228–232; as 238, as 240 and 245 Memphis; as 248–253, 15 from Defenneh, 9 from Memphis.

90. The barbed heads begin in the simplest way, without any tang or socket for the shaft (85–89), both in Greece and the Caucasus. They must have been cemented into a notch in the shaft, using the inner edge of the barb to give a longer attachment. A tang was added in Greece (90–92, 94), showing that reeds were then the material of the shaft; and this form of head with a very long tang is common to Spain, Gurob (Egypt in the xviiith dynasty 177), and Persia (96, 97). The narrow barbed arrow, 99–105, is northern, not being found south of Parma, except 216, 217 of Persian introduction at the palace of Memphis. The wider form is as old as the *fonderia* at Bologna, 108; and the same is found in Egypt (205–9), and as late as the Alaman example, 107 (see M. 2.9.5). The widest splay of barb is northern, from the valley of the Po, France, Hungary, and Siberia (112–120).

A peculiar head with a very wide edge 121, 122 is found in Hungary, also at Defenneh (122), and the palace at Memphis (236), both overrun by Persians. It is related to the larger lance head from Sweden, H 122. The use of such a form would be for cutting through leather garments, where the whole blow was wanted at once to make a single cut. A long, tapering form would lose its force by wedging in the leather.

91. A type differing in origin from all the others, is the Rhombic head, that is to say, having a rhombic horizontal section, sometimes half as thick as it is wide. It does not arise through any other form, but seems to be a fresh invention. It is dated by being found in the mortaring of a brick wall of Rameses II at Abydos, R 126, and the two from Mykenae, 124–5, are of about the same age. A peculiar feature is a triangular projection left at the base of the blade. This would act as a stopper to hinder penetration, yet the head is always barbed and was therefore expected to penetrate. The knob is therefore a puzzle. The heads are mostly of bronze, and seldom of iron. They became much changed by the xxvith dynasty, as 131, showing that the curved edge form did not descend later than 700 B.C. in Egypt. Their range may then be put from about 1200 to 800 B.C., or a little more either way. They are entirely southern, mainly from Egypt, also Mykenae and Epirus (128–9) and rarely as far north as Bologna (130). A curious feature is the unexplained mark found on three in Egypt, two bronze, 200, 201, and one of iron, 202; also on one in the British Museum. This connects these as being used together.

92. The class of spur arrow heads, 133 to 150, is peculiar. The spur cannot be merely a form of barb, as it is added to barbed heads. It cannot be for tying on the head to the shaft, as it is needlessly long, and slopes away. Possibly it is intended to catch under the clothing, and prevent the head falling away. These examples are selected from a large number collected in a paper in S.F. 12, 483.

The large iron blades, 193–4, are evidently not native to Egypt. They are nearly the same as the lance from the Caucasus, 151. The latter blade is rather longer, and more pointed at the sides, but the long tang and flange at the head of it are alike. Both of them also show the curious shift in the planes down the axis, as in the section of 152 but less pronounced. The Egyptian examples were probably left behind by a Sarmatian soldier. It is strange that the double-plane form, 152, is found at Olympia and in the French Alps; the source was probably the Gothic invasion of Greece, and the Goths on the way into Spain. The triangular lances, 154–5, from Hungary, are of the family of triangular heads which belongs to Asia, 66–72. The heavy square heads, 156–8, are probably all Roman casting spears, to which 157 is assigned. The mediaeval arrow heads for piercing armour, 159–61, are in the Museo Nazionale at Bologna. The forked arrow has certainly been re-invented; common as a flint lance in prehistoric Egypt, it appears again in an allusion to the hunting of ostriches, as imported to Rome by Commodus. This, however, can scarcely have started it in Hungary, the Caucasus, Sweden and Siberia (166–69); it is from this northern source that it was familiar to Shakespear in deer-hunting (*As You Like It*, ii, 1).

93. Pl. xliii. Dealing next with the non-metallic arrows, a peculiar form of arrow is painted at Beni Hasan, having a triple point (257). This was doubtless for shooting birds, to increase the chance of hitting. Of actual arrows there are many hard-wood long points, painted black with white bars, pl. lxix, 271, 272, and 7 others, which are probably prehistoric. Other arrows of the same style and age, but of bare wood barred with black, are 265 to 270, and 18 others. Of the beginning of the dynastic age are the ivory or bone points, 261 (and 2 others), which were set in reeds, the butt of the reed being 260. In the early dynasties a long tapered hard-wood point set in reed was usual, as 262–3 and six others. Also two from Tarkhan, S.D. 77. In all periods down to the xvth dynasty flint arrow tips were sometimes used, usually straight cross edges to cut through the hide at one blow (*Jour. Anthrop. Inst.* xxvi, pl. x.).

94. Bows have not been recorded in prehistoric graves, the earliest perhaps being the tip of a bow from Tarkhan, grave 22. It seems probable from the colouring that the bows here painted red with white lines, lxix, 273 and another, are prehistoric, linked with the prehistoric to Algerian use of red painted pottery with white lines. This would carry with it the pieces of a bare wood bow with black lines, 274, and another. There is also a horn from a bow, which was made of two horns joined. The simplest dynastic bow is slightly curved, 264 (and another), without any notch or attachment for the string. In the vith dynasty the bow is figured with recurved ends, xliii, 258. The doubly curved bow, 259, is represented as carried by the Amu from Syria. The compound bow, built with layers of horn and wood, was brought into Egypt, probably from the Assyrian invasion of the xxvth dynasty, as shown by a birch-bark coating upon it (*J. Anthrop. Inst.* xxvi, 210). A figure suggesting such a compound bow is shown as used by the Keftiu of Syria (G.W. 30), the four groups of binding upon it showing that it was liable to split.

THROW-STICKS : (V)

1 to 7, pl. xliii ; 8 to 13, pl. lxix

95. The throw-stick is a very primitive weapon, and is shown among the hieroglyphs of the first dynasty. The specimens of it, and the figures in scenes are, however, not before the xiith dynasty. Those found in Egypt are always about two inches wide, and ¼ inch thick, such as xliii, V 5, 6, lxix, 12 from Kahun, and the large one, 13, from Lahun, all of the xiith dynasty. V 11 is broken at the upper end, and had a bent continuation. Syrian forms are rather different to the Egyptian, V 1, 2, 3, xliii ; and the Libyan example V 4 has hardly any bend. The figure of the xviiith dynasty, 7, has a moderate curve.

Allied to these Syrian forms are some ceremonial sticks from Egypt ; V 8 (lxix) is oval in section, and with a handle at the end ; V 9 is well carved in polished wood, with a loop in relief near each end, and a line of cord connecting these ; V 10 has a thinner, blade-like form with a handle, broken at the top.

SLINGS AND BULLETS : (V)

14, pl. li ; 15–23, pl. xliv

96. One example of a sling V 14, pl. li was found with an iron spear head, H 175, pl. xl, at Lahun. It is probably of the same age as other iron spear heads found in 1914 (not yet published), about 800 B.C. It is finely woven, with a thick plaited cord ; another cord has been broken away. The sling is not represented in early times ; objects mistaken for it are really girdles, or lashes. At Beni Hasan in the xiith dynasty the sling is never figured in the hands of Egyptians, but only used by Syrians (N.B. i, xlvii ; ii, v, xv). In the xxth dynasty the Egyptians and the Cretans both employed slingers in the great naval battle, but they may have been foreign auxiliaries (Champollion, *Mon.* ccxxii). The sling seems to have been essentially Semitic rather than Egyptian ; and its constant use in Egypt now, is probably due to Arab descent.

No sling bullets are known in Egypt, except one of Khabbash (*Palace of Apries*, xxvi, 10) and those made in Greek times. These latter are all of one style, and many bear the Seleucid emblem of the anchor ; it seems likely that they were left by the Syrian army of Antiochos IV in 171 B.C., when he besieged and took Memphis. The types are, seven as V 15, 16, with thunderbolt ; four as V 17 to 19 with thunderbolt and star ; eight as V 20, 21 with thunderbolt and anchor ; V 22 with anchor alone ; five as V 23 with trident.

HARPOONS: (V)

24–51, pl. xliv; 52–58, pl. xliii

97. The earliest harpoons in Egypt appear to be the three-toothed bone harpoons, as V 47 of the first prehistoric age, between S.D. 34 and 38. After this the single barb head is more usual; V 43 is of 33–54 S.D.; V 46 and duplicate V 48 of 49–63 S.D.; V 45 and duplicate of 48 are from the south town at Nubt. All of these are from Naqadeh, and none are recorded from the other large cemeteries of Diospolis or El Amrah. These bone or horn harpoons must begin as early as S.D. 38, and may perhaps not extend beyond S.D. 50, belonging thus to the earlier part of the second prehistoric age. Of the copper harpoons a small one is as early as S.D. 34–38, and larger ones are dated to S.D. 54 and 61. No trace of the harpoon was found in the 2000 graves of the Tarkhan cemetery, S.D. 77 to 82. Purely ceremonial copper harpoons were in the royal tombs of the Ist dynasty, V 56 of Zer, and V 55 of Semerkhet; of the same date must be V 33, and near that age V 34, 35. Models roughly cut in sheet copper are of the close of the iind dynasty, V 36, 37 of Khosekhemui. In the xiith dynasty at Harageh two small harpoons were found, V 38, 39. The early form survived till the xviiith dynasty, as found in the Maket tomb (P.I. xxvi, 47). The representation of lancing the harpoon at fish is one of the commonest scenes in tombs from the vth to the xviiith dynasties. The truth seems to be that the harpoon as a means of livelihood ceased in the second prehistoric age; but as an instrument of sport it lasted much later, though in the latest paintings it may be only a religious archaism. Two examples quite isolated, are V 51, a large harpoon of iron, probably Roman, and V 50, a harpoon head of slate. Of duplicates of the photographed examples there are 3 of 40, and 2 of 47.

On the European side the bone harpoon was a favourite implement in the Magdalenian period, as V 52, 53; it is generally barbed on both sides, and where only on one side, there are many barbs. In Europe it was not commonly continued into the copper age, as it was in Egypt; two little ones from North Italy, V 54, 57, are all that I have noted. The fishing harpoons are very usual along the northern coasts of America; nearly all of these differ from the European and Egyptian, by being toggle harpoons, with a short head, which turned across the wound on being pulled, and so held firmly in the seal. The use of a pair of harpoon heads on a very long casting spear, is singularly alike in the Egyptian and American use. See fig. 19 in the exhaustive memoir by Otis T. Mason on *Aboriginal American Harpoons* (Smithsonian Inst. 1902).

The barbed iron objects from Defenneh, V 58, may be for some use in fishing.

FISH-HOOKS: (V)

61–87 pl. xliv; 59, 60, 88–102, pl. xliii

98. The earliest dated fish-hook is of the age of Den, Ist dynasty, found at Abydos, V 59. Probably as early is 61 (xliv), which was found at Ballas with a pottery cist burial of the Ist or iind dynasty. Next is a hook 60 (xliii) from the grave of Perabsen. This shows the beginning of the angular hook, which is seen farther in the hooks painted in a tomb of the Old Kingdom (L.D. ii, 96), exactly of the form V 62. The two delicately made hooks, 62, 63, are of the xiith dynasty from Kahun; 62 has the line still attached to it, which was wound round a papyrus letter. V 64 to 67 are of the same age from Harageh. The old polygonal type of 62–3 still remains, and no barb was yet used, in the xviiith dynasty at Amarna, 68. But the hooks from Gurob of the xviiith or xixth dynasty 71–78 are barbed, and very nearly approach the modern "Limerick bend." One of the xxvith dynasty is merely rounded, V 95, xliii. 69, 70 from Quft are not dated; 79 is unplaced. 80 is a large iron hook from Balyzeh, Coptic; it is evidently strained out of shape. The hooks 81–86 are all unplaced; the last is a very unusual double hook. (There are two duplicates from Kahun, and five from Gurob.) The great hook 87 is of iron, from Wushym in the Fayum, of Roman age. Such a size was required for the enormous fish over five feet in length, such as are still caught in the Nile (see *Medum*, xii; and *Saqqara Mastabas I*, chapter by L. Loat).

The European fish-hooks do not appear before the *fonderia* age. The statistics of the Lake Bourget finds show fish-hooks to be rarer than needles or borers. Considering how the lake dwellings must have relied upon fishing, the moderate number of fish-hooks points to their depending more on nets. The few copied here, 88–94, are merely rounded, without any peculiar form. In Greece,

96–98, and Roman Italy, 99–102, hooks are common; 100 is the usual pattern, 101 and 102 are the limits of size.

SCALE ARMOUR (V)

103–128, pl. xlii; 129–132, pl. xliii; 133, xlii

99. The earliest metal scales, apparently, are a set of bronze scales, large and thick, which were found by the temple of Amenhetep II at Thebes, V 105–8, xlii. There are seventeen of them, and each has two nails driven halfway through, at the middle of the length. These prove that these scales were not worn as armour; and, as a scale pattern is usually figured on the sides of thrones, it seems likely that these scales are from the sides of a wooden throne, perhaps belonging to a statue in the temple.

Somewhat similar are seven larger scales, also with nails, V 104, and a large hinged scale, V 103, of unknown source. The hinge suggests actual wear on the person; yet the scales are so thick, that the weight would be prohibitive, to say nothing of the projecting nails. The only explanation seems to be that they were nailed on to a wooden statue: such may also have been the use of the scales V 105–8. A limestone torso of a figure, lying at Karnak, is covered with such rounded scales, which probably indicate scale armour.

The next examples are the figures of corslets of scale armour under Amenhetep II (L.D. iii, 64) and in the tomb of Rameses III (G. W. 53a; R.M.C. cxxi). Shortly after, there are actual pieces of scale armour of Sheshenq I; the scales are of two forms, V 129, 130, with the cartouche upon them. Iron scale armour was used by the Assyrians, and found in large quantities of Khorsabad; the scales were rounded at one end, and had a mid-rib to stiffen them, as in V 115–117 (L.N.R. i, 341).

On reaching the xxvith dynasty there is abundant material, especially from Memphis (*Palace of Apries*, xvi). The series of forms kept here are eighteen of small bronze scales (V 109–14, thirty-two iron scales (118–25), bronze ridge-plate 115, iron ridge plates 116, 117, and masses of scales 127, 128. Similar examples of overlapping scales were found at Defenneh, V 131, 132. From the absence of Egyptian figures of the Saite age in scale armour, and the known frequency of iron scale armour among the Persians (*Herodotos*, vii, 61), it seems probable that both the Memphite and Daphniote armour belonged to the Persian invaders, who occupied those places. Hence we may say that it is only when Egypt was under strong Asiatic influence, or occupation, that scale armour appears, and that it was therefore of Asiatic origin.

On the rise of scale armour from leather and horn defences, and its Chinese development in metal, see *Chinese Clay Figures* by Berthold Laufer (Field Museum, Chicago, 1914); that work, though on more primitive stages of defence, only discusses post-Roman examples, except touching the Herodotos quotation. Therefore as regards date it is entirely later than the examples dealt with here. (See especially pp. 191 and 239.)

V 133 is a shield boss of iron from Egypt, with a plain short spike. It is most like the Frankish type, and was doubtless introduced by the same Roman auxiliaries who brought various Frankish ornaments into Egypt. The Ala i Francorum was stationed at Contra Apollinopolis and the Cohors vii Francorum at Diospolis (*Not. Dign.*) about 425 A.D. Other northern troops were the Sigambrians, Germans, Jutungs, Alamanni, Vandals, Rhaetians, Quadi and Sarmatians; these will fully account for much of northern origin found in Egypt.

RASPS AND SCRAPERS: (V)

134–37, pl. xliv

100. Small conical rasps are not uncommon about the xviiith dynasty. They were made by punching a sheet of bronze to throw out a rough burr, and then coiling it into a cone. Two here, V 134–5, are from Koptos, and there are five from Gurob in worse state.

Two very simple scrapers or scoops, V 136–7, are from Kahun, of the xiith dynasty. They are made by inserting a bivalve shell into a piece of reed, and then binding it around with string. The thimble and the hammer at the end of pl. xliv are noticed under Needles, N 110, sect. 147, and Hammers, M 97A, sect. 111.

CHAPTER VIII

ARTISANS' TOOLS: (M)

Pls. xliii, xlvi, xlviii, lxxviii

101. The brace has not been found in any Roman remains, although there are bits with square shanks. The earliest figure of the modern

brace that I have seen (M.1. xliii) is in a picture (28) at Naples dated 1523; that is of the pattern used with little change till the present time, cut in wood with chamfered edges. Another, M 2, of nearly the same pattern, but simpler, was used in Holland in 1694. In the group of Assyrian tools at Thebes, there were found with the bits a pair of bent pieces of iron with rounded points M. 3 (lxxviii); the wood with which they may have been connected had entirely disappeared, but it would seem as if they were parts of a crank brace of some kind for working the bits.

102. The pump-drill is not known before Roman times. It is made of a length of stout reed, xlviii M 4; this was found at Hawara. It is shown, M 5 (xliii), in a picture of S. Eligio by Roselli in the *Antica e Moderna* at Florence, probably about 1480.

103. The bow drill has been a general tool for thousands of years. Probably the earliest form was an arrow twisted by a bowstring around it. The bow form was soon modified in Egypt, much wider at one end than the other, to allow of the hand holding it at one end. Drill stocks of the xiith dynasty were found at Kahun. M 6 (xliii) is complete, with the discharge hole to eject the drill. M 7 is from Gurob of the xviiith dynasty. In M 8 (xlviii) the stock is unfinished; it is of the xiith dynasty, as well as the bow, both from Kahun,but not found together. The caps of such drills were, some of wood as M 6, 7, others of hard black quartzose stone (ten here), with highly polished holes, as M 9, 10, 11 (xlviii). It seems that the hieroglyph *t*, which is always coloured black, is taken from the hemispherical drill cap, such as M 9. The bow drill is often represented in scenes in the tombs; in some cases three drills worked by one bow, as R.M.C. lii; M.A.F. V 569, ii, both xviiith dynasty. The earliest examples do not show detail, but that of the xiith dynasty, M 13 (xliii), is more explicit, and also those of the xviiith, M 12, 14. A perfect example is in pl. li, M 15, from Hawara, of Roman age. The stock is turned; and the cap has been made in two halves, pegged together, in order to hold a ball head of the stock, so that the cap cannot be removed. The bow drill was used by the Dutch pearl borers in 1694 (M 16, xliii), and is still usual in the East, where the bow is also the regular means of turning the lathe.

104. Rimers of regular form do not seem to have been found in Egypt. An elementary one occurs in the *fonderia* at Bologna M 17 (xliii); and a well-developed octagonal rimer comes from Pompeii (M 18). A punch here, lxxviii, M 137, is from the Assyrian group of the viith century B.C.

105. Bits for drilling are found in the Assyrian group of tools of about 670 B.C. at Thebes. One is an excellent scoop drill of mild steel with an S-section, so that both of the edges should cut forward in rotating, M 19 (lxxviii). A small scoop drill of bronze comes from Peschiera, Lago di Garda, M 20, xliii. A well-formed scoop drill, like the modern spoon bit, M 23 is from the Roman camp of Newstead. Four flat drills, too much rusted and broken to show exact detail of the cutter, are of Roman age from Germany and Pompeii (21, 22, 26, 27). The idea of a centre bit was started as early as the Assyrian group, M 24, 25 (lxxviii). These have a central peg, and a scraper at each side of it. The use of a cutter to clear the outer edge was not yet brought in; but the central steadying point was used here, as also in the facing tool used to clean the cast copper discs for the Ptolemaic coinage.

106. The auger with a cross head, was apparently used at Defenneh (M 28), where it would be in great request for shipbuilding. In the middle ages it was used in France, M 29, and it is shown as a large scoop or taper auger used by ship-builders and wheelwrights in Holland, 1694 (M 30, 31).

107. The drawing knife was made at Pompeii, apparently without any wooden handles, M 32, 33. Another, M 34, from Oberolm (in Mainz Museum) is assigned to Frankish times. Much the same curve, with handles added, was the Dutch tool in 1694 (M 35). A form (M 37) with long handles at right angles to the blade, so as to get a dragging cut, comes from Auvergne, of the later iron age or Roman period. Two of the same principle were used in Sweden, M 36, 38; and this is still known as the cooper's two-hand round shave, of the Liverpool pattern.

108. The plane seems to have been a Roman invention. There are four from Pompeii, of the form of M 39. A continuous plate of iron goes from the back, along the base, over the front and top, and is rivetted to the base plate at the back. The top opening is cut through this plate. A cross bolt, run through the wooden body, serves to block the wedge which holds the cutter in place. This seems preferable to our side grooves for the purpose, and the bolt at that height would scarcely be in the way of the shavings. The Silchester

plane, M 139, lxxviii, is iron shod and faced, over a wooden block; but—though decayed—it does not appear to have had a back hole for a handle. The planes figured by Gruter and found at Rastadt have two holes through the body; one found at Cologne has only an iron body, without wood block, there is also a broken one from the Saalburg (see *Archaeologia*, 1894, 139). From Newstead is a plane iron for shooting mouldings, 40, the only example I have met, though such was obviously used for the wooden mouldings of Roman age.

The mediaeval French plane, M 41, was inferior to the Roman pattern in the clearance of it; it had the modern side grooves for cutter and wedge, and added a front handle. It is curious that modern planes should have dropped the back and front handles, and adopted for the trying plane, a handle nearer the middle, which does not guide the plane so well, or else dropped the handle altogether in the smoothing plane. In France and Germany a horn-shaped front handle still survives.

109. The anvil came into use in the bronze age for fine work; probably so small an anvil as M 42 was for goldsmiths, like the beautiful set of small bronze tools in the British Museum (C 227, C 168, two tiny hammers and anvil), found at Lusmagh in Ireland. Other small anvils of Roman age M 43, 44 are from Pompeii. The large anvil M 45 from there is of the same form as that from Silchester M 46 (lxxviii). These are strictly smiths' bick irons. Other iron anvils from there are for shoemakers' lasts, M 47, 48 (drawings are in A. liv. 139). Further examples, from Heidenberg, are in the Mainz Museum (M. v. 46). A curious kind of portable anvil used for dressing scythes in the field, was also found at Silchester, M 50, 51, lxxviii, where it is shown with exactly similar anvils, 49, 52, now used in Spain and North Italy. Probably stones were put under the side rings, to increase the bearing upon the ground.

110. The wooden mallet was a primitive tool, which has not yet been superseded. The earliest Egyptian form, pl. xlv, is a piece of a branch, thinned down at one end to give a hold, as M 53 from Kahun, xiith dynasty, 54, 55, from vth and vith dynasties, 59 of the xiith dynasty, M 60 (xlvi) from Deshasheh, vth dynasty, 61 from Kahun, xiith dynasty. A mallet of limestone, 62, from Kahun, of the xiith dynasty, is very unusual. The small mallet, 63, is a tomb model of that used for driving a mooring peg. The usual type in the xiith to xixth dynasties was a large head with cylindrical handle, cut in one block of wood. The head was usually conical, as M 64, 65, 68; otherwise bulbous, as 56, 57, 58 (xlv), 70 (xlvi), oblong as 66, 67 (xlvi), or cylindrical, M 69. The last occurs also in Slesvig, M 87 (xlv). The form with a long handle, cut from the stem and branch of a tree, is as old as the vth dynasty, M 71 (xlvi) from Deshasheh. It is also found in Slesvig (79, 80, xlv) of Roman age. The inserted handle in a socket is not found in Egypt till Greek times, M 76, 77 from the tomb of Aba at Thebes, and 72 to 75 from the Fayum (xlvi). This was the usual form in Italy, M 78, and Europe in general, from Roman times to the present, for masons, 82, 83, and carpenters, 84, 85.

111. The hammer with a handle was strangely neglected by the Egyptians. In all ages they used a smooth stone in the hand, even for the heavy work of beating out copper vessels. How they endured the shock to the wrist, in a long course of such work, cannot be imagined. Yet, though the mallet was regularly used by masons, they never used a similar tool for hammering metal. The earliest hammers of the European bronze age are pouch-shaped tools, developed from the socketted axe,—pounders rather than hammers. The true hammer only appears just before iron becomes general, in one example of bronze from South Italy, M 86 (xlv). Another of bronze (Brit. Mus.) has a heron in relief on the faces, apparently about 400 B.C. The early iron hammer of the Greeks, 87, was small and light; the larger size of smith's hammer does not appear till Roman times (92 to 97 and 136, lxxviii). A model hammer of bronze, M 97A, is shown in pl. xliv. The mediaeval and later forms in 98, 99, show the essential points of the smith's hammer, a heavy square head, with a wide edge for rivetting and detailed work.

The mason's hammer was of the mallet type, equal at both ends, as the massive ones 100, 101, which are like the sculptor's hammer, 107, of 1694. Lighter sizes were also used as 103, 104, and 105 from Silchester (lxxviii). The hammers heavier at one end, 102, 106, are peculiar, and must have been awkward to hold, from their want of balance.

The carpenter's hammer, or claw hammer, for drawing nails, is also a Roman type, 108, 109; the latter is most like a modern farrier's hammer, and that may have been its use. The claw-hammer four centuries ago (112) was made exactly as on the Continent at present. The light hammer, 110, might be for carpentry, or fine metal work, as it is not heavy enough for the smithy. 111 is the form of modern shipwright's hammer. Other forms of special trade hammers, 113, 114, 116, 118–120, are shown in the engravings of 1694. The axe-hammer, 115 (lxxviii), from Silchester, was probably for wooden building work, like a modern lath hammer. The Roman, 117, was probably a cooper's hammer.

112. Tongs are not represented earlier than on the pre-Roman coins of Malaga, where they are shown behind the head of Vulcan. None of the existing tongs can be dated before the Roman period. They were at that age well developed with special forms of jaws to hold the work, like modern box-tongs 121, 122 (xlv); 123 (lxxviii). The simple tongs of all sizes are usual, as 124 to 130. The Swedish form 126, with a locking catch, was intended to maintain the grip while the tongs were turned round and round in the left hand, to hammer on all sides. The same form, but without a catch, is found at Newstead (C.N. lxiii), and Heidenberg (M.V. 46).

Pincers are rare; one pair from Sweden, 131 (like the modern Lancashire pincers), is not dated. None seem to be known of Roman age, even from Pompeii.

Lifting tongs for light objects are shown in a goldsmith's hand at Thebes, of the xviiith dynasty, M 134. Two very slender bronze tongs come from La Tène (132), and the celebrated group of the Heathery Burn cave (133); slender tongs with the ends turned down, were used by chemists in 1694 (135).

CHAPTER IX

BUILDERS' TOOLS: (B)

1–6 pl. xlvii, 7 xiii, 8–15 xlvii, 16–25 xiii, 26–27 lxxviii, 28–29 xlix, 40–43 xlvii, 44–50 xlix, 51–63 xlvii, 64–89 xlviii, 90–93 xlvii, 94 xlviii.

113. THE trowel was probably required for the refined building of the Greek age, but the earliest that we have are Roman from Pompeii, B 1, 2, 3. The Egyptians merely used the hand as they now do in the villages; and finger marks are plain on the mortar of the great pyramid, as also on the brickwork mortaring of all periods. A small trowel comes from Sweden, 6. Smaller tools, perhaps used for smoothing wax tablets, 4, 5, are in the Kircherian Museum. A plasterer's moulding tool comes from Egypt, B 7, xiii; and B 8, xlvii, from Newstead seems to be a moulding tool with a spoon at one end to hold the plaster, though it is called an auger by Mr. Curle. The Dutch trowel, 9, used in 1694 was triangular, like our modern London trowel. The Scotch trowel has curved sides. Mortar-rakes were used in Egypt in later times. An iron model of one, B 10, was in a foundation deposit of Ptolemy II; and I bought a bronze one in Egypt, now in the British Museum, B 11.

114. Wedges for splitting blocks of stone are often found of iron, 12–14. One of bronze, B 15, is from Defenneh. The iron wedges from Egypt begin with two from the Ramesseum, B 16, 17 (xiii), probably about 800 B.C. Two are from Defenneh, 600 B.C., B 18, 19. Two from Naukratis, B 20, 21, may be 600–300 B.C. Two others are undated, B 22, 23. Two of the "feathers," or thin flakes of iron for placing between the wedge and the stone in splitting, are at B 24, 25. Two wedges are from Silchester, of Roman age, B 26, 27 (lxxviii). Two iron punches, 28, 29 (xiii), were found at Gurob.

Wooden chisels were used by the early Egyptians for excavating in gravel and marl. Many such were found in an unfinished pit at Deshasheh, vth dynasty, as B 30, 31 (xlix). 32 to 35 are of the xiith dynasty from Kahun; 36 is from Gurob.

115. For shifting large building stones the Egyptians seem to have placed them on a cradle of wood, so that they could be readily twisted round, drawn along, or rocked up an inclined plane. Models of these cradles are found, with other tools, in the foundation deposits, as B 37 from Deir el Bahri. See *Arts and Crafts*, p. 75.

For shifting the large blocks, rollers of wood were used, short, and with rounded ends, to prevent their catching. Many such were found in the builders' waste of the pyramid of Lahun, B 38, 39.

The crowbar has not been found in Egypt before Roman time, either in scenes or actual example. In the deposits of Tausert and Saptah (*Six Temples at Thebes*, xvi, 26, 27; xviii, 44, 45) were some rolled-up slips of copper bent at the end, but it is not at all certain that they were models of crowbars. The modern forms of crowbar, with forked end, and also with chisel end, are found at Pompeii, B 40 (xlvii). Also short forms of extractors for nails, 41, 42, like the French *lève-clous*. A crowbar from Memphis, which is probably Roman, is in *Memphis*, iii, pl. xxxviii (Univ. Coll.). For lifting stones with a windlass the Roman had invented the lewis, as used at present. A slit was sunk in the upper face of the stone, enlarged below at the two ends. The two tapering pieces of B 43 were then dropped in and pushed apart by the plain strip between them. A rod was then passed through the eyes on the three pieces, which thus could not be withdrawn from the stone; in this way the block could be lifted by the rod as a handle.

116. For dressing down large blocks to a true face, the system was to run saw cuts about half an inch in on all sides; the surface was then hammer dressed, nearly down to the plane of the cuts. The fine dressing—as shown in the tomb of Rekhmara (pl. lxxix)—was done by holding two rods of wood square to the face, upon the saw cut on opposite sides. A string was stretched between the tops of the rods. Then a mason held a rod of equal length on any point of the stone, and the amount which that stood above the string showed how much had to be chiselled away. Many of these rods have been found. B 49, xlix, is a set of round rods, 3·00 inches long; B 50 is a set of square rods from Beni Hasan 3·40 long; other odd rods are B 44 (2·64 inches), 45 (3·12), 46 (2·93), 47 (3·51), 48 (3·11 inches). The two end rods always have a hole from the side coming out on the top, for the string; the third rod is plain.

For dressing the faces of stones the Egyptian used an adze, from the pyramid times onwards. The result was tested by laying on it a true plane—or facing plate—covered with red ochre. The claw tool or comb-pick was invented in Greece (B 51, 52, xlvii). The pre-Persian masonry at Athens shows the characteristic grooving due to it, according to the late Prof. Hayter Lewis. This comb-marking is the token of Greek and Roman work in Egypt, both in rock-cutting and stone-dressing. The tools then used have not been recovered; the forms given here are those used in the xiiith century in France, and 51 is the common form to-day in Egypt, where the tool is generally used. It is to be noted that Viollet-le-Duc states that the marks of this mode of dressing are only to be found in Europe in the xiith, xiiith, and early xivth centuries, that is, the period of the crusades. Doubtless the mixture with the east at that time brought these tools, as well as much else, into western use.

117. The Egyptian used the hand for spreading plaster in early times. But the need of finely stuccoed walls for tomb painting, and probably for houses also, led to the use of the plasterer's float. B 53, 54 are two forms of plasterer's float of the xiith dynasty, found at Kahun. They are very rarely found, for I have not seen any others.

Brick moulds must have been in use in the later prehistoric times, as brick building was then common. The only examples that I have seen are one of the xiith dynasty found at Kahun, B 55, and a model, probably from a foundation deposit, pl. lxxvii, B 56. The modern mould is much like it, but not so well made, being only nailed at the corners, and not mortised.

118. The use of the plumb line must have started with Egyptian building, and the plumb bob has been found at the end of the iiird dynasty, B 64, xlviii. The mode of using the plumb line is shown by a mark on pottery of the xith dynasty (*Gizeh Rifeh*, xiii, J. 5), and the model B 57 of the xixth dynasty. This, with the squares and level, 58–60 (xlvii), all come from the tomb of an architect Sen-nehem, a group now in the Cairo Museum. These were not the actual working tools, but copies of them made to place with the burial. The **A** form of levelling plumb line (B 59), and the square with a foot (B 60), were both used in Roman work, as shown on the stele of Aebutius in the Capitoline Museum, Rome.

The plumb bob in Egypt was first made with a groove round it, in which to tie the line, see B 64 from Meydum, and B 65, both probably from the end of the iiird dynasty (pl. xlviii). The square bob of hard brown limestone (B 66), with a hole through it for the line, was found at Gizeh; it bears the name *Khuf*, and is doubtless of Khufu. B 67, 68 are without a history, but belong probably to the vith or xiith dynasty. B 69 is from Quft, undated. B 70 is of limestone, 71 of alabaster. B 72 of limestone, and 73 of marble, are from Kahun, of the xiith dynasty; the system for the line was to have a short vertical hole in the axis, and across this a hole from side to side; the line was put through the axial hole, the end pushed out to one side, and knotted to retain it. 74 is of limestone. 75 is of yellow limestone, 76 of wood, and 77 of shelly limestone, all three from Kahun. 78 is of limestone, 79 of steatite, 80 of limestone, 81 from Kahun of limestone. 82, 83, 84 are of lead, probably of Greek age. 85 is of steatite, 86 of diorite, 87 of limestone, 88 of black steatite. B 89 is a remarkable Roman cubic plumb bob of nummulitic limestone, with figures of gods on the sides; Horus, Hathor, and Amen ? can be distinguished.

The Roman bobs on pl. xlvii are B 90, of marble with a bronze loop; 91, 92, 93 of bronze. 92 is of the form on the stele of Aebutius.

119. The square was doubtless used in early times in Egypt, but no example occurs until the model from the tomb of Sen-nehem, B 60. A similar form, with a foot, is figured in the tomb of Rekhmara (xviiith dynasty) and on the stele of Aebutius. The plain square of wood, B 94 (xlix), was found in the destroyers' rubbish at the pyramid of Lahun, probably Ptolemaic. Another plain square, from Pompeii, B 61, is of bronze.

The need of a mitre square was naturally felt in Egypt; a carpenter of the xviiith dynasty has the form 62, with a foot to slide along an edge; a bronze square with a foot, and mitre slope comes from Pompeii; and another without a foot is represented on a stele, 63.

CHAPTER X

THE SAW, SICKLE, AND BILL-HOOK

THE SAW: (S) PLS. XLVIII, L, LI

120. THE saw is certainly as early as the beginning of the first dynasty. The large number of wooden coffins of that age must have been sawn, and on one piece the varying directions of the marks show how troublesome the work proved to be (*Tarkhan*, i, xxiv). Beside that use of sawing, the great amount of boards, required for the wooden architecture, also must have required much sawing. The oldest saw found is a model early in the iiird dynasty, S 1. A piece of a roughly notched saw of copper was found at Meydum, of iiird dynasty, S 2, xlviii. In the vth and vith dynasties are many scenes of sawing, from which may be quoted the two types of saw, with a handle in one with the blade, S 3, and with an added handle, S 4. A model is of the xith dynasty, S 5. Another model of about the same age is S 6 (xlviii). In the xiith dynasty the handle is of the old form, S 7; and also turned more away from the blade, S 8, in order to get a larger surface for pushing, exactly like the modern French miner's saw. This same idea of the handle remained in the xviiith dynasty, as S 9, and saws figured in the tomb of Rekhmara. The rudest kind of saw was merely a blade notched by chopping on it, as S 10 (xlviii), and S 11, pl. l. All of the preceding blades were probably of hardened copper.

121. Of bronze saws the earliest European is perhaps that from Knossos, S 12, which is a very slightly notched blade. Another roughly made saw is from the lake dwellers, S 13. So far there does not seem to have been any distinction in the direction of the teeth. The saw was simply an abrading instrument for scraping out a groove equally by pushing and pulling, like the tenon teeth of a modern cross-cut saw.

The true cutting saw is that in which the teeth all have a rake in one direction, and are a series of cutters, while in the back stroke they do not act. The first such saw appears in the *fonderia* group at Bologna, invented apparently at the same mechanical outburst which produced the perfect tang and socket chisels. Among the small pieces of bronze saws, S 14–18, one of them, 15, has the teeth all pointing one way. From the thinness of these pieces it seems that they were framed saws (as S 42 to 45); but there is nothing to show whether the true saw was pushed or pulled. The Spanish copper saw, S 19, was clearly a pull-saw. The pieces from El Argar, Rome, Felixstowe, Moeringen, and Naples, S 20 to 24, were all worked both ways. Other bronze saws of small size have been found in the Jura, Charente, Hautes Alpes, Spain and Portugal, see D.M. ii, 274. Two beautiful and delicate saws are from Reggio and Ephesos (S 25, 26). Near the butt, where it has not been spoilt in sharpening, the Reggio saw shows that it was a pull-saw; and the Ephesos saw is so slight that it must have been pulled. These are supposed to have been for surgery, and are the latest of the bronze saws.

122. The iron and steel saws begin at least as early as 666 B.C. In the Theban group of the Assyrian armourer (lxxviii) were three saws; one double edged and narrow, probably a framed saw, S 27; the other two blades have a decided rake in the teeth, and both of them were pull-saws (S 28). Half of a large saw from Nimrud (29) has the teeth equal, without any rake.

In Europe the saw had another development with triangular teeth, cris-cross, S 30; this same form was used for the saw backs of the Russian swords, in the Crimean War. Plain pull and push teeth were made at La Tène (31, 32) and the Roman saws from Newstead (33) and Pompeii (34). The little saw from La Tène (32) shows a neat handling, with a disc to hold between the thumb and finger of the right hand, and a turned-up end for the left hand, so that a firm pressure and direction could be applied. In the Pompeian saw, S 34, the teeth show it to have been pushed, if the lower end is the handle; but it may have been one end of a framed saw. The teeth are almost like a pit saw. On pl. li is a large framed saw, 35, complete with the bentwood frame. The band saw was originally held by a pin at each end; but the frame contracted with the pull, and so the surplus length of blade was taken up by giving it a turn half round the end of the frame. The teeth have a moderate rake. This comes from the Fayum. Another blade of a framed saw, 36, has deeply raked teeth, at the lower end where not spoiled by sharpening. S 37 is a roughly notched iron blade, from a handle saw. Two pieces of a very coarse band saw, 39, 40 (xlviii) are from Oxyrhynkhos. Thus it seems that the pull-saw with raked teeth began at about 900 B.C.; that there is no evidence of a push-saw in Roman times; and there is no trace of setting the teeth alternately to one side and to the other, so as to cut a wide kerf, in any ancient saw. The Dutch saw of 1694 shows the earlier form of the curious little notch on the back, which is still continued in modern saws, without a meaning. It seems originally to have been a tapering of the blade to the end, interrupted by a projection, with a hole in it for hanging up the saw, S 41.

123. Of framed saws the modern bow saw descends from a Roman form, S 42. In this there was apparently no means of tightening the saw; that may have been done by a little hammering inside the bow. The handle was attached too far from the saw, so that the push was indirect. The framed saw is often represented on Roman sculptures, as S 43. The Dutch carpenter's framed saw for wood is S 44, and mason's saw for stone is S 45. This is provided with a handle at the end, as the end pieces were too large to grasp.

124. The coarse file is a form of saw, which seems to have begun about 900 B.C., as it is found of bronze at Bologna and at Hallstatt, S 48. This is a combination of a broad and a narrow file. Of iron there is the crippled file from Auvergne, 50, and a good one from Silchester, S 47 (lxxviii). A half-round file of iron comes from La Tène (Volk. Mus. Berlin). The fine-cut file begins with the Assyrian group, lxxviii, S 46. This is like a thick-backed knife, hatched with fine parallel cuts on both faces. It seems to be the parent of the modern three-cornered file, or saw file. The cross-cut file was known in 1417 at Nürnberg. The rasp is found in a perfect form in the Assyrian group (S 49), exactly of the modern shape and detail.

125. The very important work of Egyptian hard-stone cutting is only known by the results, as unfortunately there are no tools left; but the abundance of pieces of waste showing the methods employed, and the marks upon the finished work, are enough to prove the general methods. Only a small selection of the specimens are illustrated here. On pl. lii, 51, 52 and 53 are plain faces of saw cuts; 51 is a piece of waste of grey syenite; 52 is part of the face of a basalt block of Khufu's temple; 53 is a cast of the face of the granite sarcophagus of Khufu, where the cut was running too deep, and was brought further out. Nos. 54 to 57 show the breadth of the saw, which varied from $\frac{1}{30}$th to $\frac{1}{5}$th of an inch; 54 is a cut across a slice of basalt (Khufu); 55 is a row of cuts in hard quartz rock, the piece here being the heel left from slicing up a block; 56 is a piece of Khufu's basalt paving, where the saw had run much askew, and been backed out to a fresh face; 57 is a cast of the side of the portcullis in the great pyramid, showing the marking out of work in granite by a saw cut, to limit the hammer-dressing of a face.

These specimens amply prove the use of saws which could cut granite. The saw cuts ran from end to end of the sarcophagus of Khufu over $7\frac{1}{2}$ feet long. Allowing for the throw of the saw in cutting, the blade must have been about 9 feet long. The material of it was doubtless copper, as no other metal was common at that time. The actual cutting was certainly done by some hard stone; in what way we shall consider further on.

126. Another application of the same method of working was by the tubular drill. This is illustrated by the alabaster vase, 64, with the drill core still in it, and the split vase, 65, in which a drill core is now laid. 66 is a plaster cast of a drill hole in a lintel of the granite temple at Gizeh, showing the stump of the core left in it. 63 is a scrap of hard limestone, on which drills have been tried. The most perfect core is of red granite from Gizeh, 59. On this a continuous groove of the drilling point can be traced for several rotations, forming a true screw thread, and showing a rapid descent of the drill. The grooves run continuously across the quartz and felspar crystals without the least check; as the felspar is worn down (by rubbing) more than the quartz, the latter crystals stand highest;

yet the grooves run with an even bottom through a greater depth of quartz than of felspar. Every mechanician who has examined this agrees that nothing but a fixed point could have cut such grooves. A loose cutting powder might wear grooves, but they would have been slighter in the harder crystal, instead of deeper, and they could not pass across the fissures between varying crystals without a check. Another core of granite has finer grooves, 62. No. 61 is a core from an enlarged hole in basalt; a lesser hole had been cut and found too small, and then a larger hole was made, detaching thus a tube of basalt. 60 is a piece of the outer side of a drill hole in diorite. 63 to 65 are noted above. 58 is a block of red quartzite sandstone, with a curved surface, which looks as if it were the outer side of a drill cut. The diameter of 28 inches seems impossibly large; yet no other motion would produce a cylindrical surface with perfect parallelism of the grooves, and the circumference would not be longer than the straight saws.

67 is a drill core of alabaster. 68 is a core of black and white porphyry, a stone which is only known to have been wrought in the beginning of the 1st dynasty; it implies that tube-drilling was already then developed with extremely hard fine cutting points. 69, 70, 71 are cores of alabaster from vases, showing the different sizes.

Nos. 72 and 73 are borers of sandstone, used along with sand for boring out the interior of vases. The hour-glass form of 73 was to enable it to be slipped through a neck, and then turned flat to drill a wider hole. It was rotated by a forked stick holding the contracted part.

The tubular drill was used for all the hollowing out of granite sarcophagi; the traces of the sides of drill holes are seen inside the sarcophagus of Khufu. Rows of holes were cut, and then the material that was left was broken away. Similarly statuary was rough sawn, and the hollows cut out with tube drills. The base of such a drill-hole remains between the feet of the great statue of Khofra at Cairo, the space between the legs having been hollowed by a long drill hole. A small statuette of quartz crystal, at University College, has been begun by the profiles of front and sides being cut out by a saw, as the first stage in working it. See *Arts and Crafts*, fig. 89.

127. Lastly, what were the cutting points used on hard stones? That they were fixed points is shown by the grooves in quartz and felspar noted above. That they were extremely hard is proved by a point cutting through quartz crystal, and the very fine grooves on the black and white porphyry core. The same is shown by the lines graved on diorite with a cutting point, for hieroglyphs. These are not scraped, but ploughed out with a single cut. The line is only $\frac{1}{150}$th of an inch wide, so a very strong and tough point would be needed. That emery was familiar to the Egyptians at that time is certain, as it was used long before that in the prehistoric age. But could any emery point stand such pressure on a fine edge? The difficulty would be settled at once if we could find any bort or diamond known at that age. Engineers with full experience of the subject, do not believe that emery could do the cutting. Sir Benjamin Baker remarked that any engineer now would be proud to turn out such drill cores as the Egyptians did. Certainly modern diamond drill cores are clumsy and smudged work, when compared to the Egyptian cores. If this is the best we can do with diamond, can we suppose the Egyptians beating us with only emery?

For the irregular forms of hieroglyphs, tube drilling was used at the corners, and sawing out with blades fed with emery around the outlines. This is proved by the scratches on the surrounding polished surface, where the tool has slipped and scored over the face. The inner mass was broken away, and the hollow polished.

128. The method of hard-stone sawing was not unknown elsewhere on the Mediterranean. At Tiryns the hard limestone was cut with saws as in the Egyptian work. In one of the saw cuts I saw a lump of green material. This seemed likely to be a bit of a saw, broken off and jammed in the cut. I called Dr. Walter Leaf as a witness, and removed half of the green material. It had every appearance of corrosion of copper. In the powder were small rectangular lumps of a black material, about $\frac{1}{16}$th inch long. These were determined to be emery, at the Mineralogical Department, British Museum. Such lumps of emery could not possibly be used as a loose powder; by their size they must have been set in the copper saws. The Tiryns example therefore proves the use of set-stone saws; being only for cutting hard limestone, emery would there suffice, but this does not at all prove that emery was used for the Egyptian granite work.

For cutting the soft alabaster, plain sand was amply hard; and where alabaster vases have been cut, of the early dynasties at Hierakonpolis, and of Greek times at Memphis, large quantities of sand and alabaster dust have been found.

129. On pl. liii are the mauls used for dressing down surfaces of stone. They were regularly employed in the pyramid period, all the hard stone that was not sawn being bruised down to a flat face, and afterwards polished. This was the method for the whole of the king's chamber in the pyramid of Khufu, and for the statue of Khofra, on which the stunned marks of blows may be seen not completely ground out. No. 74 is from Meydum, iiird dynasty. 75, 76 are of syenite from Gizeh. 77 is of basalt from Gizeh. 78, 79, 80 are quarry tools of basalt from the Sinai mines, used in cutting the sandstone at Serabît. Others are published in *Researches in Sinai*, figs. 56–58. Besides these, flint flakes were largely used there for graving out nodules from the sandstone, see *R.S.* fig. 60, p. 159. No. 81 is from the alabaster quarry of Khufu at Amarna, chipped in hard silicified limestone. The same stone was used at Beni Hasan, 82 to 85, for the regular implements for dressing down the walls of rock chambers of the Middle Kingdom, and similar ones were used at Qurneh (*Qurneh*, ix). 86 is a similar tool chipped in brown quartzite sandstone.

No. 87 is a block of limestone from the pyramid waste at Meydum. Such pieces were probably used to pivot wooden levers upon, which served in moving large blocks of stone.

Nos. 88, 89 are examples of hammer dressing, as used in the process of sculpture. 88 is a head of a canopic jar of silicified limestone. 89 is part of a kneeling figure in durite.

Nos. 90, 91 are unfinished bowls cut in soft limestone, of Ptolemaic age, found in the waste around the pyramid of Lahun. They were cut with a chisel. 91 shows how the middle was hollowed by flaking out large lumps, but in this case a blow has struck away part of the bowl, and it was abandoned. 92 is of similar working, begun and spoiled, for a bowl of brown basalt, from Gizeh. Specimens of different methods of dressing surfaces of stone are also in the collection, but they cannot be suitably illustrated here.

THE SICKLE : (F) PLS. LIV, LV

130. The sickle is often represented in harvest scenes, on the walls of the tomb chapels. The form seems to have varied a good deal. Sometimes very flat, as F 1, 5 ; more curved as F 2, 3 ; with a marked heel as F 4, or a deep semicircle as F 6. In any case the Egyptian (like the early English) only cut off the heads of corn closely, and put them in a bag, which was worn on the hip, or on the shoulder, where it was held by a band passing across the forehead. The long straw was left to be pulled up whole, being too valuable to be knocked about. As we have in modern times given up thatching and straw-work, we now cut the whole plant and crush the straw merely as litter or packing material.

Though the sickle-flints are found of the prehistoric age, the earliest actual sickles preserved are of the xiith dynasty, from Kahun, F 7–9, lv ; 10 ; there is also one in the British Museum, undated. They are carved in wood, sometimes in one piece (7, 8), sometimes built up (9, 10). A groove held the notched flint flakes, which served as teeth, cemented in place with Nile mud and glue. The flints which have been used for this purpose can always be identified by a very high polish along the cutting edge, produced by the siliceous straw, and a dull face elsewhere. An unusual form of blade is figured in a drawing (11) ; it is so closely like a bronze blade from French Switzerland (12) that it is hard to believe an independent origin. As there is also a link of about the same age between Swiss tanged daggers, D 112–114, and Cypriote, D 119, the influence of European on Eastern forms at that period seems corroborated.

A small semicircular sickle of copper, with hatched toothing (F 13), seems early by the style of it. It is rather small for work, and is perhaps a funereal model.

131. A much slighter curve is seen outside of Egypt, in the Turkestan sickle, 14, Mykenaean, 15, 16, and Swedish, 17. These lead into the scythe type, 18–22. It seems likely that all these flatter curves are for cutting close to the ground, where the stems are fixed, and have not to be bunched in the hand. The angle of the handle varies much. In the La Tène and Swedish, 17–20, the handle makes an open angle with the tip. These must be for holding in the hand, with a sawing motion. The Idria type, 23–25, has the handle at a close angle with the tip ; these are more for a dragging cut. The Roman type, 21, 22, from Newstead and Heidenberg, is the true scythe, to use with a long handle standing up from the ground ; in these the sawing cut was given by rotating the handle. The Egyptian (26) and Pompeian type, 31–34, has a

large gathering curve, and half the blade lies in almost a circle around the hand, so as to give a sawing cut from the wrist. The large curve was to gather in a bunch to be held by the hand. The open angle of 31 is like the Spanish sickle, and the closer curve of 32–34 like the South American sickle. The Hungarian 35 is probably of the Roman type. The Russian 36 seems to come from the open La Tène or modern Spanish type. The mediaeval sickle seems to have been socketted (37), descending from the western bronze age form. The detail of the Roman sickles in Egypt, 26 to 30, is quite peculiar to that land. They descend from the wooden sickles with flint teeth; the body is of iron with a groove along the whole length; in that groove a strip of steel with teeth is inserted, and can be renewed as often as needful. This is one of the curiously isolated forms of tool which seems never to have spread beyond Egypt. The sickles 23–35 are placed here with the handles upright, so as to show the angle of cutting.

THE BILL-HOOK OR PRUNING-HOOK: (P) PLS. LVI, LVII, LIX

132. The sickle, as we have seen, is the scythe on a lesser scale, intended to cut a large quantity of stalks, by a sawing motion. The bill-hook, on the other hand, is intended to cut by a blow, struck at only one or two stems of firmer growth. In a sickle the hand must be either near the centre of curvature, to sweep from the wrist and elbow (as F 26–34); or in the line of curvature, to sweep from the shoulder (as F 16–20); or the handle must be at right angles to the plane of the sickle, to sweep from the wrist (as F 7, 10). But no sawing motion could be simply given to any of the forms of the hooks on pls. lvi, lvii, excepting perhaps P 17. Therefore, though the size of some—as P 1—overlaps the sizes of the sickles, yet they cannot be reckoned with true sickles, as the direction of the cutting edge prevents a sawing motion from the handle.

In the form of the pruning-hook there are two different families. The Mediterranean family is mainly required for the vine, and is therefore of a large curve, and a gathering-in shape, in order to catch and lop sprays out of reach. The northern family is straighter, as it is mainly for cutting brushwood, for fuel and for basketry. In the modern Rodding bill-hook, or the Scotch cutting-over bills, a perfectly straight edge is reached. The Romans recognised many varieties of *falx* by different names, both with a sawing and a chopping action, as *foenaria* for hay, *messaria* for reaping, *putatoria* for pruning, *vinitoria* for the vine, *arboraria* for the orchard, and *silvatica* for the woodman. The *culter* had a straight edge, either as a knife or chopper, or to rip up the sod by a plough.

The earliest European bill-hooks are of bronze, starting with a large size in the *fonderia* at Bologna, P 1, and others with a back chopper for cutting hard stems, P 13, 14. The French (P 2, 3), South Italian (P 8, 9), and Assyrian (11) forms are probably for the vine. The Saxon forms (P 4–7) would not make a sweeping cut, but are, like the English, P 10, adapted for brushwood. The form with back chopper was usual in the middle ages, P 15, 16.

In the iron examples the hook from Egypt, P 17, is well dated, having been found by Belzoni underneath a sphinx of Rameses II (Belzoni, *Researches*, p. 151). At the handle end the grain of wood is marked in the rust. The form might be for a sickle or a pruning-hook; at present it stands quite alone, no other such hook has been found in Egypt, or elsewhere. It must certainly be early, as all Greek and Roman hooks have a tang or socket; this has the weak hafting of the bronze age, as P 2, 3, 8, 9. Looking at the curve, and the metal, it seems more likely to be an importation of Norican origin (see P 14, 18, 20). Another dated form is the sickle or pruning-hook in the Assyrian group, P 37, pl. lxxviii. This is between P 17 and the Norican, P 20, and is probably of northern origin. P 18 is of an early type, copied from the bronze P 13.

133. The straighter forms P 21 to 25 are rather choppers than bill-hooks, the breadth of the blade being evidently for heavy work. The broad blades with a short hook, P 41 to 45, and 50, appear to be woodmen's tools, to cut through saplings, and to hook in branches, 41, 42 like the modern Berkshire bill, 44, 45 like the modern bush-hook. The very short, wide blade of 54 must be for some other purpose; being only fastened by two rivets into a bronze plating, any heavy blow would have sheared the rivets, or torn the plate. Perhaps, like the hook with a carved ivory handle, P 59, it was a fancy tool for retired leisure to trim city gardens. The sharp bend of 57, 58, is like the modern pea-hook.

The Egyptian pruning-hooks, P 30–36, lix, and

52, are all of Roman age; they were probably for vines and fruit trees, as there are no copses in the Nile valley. The nearest comparisons for the socketted forms, 30 (Tarkhan), 31 (Wushym), and 35, are the Pompeian 48, 49. The tanged forms, 32, 33, seem more northern, like the French and Carniolan, 19, 20. Again, 34 is of the same curve as the Carniolan 53, and 60 from Defenneh is closely like 20. Probably these northern forms were manufactured in Noricum, and imported into Egypt. The little hook 36 is very carefully made, with deep serrated teeth; it has a Coptic twist-pattern engraved on one side, and the name APA PAMOUN on the other side of the handle, which is also given here. It seems as if intended for some religious purpose, perhaps for cutting ears of corn to make sacramental bread. A similar knife, inscribed APA POLLO, was found at Balyzeh (P.G. xxxviii, A, B).

The small, deeply curved hook is specially northern, and mainly British, 61 to 67. The size is too small for wood cutting, and the people of Wookey Hole hardly cultivated fruit trees. Perhaps these were for osier cutting, to make basketry. The modern osier hook is similarly curved, and smaller than for other purposes.

CHAPTER XI

SHEARS, CUTTERS, TOILET TOOLS, AND THREAD-WORK

THE SHEARS: (Q) PLS. LVIII, LIX

134. SHEARS appear to have been of Italian invention, at about 300 B.C. No bronze shears are known, except an ornamental pair from Caerleon, Q 25. The earliest are those from La Tène (1, 2, 21, 22), and from Bologna in tombs of the Gallic age (3). They are classified here by the form of the spring. The plain curve was usual at all times, down to the mediaeval Q 8. In Pompeii blades of iron rivetted to a bronze spring were not uncommon (Q 12). In Egypt the simple shears are found, as Q 17 (lix); but the more usual form there is quite peculiar to that country. One limb is made as seen on edge in Q 14, with a slot hole, and a hook catch. The slot passed over an oblong pin on the spring, and on turning the limb round it was secured, and at the same time the hook caught a second pin. Thus the limb, when its edge was put past the fixed edge, was as completely fixed as in ordinary shears; but it could be disengaged in a moment, in order to sharpen each limb separately. It is very strange that such a great improvement in shears should never have been copied in any other country, ancient or modern. The wish to get more range for the spring, so as to equalise the force of it, without increasing the size too wide for the grip of the hand, led to the expanded spring, where the limbs are brought closer together for the grip, as in 18 to 26.

The blades Q 27 to 29 may have been intended as separate limbs for shears, or they may be simple knives, as K 48, 49. The breadth of the blade seems more like shears, where a large sliding motion is required. The great shears, Q 30, can hardly have been purely for use. They would be impossible for sheep shearing, or cutting hair or cloth. Some ceremonial purpose is suggested by the size, perhaps carried in a sheep-shearing festival.

Two-handed shears for cutting metal are rarely found. Q 31 (lxxix) from Mainz is the only Roman example, and Q 32 is Anglo-Saxon. The form remained in the Dutch tinman's shears, 1694 (Q 33), and in the same of modern times. Perhaps the Swedish, Q 34, is to be considered as shears, as requiring two hands, though the blades are of a scissor form.

135. Scissors worked by separate fingers are not dated earlier than the first century, Q 36. Those from Priene, 35, South Italy, 37, and Egypt, 38, are of Roman age, but not dated more closely. The snuffers are a special form of scissors, and are found in Egypt, made of bronze, Q 39. From the metal these can hardly be of very late date; the thin, weak form of the legs is inferior to the usual scissors of Roman time, and they are probably Ptolemaic. Neither of the two words in the Pentateuch rendered as snuffers imply this form. One is *mezammeroth*, from *zahmar*, to prune the vine, implying a small knife to cut a lamp wick; the other word is *malgah-khaym*, from *mahlag*, to pinch off, implying tweezers for trimming the burnt part, like the lamp trimmers on pl. lxiv, Nos. 54 to 59.

The Dutch shears, Q 40, are much like those of modern tailors, in the depth of the hinge pin. Spring shears were also used in 1694, for cutting out clothes (*Het Menselyk bedrye*, pl. 2).

HAIR CURLER AND RAZOR: (X) PLS. LX, LXI

136. A curiously shaped utensil is found in burials and towns, X 1 to 20. It is formed of two

parts; a small knife, as seen separate in X 2; and a trough of sheet copper, into which fits the projection of the knife back, retained by a pin on which the parts hinge together. Thus the pointed butt of the knife can be recessed into the trough, as in 5, 6, 7; or else the back of the knife can be recessed as in 9. The knife is sometimes sharp on one side, as 2, 3, 6, 7, 8, 9, 10; in other examples it is sharp at a wide end, as 1, 4, 5, 11, 12, 13. These utensils are found at Mahasnah (grave 395) as early as the vith to xth dynasties (1); in the xiith dynasty at Kahun (2, 3); in the xviiith dynasty at Gurob (5 to 8) and Amarna (4); and about the xxiind dynasty at the Ramesseum (11). That these were not merely trade tools is obvious from the beautiful designs on them in the xviiith dynasty. 14 is a running jackal; 15 is a running panther; 16 is a galloping horse; 17 is a crane, with the hinged opening made to represent the jaws; 18 is a group of a dog chasing a gazelle; 19 is a galloping horse with plumes on the head; and 20 is a figure of Taurt. These figures are of the best style, and they are some of the most charming and spirited work of the xviiith dynasty.

As to the utility of these articles, the knife was the less important part, as it is diminished in some figures, and entirely suppressed in 17, 18, 19 and 20. Hence the two points, hinging open or shut, are the essential part. From the care and delicacy of the decoration it is probable that these were toilet articles; and we may guess that the two hinging points were for winding the little curls of the wig. If the points were slightly heated, and the curl was then wound, and stretched upon them, by using them like a glove stretcher, the curl would take a set. The wigs of two centuries ago were curled by winding the hair on heated cylinders of pottery. So the much closer curl of an Egyptian wig would be set by the stretcher of warm metal. The small knife would be required to cut off any straying hair, but it was less important than the curler.

137. Ancient razors are of two types, to scrape like a modern razor, or to saw to and fro through the hairs with a rotary motion. In the scraping razor the hand is at the end of the cutting edge, which is along the side of the blade. In the rotating razor the edge is an arc of a circle around the grip, and it can be rotated around the grip, to and fro.

The scraping razor must have been used from the beginning of the 1st dynasty, as the earliest dynastic people were shaved, while the predynastic race was bearded. The razors 21, 22, are sharpened at one edge; from their form and the slightness of the handle they may have been derived from the flaying knife, K 1 to 4. These are probably of the iiird to vith dynasties. The projecting edge, X 23, 24, was certainly used in the xiith dynasty, as dated at Dahshur to Amenemhot III, X 25; and it continued in use till the xviiith dynasty as dated to Hotshepsut, X 26. After that the rotating razor superseded it in Egypt.

The scraping razor was made in slightly varied forms in Crete and Rhodes, X 27–30. Much the same form occurs in iron at Madras, and bronze at Mantua, X 31, 32.

Another form, having a point, looks as if it were copied directly from a flint knife. It starts at La Tène (X 33, 34) and is always of iron; variants are 35 from the Ardennes, and the Roman examples from the Milanese (36), from Pompeii (37, lxxix, with marks of a wooden sheath rusted on it) and from Mainz (38).

138. An entirely different type of scraping razor, X 39 to 63, seems derived from the flaying knife. The earliest examples are X 39, 40, 41 from Crete, belonging to the close of the Middle Minoan and beginning of Late Minoan period. A broader form became usual rather later in Italy, from the middle of Etruria northward, 42. An unexplained variant arose in Sicily, having a notch in the end; this comes from post-Mykenaean cemeteries, but without any trace of iron, perhaps 1100 B.C. The notch appears most certainly in the largest razor, 43, which is probably the earliest of this group. The notch dwindles in 45–47, widens in 44, leading to a slightly concave end in X 48, 49. The purpose of it is quite obscure. X 49 has an unsymmetric ridge on each side, making the rhombic section here marked in the middle of it. As the skin would be held by the left hand in shaving, the right would move outward away from the left, hence this section gives the broader side of the edge outward in use.

This type had remarkable travels. The Sicilian form, 48, 49, seems closely copied in the Rhine type, 50. The notch at the end cannot be dissociated from the split end of the Syracusan form 51. This peculiar form again cannot be separated from the Yorkshire form 52, from the Heathery Burn, and similar forms from Wallingford, Dunbar, and Ireland (Evans, *Bronze*); these must go with the Wiltshire 53. The other West of England razors, 54 and 55, probably are of the same stock. The type penetrated to the Continent; the Flemish form, 56, with a split end, is too peculiar not to be connected with the Yorkshire 52. An enormous development of the end notch seems to have arisen in Switzerland, South Germany, and France, in the forms 57 and 58, which have not apparently any other origin. In South Italy an entirely different line of development was followed, leading to a square razor, 62, 63. The notch at the end in 59, 60, links these to the Sicilian type; the notch recedes into the blade, as a hole, in 61 from Athens, and an echo of it may remain in the circle pattern on 63. In looking over the whole series it is evident the Cretan flaying-knife razor is the earliest in actual dating. Only from that type could the Sicilian form be derived. From the Sicilian notched form three other branches come, the split in England and Flanders, the lunate razor of Germany, and the square razor of Italy. It seems impossible, from the progress of type, and the relative ages of the groups, to arrange them in any other historical sequence. This throws much light on lines of trade; the English and Flemish forms arrived by some other route than Italy, and probably the German forms by a third route.

139. The rotating razor begins as a strip of metal sharpened at the end, X 64, pl. lx, from Dahshur, X 65, lxi, from Kahun, both of the xiith dynasty. This type had a loop added in the form of a goose's head, X 67, in the xviiith dynasty; and perhaps from this may come the northern razors, X 68, 69. Another such form is that with Taurt, X 66. Plain strips were also used, as X 72, 73. As these strips were grasped at the middle, and the end worked with a sawing motion, it was a simple step to hold them by the thumb and finger, and rotate them to and fro. The whole razor of this type, as fully developed, is X 78, 79 (two duplicates of 79). Holding the middle of the blade between the thumb and finger, the little finger and third could hold the projecting spur and vibrate it to and fro, thus rotating the razor and working the edge in a saw-fashion. Other examples here have lost the handles, as X 74, 75 (two duplicates), 76, 77, 80, 81. No. 75 is the only inscribed razor that I have seen, belonging to the "guardian of the door of Rannut, Pasar." Nos. 80, 81, are of the reign of Tehutmes III, 78 and 79 are probably about Amenhetep III. From La Tène comes 83, an adaptation of the same form; by holding it on the straight part of the stem, and vibrating the ball, the edge would be rotated to and fro.

This type was evidently copied at Carthage, X 82; but modified by providing a ring to hold as the centre of motion, and a long neck and head of a goose for the little finger to vibrate.

The ring in the previous example shows how the ring handles of Italian razors were to be held, X 85 to 94. In the best formed, 93, 94, a large part of the edge nearly centres on the ring handle, and would be worked to and fro by rotation round the ring. The little spur at the base of the blade in 86, 87, 88, looks as if it were to be worked on by the finger. Without actual experiment and practice the mode of handling these razors cannot be settled.

The latest razor is a steel-edged blade, X 84 from Oxyrhynkhos, which was worked like a knife.

LEATHER CUTTER, AND CUTTING-OUT KNIFE: (L) PLS. LXII, LXIII

140. The short blade used with heavy pressure for cutting leather, has always been of much the same shape. An example in the Cairo Museum, L 1, is closely like one figured in the tomb of Rekhmara, L 2, of the xviiith dynasty. The bronze L 49 from Memphis is probably a leather cutter, but without a wooden handle. The modern Greenland form, L 4, seems to be for the same purpose, and is like the present saddler's knife. A very simple knife on the same principle is the rough bit of iron set in wood, L 3, which I owe to Dr. Seligman, who informs me that it is used for cutting maize stalks in Kordofan.

For detailed cutting a smaller blade and longer handle are needed. These appear in the iron age at La Tène and Stradonic in Hungary, L 5, 6. A later, and more decorated, form is from Auvergne, 7. The square-ended blades, 8, 9, of Roman age, might be used for long straight cuts. The slope-ended blade of Pompeii (10) is of bronze, and is called a paste-cutter; that from Heidenberg (11) might be a form of socket chisel. The socketted cutter, 12, from the Roman camp at Newstead, has been called a turf cutter. The ornamental cutting in a garden is an unlikely purpose, and for cutting peats or turves a long blade is needful. This might be a small spud, but it is so much like No. 6 that they are classed together here.

141. Another tool akin to the leather-cutter is the cutting-out tool for linen. Before scissors were started in the Graeco-Roman age, or shears in the late iron age, some special form of knife was required to cut out linen garments. The type of knife L 17–26 is often found with burials of women (*e.g. Illahun*, xvii), and it is exactly adapted to cutting out on a flat board. The convex curves at the top and at the butt are the only sharp edges. The top curve would be for making a running cut, and the butt for chopping through any tough threads, or parts that dragged in the long cut.

The earliest cutting-out knife is from Abydos, just before the 1st dynasty, L 13A, pl. lxxix; the next is that found in the tomb of king Zet, first dynasty, L 13; another of the same form, L 29 (lxiii), is without locality, but obviously of the same age. Only the two convex curves are sharp. The large flat knife, 28, apparently for cutting out, is like one of the vith dynasty from Mahasnah (G.M. xxxiii).

The beginning of the single-curved end is seen in L 30, 31, 32; these are probably of the xiith dynasty, compare K 95, though a further form of this lasted till the xviiith dynasty, L 21, 22. Also of the xiith dynasty is the beginning of the notch, as in L 14 from Diospolis and L 33 from Ballas. Of the photographs none of the remainder are dated, except 43, 44, of xviiith or xixth dynasty, from Gurob. The drawings are all of dated examples from tomb-groups. Under Tehutmes I, No. 15, the form is like L 34. Nos. 16 to 22 are all within the long reign of Tehutmes III; with these go L 35 to 42. The later cutters are narrower in the handle, as 23 of Amenhetep III, with which goes 43, 44. The xixth dynasty is marked by the projections of the butt edge, as in 24, 26, and with these go L 45, 46, 47. The only inscribed specimen is 45, reading "Uab-priest of Anhur." L 27 is probably about the time of Tehutmes III; it combines the wig curler with this form of knife.

After the xixth dynasty no examples are known with any dating. The knife L 48 is of the same form of cutting edge, but quite different in the stem. It seems of later date, as it has a tang for a handle. The strange little knife, L 50, is covered with punched patterns. It was bought in Egypt, and cannot be dated. Above the last are three curved slips of bronze; they may be models of some tool, or possibly eyebrows from a coffin.

TWEEZERS: (Y) PLS. LXII, LXIV

142. The two main uses of tweezers are for removing hairs and extracting thorns. For the former purpose wide jaws were usual; for the thorns, narrow or pointed jaws, to press down into the flesh. Where wide jaws are used there is no need for a wide hinge, as a little side play is of no consequence; but with pointed jaws the hinge must be wide, to prevent the points slipping aside, one past the other.

No tweezers have been found in the prehistoric graves; but by the middle of the first dynasty, in the tomb of Semerkhet, there was an admirable pair of tweezers, Y 1. This has a very wide hinge, thin and flexible, with stiff legs, so as not to flatten out with pressure. From this we may similarly date Y 23, 24, pl. lxiv. Though 25 is like the Pompeian Y 20, yet the style of manufacture, and its being apparently of copper, show that it is early dynastic. Y 26 has pointed jaws, so that it would be difficult to grasp anything. Next after these come the tweezers from Mochlos, of early Minoan II period, like 28 (S.M. 35).

In the xiith dynasty wide jaws were usual, and a narrow hinge, Y 2, 3. In order to keep the tweezers in proper order, when carrying them hung from the girdle, they were often set on a block of hardwood, or of ivory, as Y 27, 28. Similar blocks were used in Denmark (S.A.N. 1908–9, p. 89). To the same period belong other wide-jaw forms, sometimes strangely decorated, as Y 2, 3, 30, 31, 32, 33; 29 is from Rifeh, and 30 from Kahun. In the xviiith dynasty tweezers were very poorly made as Y 34, 35, 36, 37. There are six duplicates of 35, and two of 36; also duplicates of 29, 39.

In the Roman age there are many forms; simple loops as 41 (and duplicate), 42, with wire hinge and flat legs. Y 43 has a term bust at the hinge, and depends entirely on the spring of the legs. Y 44 has an openwork head. Y 45 has a slot in each leg, for a sliding pin to clip the legs together.

In the late Roman and Coptic age sets of thorn tools, to hang at the girdle, became usual. The set generally consisted of a minute knife to open up the skin, a point to press below the thorn to raise it, and small tweezers to extract the thorn. The frequency of prickly plants on the desert edge made such tools to be more required in Egypt than in other lands. The earlier stage is seen in the xviiith dynasty, when slips of bronze were made with long sharp points, and kept sometimes in a bunch of half a dozen; but they were not fastened to the tweezers.

Y 46 is a bunch of a knife, a point, a presser (?), and other indistinct pieces. Below it is a simple point, 47. 48 is a bunch of tweezers, pricker, and knife. 49 is a knife separately. 50 is a ring with tweezers and point. Y 51, from Lahun, and 52 are bunches of all three tools. Y 53 is a pair of tweezers, with a point hinging on a rivet through the tweezers, so that it can be turned out sideways, or else carried between the tweezers for protection. Y 54 to 59 are large weak tweezers of iron, sometimes with a long point (57, 58); they are all from Oxyrhynkhos, and seem to be a local form. Duplicates are here of 55 (4); 57 (2); and 59. They are far too rough and weak to grip thorns, and seem to be probably for lamp trimming, like the pinchers—translated snuffers or tongs—mentioned in the Pentateuch. The length of them was required to keep them cool enough to hold, when engaged in a hot flame.

143. Turning now to the European forms, we see that the La Tène form (M.L. 291) is closely like that of Y 30, and large sizes do not appear until the iron age. The early forms are small, simple, and not well made, being narrow both at jaw and at hinge, Y 4, 5. A grip clutch was often used, Y 6–8, which is scarcely needed for thorns; this suggests a surgical use, to secure a hold on internal tissues when operating. Very wide jaws were used in the north, as Y 9, 10. At Pompeii the skew form, Y 12, 13, was favoured, in order to get a clearer view when in use. Simple and rude forms are found widely spread, as Y 14 to 19, probably the earliest stage on the European side. The bunch of thorn tools occurs in the north, Y 21, and a similar set from South Germany has an earpick also (M. V. 69); these are attributed to the late Hallstatt period. This would suggest that the Egyptian examples are not Roman in origin, but were brought by the northern garrisons, which have left so many Frankish and other remains in Egypt.

Yet a much earlier source of the type appears in the copper age of Mesopotamia. Banks found "little funnel-shaped cases containing four instruments held together by a key ring . . . . a pair of tweezers and three knife blades of different shapes" (*Bismiya*, p. 310).

The pair of pincers, Y 22, was doubtless for surgical use.

BORERS, PINS, AND NEEDLES: (N) PLS. LXII, LXV

144. Early borers are always mere expanders for forcing and enlarging a hole in skins; it is not till later that the advantage of a square form to cut the hole larger, is adopted. The simple squared borers here are N 29 to 32 from Naqadeh, of prehistoric Egypt; N 1 of the 1st dynasty; and 33 to 35 of the xiith dynasty, from Kahun. The figure of a borer in a handle, N 2, is of the same date. N 36, 37 in handles, both round, are without a history. N 38 is square, and 39, 40 are round, from Harageh, xiith dynasty. N 41 is square, and 42, 43, 44 round, from Amarna, xviiith dynasty. 45–47 are square, and 48–51 are round, of the xviiith–xixth dynasties from Gurob. 52 is square, and 53 round, from the Ramesseum. 54, of unknown site, is of iron and square. 55 to 57 are flat copper bodkins. There are five round and two square borers without a history. From Europe there is a round borer from La Tène, N 3; from Susa, N 4 is a round borer with a square shank showing that it had a fixed handle.

145. Two interesting tools are 58, 59, of bronze. They are both very thin, and incapable of being used with force; they can only have been worked with very delicate handling, and they seem to exactly agree to the requirements of the needle used for splitting papyrus (Pliny, xiii, 23). The length would allow of taking off the breadth for a roll, the double edge of 59 would work in either direction, the thinness would prevent straining the leaf, and the lightness would enable the hand to feel the way between the leaves without cutting through them.

146. The pin may be regarded as the prototype of the borer, being left in the hole to secure the garment. To turn over the end of the borer so as to tie it on, and prevent its loss, was a common stage in most lands. In Egypt the copper pin with loop head is found in the oldest graves known, S.D. 30. The examples here are on pl. lxv, N 102, of S.D. 71 (Naqadeh 485); 103 (Naq. 1460); 104, 107 (Naq. 63); 108 (Naq.); 109 (South town, Naq.); and two unplaced, 105–6. A simple form of loop head is found down to the xiith dynasty, N 12, lxii. Outside of Egypt the simple turn-over head is found in Western Persia, N 13; and the turn-over and twisted heads are found in many parts of Europe, as N 5 to 11, which are from drawings kindly sent by M. Siret.

The toggle pin is dated in Egypt to the xviiith dynasty, as in N 15, 16, 17. It is found in Mykenaean Greece, and also in Western Persia, N 14. The history of pins belongs rather to toilet and personal ornaments, and will be dealt with more fully in the volume on that section.

147. Needles of copper begin to appear in the earlier part of the second prehistoric civilisation, S.D. 48 in Egypt. Four here, N 66 to 69, are from a prehistoric grave, Naqadeh 63. Some of them are pointed at the butt, which is not the case later. From Kahun are N 70 to 74 of the xiith dynasty. Similar needles, N 75 to 79, are from the opposite site of Harageh, of the xiith dynasty. The very long and thin bronze needle, 80, is one of a group found stored in a bird's bone, site unknown, probably of the xviiith dynasty. The needles 81 to 84 from Gurob, and 85–87 from Amarna, are also of the xviiith dynasty. 87 is peculiar for having two thread holes at right angles, to sew two threads at once. All these are of bronze. The total of the copper and bronze needles at Univ. Coll. are, prehistoric 3 from Naqadeh, iiird dynasty 3 from Meydum, xiith dynasty 31 from Kahun, 24 from Harageh; xviiith dynasty 57 from Gurob, 11 from Amarna. Undated 5 from Koptos, 17 unplaced.

The great coarse needles or bodkins are later; 88 is of bronze undated, 89 is from the Ramesseum, perhaps 800 B.C. Of iron, 90 is from Memphis; 91 from Gurob; 93 from Hawara; 94 from Lahun; 95 from Oxyrhynkhos; 96, 97, pl. lxix, are from Rifeh; all these are probably of Roman age. A set of late Roman needles from Hawara are N 21 to 25. Similar needles of the Coptic age were found at Balyzeh (P.G. xxxviii, A, B). Of European needles, N 19 is from Bologna, about 500 B.C.; N 20 is a bronze bodkin from Athens, pl. lxix.

Netting needles are found from the xiith dynasty, of wood. N 98 is a bronze one from Harageh, of the xiith. N 99, 100 are bronze netters undated. Two of wood are among weaving implements, 130, 131, in the next plate. The end of an iron netting needle, N 26, is from Defenneh. N 27 is a bronze netting needle from Athens; the eyes are at right-angles one to another. Netting was greatly used for fishing nets at all periods in Egypt.

A bronze thimble, open at both ends, was bought in Egypt, N 110, xliv; the date is not known, but probably Roman.

SPINNING AND WEAVING: (N) PL. LXVI

148. The simplest method of using thread was in a ball, or on a reel. In the xiith dynasty little balls of thread are often found, wound on scraps of pottery. In the xviiith dynasty reels of clay are common, as N 111, 112 (Gurob); sometimes they are larger, of blue or green glazed pottery with a pattern, N 113, 114, which are probably of the xxiind dynasty. Larger reels, 115 (blue paste) and 116 (wood), were made from the xviiith dynasty onward. Probably these reels were used for net making, instead of netting needles. A turned reel of polished wood, 117, has thread on it still; it is probably Roman.

Bodkins of wood are often found, as 118 to 122.

Bobbins for pillow netting, like pillow lacework, were made of bone, 123, and of ebony, 124, in order to distinguish two classes of thread (Gurob); these are probably of xixth dynasty, but might be Roman. Similarly bits of reed were used for the thread, as 125.

Netting was generally done with pointed rib bones, 128, 129, on which thread was wound. These are from Gurob, and such netters abound in sites of the xviiith and xixth dynasty, and were likewise used in Assyria. Netting needles of wood are sometimes found, as 130 (Kahun) and 131 (Gurob).

149. For spinning, the small rounded limestone spindle whorls abounded in the prehistoric town at Naqadeh. The domed limestone whorl, 138, and coned wooden whorl, 139, are of the xiith dynasty from Kahun. 140 is the typical cylindrical whorl of the xiith dynasty; there are also many others here from Kahun. The thread notch in that age was a deep spiral groove round the shaft. N 141, 142 are the typical domed whorls of the xviiith dynasty, found with many others at Gurob. The thread notch is a cut across the shaft near the top. N 143 to 147 are the Roman spindles, with iron hooks to retain the thread. A beautiful spindle of bronze, pl. lxii, N 28, is at Athens.

150. Shuttles are rather rare. N 126 has the stock of thread wound on it, and retained by cross binding. N 127 had a reel for the thread in a middle gap; it is weighted with plugs of lead, to enable it to be thrown with better effect.

Pieces of looms are sometimes found. 137 may be a weaver's warp beam with pegs for the groups of warp threads; or it may be part of a harp. 133, 134, 135 (Gurob) are bars for spacing the groups of warp threads. 132, 136 (Gurob) are slays or beaters-in for driving up the thread between the warp.

Weavers' combs were introduced in late Roman times to push up the woof thread into place, instead of putting in the long slay between the two sets of warp threads. These combs are often much worn between the teeth by sliding on the warp threads. N 148, 151, 153 are the usual combs. 150, from Wushym, is a bit of comb-teeth cut to renew a comb, rather than throw it away when worn out. 152 has a curved handle. 153 is from Gurob. 154 from Wushym, is of a very small size, probably for weaving bands. N 148 has two Arabic words roughly cut upon it, perhaps reading *qelateh 'ayat*: possibly a man of Kafr el Ayat.

A large number of iron pegs, N 61 to 64, pl. lxv, were found together. The lower parts are in good state, only the top inch or so is rusted. On some of them near the point are worn fine cross grooves. It seems as if these were the stock of pegs for a ground loom. They were driven into the dry earth, and were only rusted at the top where exposed to the dew. The pegs were also used singly by hand to push up threads or to disentangle them, and hence the fine grooves worn near the point, by slipping over threads covered with grit. With these was a chisel of iron (60) with the letters *alpha delta theta* incised. For a study of ancient weaving see L. Roth, *Ancient Egyptian and Greek Looms*, 1913.

CHAPTER XII

AGRICULTURAL TOOLS: (G) PLS. LXVII, LXVIII, LXIX

151. THE simplest of all means of cultivation is the natural hoe, cut from a forking branch, such as G 57 (lxviii). Such hoes are still used among the hill tribes in Central Africa; and from the specimen here from Kahun we see that it continued in use through the high civilisation of the Old and Middle Kingdom. A bronze model of this type is here, G 70 (lxix), and a wooden model is copied, G 77, pl. lxxii.

The next stage was the compound hoe, with a wooden blade, the tenon at the top of which was inserted through the wooden handle. To resist the strain in working, a cord tied the blade back to the handle. This cord was kept in place usually by notches in the sides of the blade, as G 59 (lxviii) from Kahun, or the bronze funerary models, G 68, 69 (lxix). In other blades holes were cut, through which the cord was passed, as G 62 from Herakleopolis, 64 (lxviii), and 78, pl. lxxii. Wooden models are found in tombs (58, 60, 61, lxviii).

The Egyptian plough was developed from the hoe. The ox was tied to the long handle, and the ploughman held the forking of the hoe. The large blade, 63 (lxviii), must, by its size, have been used as a plough.

152. Winnowing fans are often found, and are shown in use on the tomb scenes of the vth dynasty. A pair such as G 65, 66 (lxviii) were held by the rounded backs, one in each hand. The trodden grain and chaff was scraped up from the threshing floor, upon the boards, and lifted up till it could be tossed on high for the wind to blow away the chaff. Some boards, as 66, have an equal rounding on each side, so that they could be held in either hand; usually they are only right- or left-handed.

Other agricultural implements on pl. lxix are the rakes, 74, 75, which are often found of the xiith dynasty; these are from Kahun. They were usually but slightly notched, being for dragging the mud over the seed, when sown on the retiring inundation. The mud, when once dried, is far too hard to be broken up by a rake, like lighter soils; the only use of a rake is upon the soft mud.

The yoke was used from the iiird dynasty, but 71 is of Roman period, from the Fayum (see G.W. 466). The bar next to it, 72, is a light carrying yoke to put across a man's shoulder. Though this was used anciently (see G.W. figs. 112, 144), and is so common in China now, it has entirely disappeared from modern Egypt.

The heavy club, 73, was for beating out fibre of some kind; it has been much polished by wear. Another kind of bat, perhaps for beating flax, is at the base of pl. xlix, W 240. The remainder of the objects on pl. lxix are weapons described under R and V.

The Egyptian agricultural tools being all of wood have been taken here together, leaving the European tools to be next considered, pl. lxvii.

153. In the light volcanic-ash soil of Pompeii the hoe was the usual tool, taking the place of a spade in heavier soil. The same use of the large hoe is continued about Naples at present. The very wide hoes, G 1, 2, 4, 8, used at Pompeii, and for the ash soil of the Campagna, were partly retained by the Romans elsewhere, as in Egypt, with a deep socket,

5 (lxxix); but the edge was narrowed, and a pick was added to break up the earth, in the tools used in Germany and Britain, 3. A pointed form was adopted, as in Germany, 12, and Spain, 11; or a smaller blade altogether, in Hungary, 7. The socket was very clumsy and heavy in many Pompeian tools, as 1, 2, 8, 9, but was much reduced in the form from Rome, 10, where it is ribbed to be as strong and light as possible. It may be that the needlessly heavy tools were for the slaves of the *latifundia*, and made too strong to be easily spoiled, while the lighter tool was the choice of the free cultivator.

An entirely different type of hoe, very narrow, long, and pointed, 13, 14, 15, comes from Athens, and was used in mediaeval France. The purpose of this is evidently for work in stony soils, on which the broad hoe would be checked and broken. The point would glance off the stones, the narrow blade pass between them, and the concave form of the blade gave strength to lever the stones out of the ground when required. It is like the modern ox-tongue grubbing hoe. The broad hoe, with a long tubular socket, was used in France on lighter soils, 16.

On the slopes of the Apennines a narrow and heavy hoe was preferred, 17, 19, with a double pick for breaking up clods, like the modern fork-end hoe; these come from the ruins of Velleia, south of Piacenza. The type was brought into Britain, and is found in Gloucestershire, 18.

154. The spade is a much later tool than the hoe, and none are preserved before Roman times. Both the pointed and the square spade were in use at Pompeii, 22, 24. The pointed spade is made with an internal socket block, pointed at each end, and the outer plates rivetted to it. Small spades as 25, 26, run down in size to the spuds 28 to 31. The shovel with raised sides, 27, is much less usual. In Norman times the spade, 20, was only one-sided; it was cut in wood, and shoed with sheet iron. Similar iron shoes are found in Roman times, so that the wooden spade may well have been the primitive form. The Normans also used the broad shovel, with the eye or box handle, 23. The crutch handle, 21, appears with the pointed spade in Dutch use, 1694. It might be expected to be earlier than the box handle, but I have not come across it.

155. Ploughs in Italy are shown in detail by two bronze models, 32. 33. They are of different form; in 32 the plough is simple, like a hoe, and the yoke is not fashioned to keep the oxen apart. 33 is more advanced; by the share resting flat on the ground it seems likely that it turned the sod over, though there is no mould-board to it; the yoke is shaped to a fixed distance of the oxen. Neither plough has a coulter. A bronze plough-share, with a socket and three projecting ribs, comes from Egypt, top left, pl. lxxi, G 76. The share of Greek period in Egypt, G 37, was a stout plate of iron, with the corners lapped round to form a socket. A similar design is widely spread in Pompeii, Italy, Sweden, and Russia (34, 35, 36, 38). It seems defective in preventing the metal from being pushed back when in use; a grip around the wooden stem would seem needful. Perhaps these were all used flat on the ground, like the flat foot of fig. 33. A form of two-handled plough was used in Roman Egypt (40) with a flat sole, and no means of throwing the sod aside. Probably it was for sandy ground, in which there was no solidity in the sod. The ploughshare and coulter of mediaeval France is 39.

156. Forks for lifting and tossing straw or hay were used early in Egypt. The form 41 is cut from a naturally forking branch. The form 42, singularly like the Etruscan 43, seems artificial. The Egyptians, however, had such elaborate training of wood to grow in required forms, that this might be all due to growth. 48 is a late form of iron fork from Defenneh; this and 47 might be fish-spears. 44 is so short that it seems rather to be a double dibble. 45, 46, 49 and 50 are probably agricultural forks.

The iron rake for breaking the soil, G 51 to 56, was a common tool, with two, three, or four prongs. Probably all are of Roman age.

THE HORSE-BIT: (W) PLS. LXX, LXXI

157. There appear to be three stages in the types of the bit; first the simple snaffle—a plain bar or jointed bar, acting by merely holding the mouth; secondly, the protected snaffle—with a large ring or a bar at each side to prevent the rein from slipping into the mouth; thirdly, the curb, with the bars lengthened and linked together behind the jaw, so as to exert a leverage on the jaw when pulled back.

The solid bar bit is found in Egypt at Defenneh about 600 B.C. (10, 11); also in North Italy (14) and South Germany (5), and later at Pompeii (21). The advantage of the linked bit in compressing as well as holding the mouth, caused it to become general. The side ring may be in one with the bar, as no. 1 from Trentino and Siberia. The rings, however, are generally loose; sometimes small, just for attachment, as in the Bologna (2) and Sarmatian (4) form; or else large, to prevent biting the reins, in the German (5) and Celtic bits, as in Spain (3), La Tène, Lochlea, Ireland, etc. The large rings with a twisted bit are also found in Denmark.

The bit with side bars arose from using tusks or horns at the side to prevent tricks with the reins. These are often found in the lake dwellings. In the side bars of the Belgian bit, 7, we probably see the copying of leg-bones of a dog or other small animal. The plain side bars, 6 to 13, belong to the north, none being south of Belgium; the Egyptian bars, 9, are too much decayed to show the ends. Ivory side bars with iron links were made by the late Merovingians (M.V. 36).

158. The curb begins with the connecting of the side bars by cross-ties through eyes on the bar. This is a more southern form, between Moeringen and Georgia on the north, and Bologna and Spain on the south (14 to 18). The S-shaped side bars are further south, in Epirus (19, 20) and Pompeii (21). The long bar with teeth on the inner side is found in Egypt, W 40 (lxxi) and two others. Exactly the same form occurs in the later graves of Mykenae (A.C. 2553), probably about 1000 B.C.; and this indicates the most likely source of the Egyptian form, as only the plain bit without rings or bars appears in Egyptian sculptures.

Elaborate open-work plates, instead of side bars, came into use in the later bronze age in Italy. The simplest is the triangle hung on the bit (22), with a bronze link to attach the rein. Various decorative forms were used, 23 to 29, throughout Etruria, but not beyond.

Another type adopted, to keep the side bar from being bitten, was the curved side bar. This very likely originated in using boars' tusks for the sides. It occurs with a solid bar, as a snaffle, in the iron age in Italy, 30; also in Spain, 31, 32, both as snaffles. Converted into a curb, it is a Central European form, at La Tène 33, Sarrelouis 36, Stillfried 34, and Bohemia 35. It is also eastern, as it is found in Georgia (38) of the first iron age, and of about the same date at Nineveh (37). This oriental type is that of the Egyptian example, 39 (lxxi), which may have been left behind by an Assyrian invasion.

The heavy bit, 41, is of an entirely different kind, depending on hurting the inside of the mouth, and not on holding the jaw. It is of classical Greek age, being described by Xenophon. A short chain is in the middle, on either side of it a sharp three-pointed star, so that one point must press cruelly on the tongue or the palate; next a sharp-edged disc, then two wide rings covered with points to press the lips. The whole was so heavy that two lyre-shaped loops of iron held it up by straps to the head-band. Outside of all are the two long hooks for the reins.

Another entirely different form of bit is the broad plate across the nose, found at Pompeii (N. 75576), and still the usual form in Naples.

SPUR

159. One iron spur has been obtained in Egypt, W 58, pl. li. The plain form of the prick, without any enlargement, is peculiar. All of the spurs after the thirteenth century have rowels; and before that nearly all have enlarged points on a narrower neck, as W 59, lxxii (D.W. 344–9). In the eighth century German spurs have thick points without a neck; and a Greek bronze spur, 60, from Naples (now in Paris) has a plain point on a disc base (D.W. 115). This Egyptian example is most like the last mentioned, and may probably be Roman in date.

BRAND: (W) PL. LXXI

160. The brands or stamps are shown on pl. lxxi in side view, with the front view above, reflected in a mirror, and therefore in the same direction as the impression. How they were used, and on what material, are speculative questions. No impression of such a stamp has been found. The isolation of the stamp, as open work in most cases (43, 44, 47, 48, 49), and on a long stem, strongly suggests that it was heated, and acted as a brand. Some are solid-body stamps (42, 45, 46), and of a smaller size; both these characters would prevent use as brands, and we must regard these as colour stamps, *pintaderas*. That they were not used on permanent material, as clay sealings, or branding wood or linen, seems proved by our having here eight brands, each of which was probably used dozens or

hundreds of times, while not a single impress of such a stamp has been seen. They were probably used on perishable articles, animal or vegetable.

The subjects are the royal name (Aohmes I, 43) or emblems of divinities, Hathor 42, Set 44, 46, Mut 45, and the goose of Amen 47, 48, 49. With the goose in 48 is the sign *men*; though *smen* is a kind of goose, there would be no object in putting part of the bird's name; this must, rather, be connected with the usual abbreviation of Amen as Men in the cartouche of Pamay, and taken as meaning the name of the god. The period of them must be from the beginning of the xviiith dynasty (43), through the devotion to Set (44, 46) in the xixth dynasty, to the time of Pamay, xxiind dynasty. It seems probable that the open-work brands were for marking slaves or cattle dedicated to a god, and the smaller solid stamps were for a colour stamp on devotees at the festival of the god.

CHAPTER XIII

DOMESTIC

FIRE-HOOKS: (W) PLS. LXXI, LXXII, LXXIV

161. THE form of a hand on a long rod of bronze is known in Greek usage as a fire-tender. The charcoal or wood in universal use only required gently shifting, as it burnt away on the brazier. In Egypt the same form occurs, probably beginning with Greek usage, as 120 (lxxii) from Naukratis, 119 from Defenneh, and 118, pl. lxxiv. Possibly the copper rod with plate at the end, 121, may be a form of the same tool. Another form combined a hook and point with the hand; this is shown on the usual half scale 51, pl. lxxiv, and smaller to include the whole object as 51, pl. lxxi; at the butt it has an animal head, and a long chain, by which it was attached to the brazier. The smaller plain hook and spike, 50 (lxxi), is for the same purpose. It is given of the same scale as the rest of the plate, at the left; and at the right it is of the scale of the large fire-hook. Two unexplained objects may be here noted; 122 (lxxii) is a pointed strip of bronze, rolled up at the end; 123 is a large iron blade with socket handle, the form rather suggests a "beater-up" for a loom, perhaps for woven rush mats.

MANACLES

162. The pair of bronze manacles, W 52, lxxi, is of a rather clumsy pattern. One side of the lower grip can be unhooked in the middle; but there is no means of opening the upper grip, perhaps it was slipped on to a post or beam.

STAFF HEAD

163. The wooden walking staves were sometimes shod or tipped with bronze. This tube, W 53, lxxi, is from such a staff, and inscribed with unknown signs. From the figure of a standing man at the end, it appears that the signs are here upright.

FISH SPEAR

164. The trident, or fish spear of Neptune, as a coin type occurs at Messana before 400 B.C., and after that often in Greece and Italy, and is a common type of the coinage of Hiero about 250 B.C. It was probably introduced by the Greeks into Egypt, being found at Defenneh, W 54, lxxii. Other forms with barbs are found in Switzerland and North Germany, 55–57.

FLESH-HOOK

165. The use of flesh-hooks for removing meat from a boiling pot, was of the early iron age, or before that, as we read of a flesh-hook of three teeth being used, in 1 Sam. ii, 13, and there is one here of bronze from the *fonderia* of Bologna. There were various types of branching of the hooks. The earliest, W 61 (lxxii), has the hooks all branching from a middle stem. The bronze, 62, from Naples, and the iron, 63, from Perugia, have a ring from which the hooks start. Later the form is rougher, of crossing strips rivetted, as 64 lxxii, 66 lxxiii. The simplest three-toothed hook was combined with the ladle for the broth, as 65 (lxxii) from Alesia, and 69 (lxxiii) from Egypt; probably 67 from Oxyrhynkhos is part of the same form. For a similar one from Ehnasya see P.E. xxix. What seems to be an ornamental two-pronged hook is the gazelle head on a socket handle, with very long twisted horns, 68.

SHOVEL

166. Shovels are found of the later bronze age in Cyprus (D.C. 250) and of Roman age at Pompeii, but they obviously were needed at an early date, especially in temple services to remove ashes of sacrifice; this is recorded of the Jewish *sacra*, from Exodus to Jeremiah. The Pompeian examples are

none of them large, 78 to 81, and are domestic rather than for trade uses. One side-shovel like a crumb scoop, 77 (lxxiii), comes from the Fayum; it was for the left hand, and may have been used to scrape up grain or flour, to place in some vessel held with the right hand. Two little tools, 75, 76, lxxiii, like the modern smith's shovel, may have been shovels for braziers; 76 is now partly broken.

LADLE

167. Ladles seem curiously scarce, considering how usual they must have been for cooking in all countries. I have only met with four from Egypt, and none elsewhere. The Egyptian ladles are all of iron, and probably of Roman age. 69 is a ladle and flesh-hook combined, so as to serve the broth and the meat from the pot. 70 is a hingeing ladle, made to pack up short; I have a suspicion that it may be a Bedawy coffee-roaster, as the bowl is shallow. 73 and 74 are small ladles.

SPOON: PL. LXXIV

168. The use of spoons begins with the second prehistoric civilisation in Egypt. They continued to be common down to the beginning of the dynastic age. Then they entirely disappear, unless a bronze spoon, 97, from Gurob may be of the xviiith dynasty. In Roman times the spoon again became common.

The prehistoric spoons are mostly of ivory, as 84, 85, 87, 88, 89, 90; rarely they are found of slate, 86, of wood, 91, of silver (P.Q 46), or of slate with a handle of stone beads (P.Q. lxi). A distinctive mark of this age is the small hole in the end of the handle, for hanging up the spoon, and often a flattening of the end, sometimes widened out as in 88. The bowl is usually circular, the handle joining it below the brim. Of later spoons, 92 is from Rifeh of Roman age; 93 is from Gurob, probably Roman; 94 is a flat disc, perhaps used for dry food; 95 is a bronze spoon; 96 is an unguent spoon, with an ear-pick at the end of the handle. The flattish bronze spoon, 97, from Gurob may be of the earlier age of that site, xviiith–xxth dynasties; it does not look like a Roman form. 98 is the usual Roman unguent spoon, from Oxyrhynkhos. 99 is the small Roman spoon, used for shell-fish. The form of 100, from Rifeh, is very unusual for late times, being more like some of the fancy spoons of the second prehistoric age. 101 is an unusual combination of large and small spoons. 102 is one of the largest size of Roman spoons. A dinner tool of combined spoon and knife was made of iron, 71 (lxxiii). 83 (lxxii) shows that the spoon was well formed by the lake-dwellers in North Italy. A lead spoon, 82, is probably Roman. A long paper on the spoons of later ages is in *Archaeologia*, liii, 107.

POUNDERS AND GRINDERS

169. The large bronze pestle, 103, lxxiv, from Memphis, is probably of Roman age. Earlier models of pestle and mortar, W 104, pl. lv, were in the foundation deposits of Saptah, xixth dynasty. The mortars are not commonly found until Roman times; the form then is conical, with a neat lug on either side at the level of the brim.

Corn grinders in Egypt were slightly concave slabs, on which a long stone was slid to and fro. Such are represented in the models of women grinding corn, dating from the ivth and vth dynasties. Such a slab might be mounted on a stand, as shown in the wooden model here, W 105, where a trough at the end is provided to hold the meal when ground. A usual place for this corn grinding was beneath the staircase in the courtyard; see the house models of the ixth to xiith dynasties in *Gizeh and Rifeh*, xviii, 118; xviii, B, 83; xix, 77; and xxii. Model corn-grinders were placed in the foundation deposits of Saptah, W 106, and full-sized grinders deposited at Defenneh by Psamtek I (P.T. xxii). In Roman times a different type came into use, of which a stone model is here, W 107. This is a slab of trachyte, with a funnel to hold the corn, opening below in a long slit, to let the corn work down between the upper and lower stones as it became ground. A notch at each end served to hold a cross bar by which it was slid to and fro. There is a whole one at University College, but these blocks were almost always broken in use, and generally only quarters are found on the late Roman sites in the Delta (see *Tanis* ii, Nebesheh vii, 21). Rotary milling was not used in Egypt till later times. The granite columns of temples have been mostly cut up for heavy millstones; and at present the circular quern is the regular Bedawy mode of corn grinding. Neither of these are yet proved to be older than the late Roman period, and probably are of Arab age.

FIRE DRILL

170. The mode of making fire is not represented on monuments; and strange to say, it is only from

Kahun in the xiith dynasty that we have the fire-sticks, W 108, lv, and drills (see P.I. vii, 24–26). These fire-sticks are exactly like those used in some lands at present, with a notch in the side of the drill hole, for the heated wood powder to fall out and catch alight. The drill stick was doubtless worked by the bow. Both the fire drill and bow drilling probably originated from the use of the bow and arrow.

STRIGIL

171. The use of the strigil is essentially Greek, adopted by the Roman. Those found in Egypt are all due to the foreign influence. The iron strigil, 109, lxxiv, is slightly curved; the bronze strigils, 110, 111, are bent at right angles. There is one of iron from Egypt in the British Museum.

BENEDICTORY CROSS

172. The small iron crosses of Coptic age, 114 to 117, lxxiv, end in a rounded handle; it seems probable that they were used by priests to hold up in benediction.

The group of bronze tools from Central Syria, O 119, A 95, 170, 171, lxxiv, have been described under axes. The iron object, 113, pointed at both ends, with rings through the middle, is of unknown use.

BOLT, LOCK AND KEY: PL. LXXV

173. The wooden bolt was used to fasten doors from very early times. It was of two forms, the plain bolt, with a head to prevent it shooting too far, W 124, which fitted in a holder, W 125, that was fixed to the door post by a tenon. Another form, 126, 127, slid in holders on the door, and had a groove across the middle by which a string could be put round it and sealed, so that it could not be withdrawn, without breaking the seal. This form is usual as a hieroglyph from the first dynasty (P.R. i, xxix, 86) showing that the sealed bolt was then familiar.

A peculiar form of opener, for thrusting back a door bolt from the outside, is used in Abyssinia. It is evident that the rods 128 to 131, with a hole at each end, were thus used as door openers. The action is fully explained, with a series of diagrams showing the positions of action, in *Zeits. Aeg. Sprache*, 1906, 60-65, where similar examples from the Berlin and Leiden Museums are published.

174. There were various forms of lock in the Roman period, depending on lifting up concealed pins, which fell into the bolt, and prevented it being moved; these precede the rotating key. The simplest type is that in which a key lifts up the pins or tumblers, so as to liberate the bolt, which is then moved by the other hand. This is form W 133; the key is here in place toward the right, the tumblers or vertical pins have been lost, the bolt is below toward the left. On lifting the key, the studs on it would lift the tumblers in the vertical grooves; the tumblers being twice the breadth of the key, and notched out to let the key pass them. Below is a bolt for such a lock 135, and keys 136-7-8-9, and 211, lxxvi. This type of lock is still used in North Ronaldsay, Orkney. For this, and a general classification of types of lock, see Romilly Allen in *Proc. Soc. Antiq. Scot.* 9 Feb. 1880.

175. The more advanced type of lock is that in use still in Egypt, W 132. The key lifts the tumblers out of the bolt, by pins on the key which rise into the bolt, thus the key engages the bolt and can slide it without requiring a second hand. Below is a bolt for such a lock, 134, and keys 140-1-2, also made in bronze and iron, as 155 to 165, 193 to 202. This type is also used in Persia. It would be capable of much refinement by having varying thickness of bolt and lengths of peg on the key; thus too long a peg would engage the block over the bolt, or too short a peg would not lift the tumbler clear. All the Egyptian locks have pegs of equal length, so that the hidden pattern of the peg holes is therefore the only security, and that could be easily copied from an impression.

Somewhat similar is the Juellinge key, W 204, lxxii, which lifts the tumblers so as to disengage the sliding lid of a box.

176. Another, and perhaps the earliest, type of lock, which has not yet been found in Egypt, is the "Homeric lock" (Brit. Mus. *Greek and Roman Life*, fig. 170). This has two tumblers, which are lifted by putting a key like W 203, lxxii, through a vertical slot between them, and then turning it round to engage them and lift them. This type is usual in Roman and Saxon times, and still used in Norway and China (*P.S.A.S.* 11 June, 1883).

177. The lifting lock is still commonly used for garden gates, depending on the wards of the key passing obstructions, and reaching the latch; this is apparently the type of the key, 166, lxxvi, and it is the usual type at Pompeii.

178. The next principle adopted was to rotate the key with wards, as in a modern lock. This was very usual in Roman times, as 167 to 192, lxxvi, from Egypt, and 205 to 210, lxxii, from Pompeii. As the pipe of the key was difficult to make, and liable to get choked, a split pipe was sometimes used instead, as 175. The peg key was also used, 189-191 (lxxvi), but in a very rudimentary form without wards, like most Italian locks of modern times.

The sources that are known of the keys are, 165, 170, 177–79, 181, 182, 185, Oxyrhynkhos; 180, 191, Balyzeh; 189, Gurob; 192, Qanadleh. The large keys with wooden handles are from the Fayum. The key 192 has a beautifully plaited handle of red leather work.

PULLEY AND TOGGLE

179. Pulleys are rarely found of Roman age, the few I have seen are of wood, as 143 (Roman?), 144 (Kahun), pl. lxxv.

Toggles were not unusual. In the first dynasty they were made of green glazed faience (*Abydos* ii, I; viii, 141–3), and probably used to fasten dresses, as is still usual on heavy cloaks. Many of Roman age are made of wood, as 152, 153 Kahun, and 154 Wushym, and used perhaps, as now, for tent buttons, or for attaching ropes in shipping. What seem to be forms of toggle of a large diameter, are the blocks, 149, 150 Kahun, and 151; they are much worn, and are made askew, probably to accommodate two loops passing over the stud ends into the middle groove, and dragging against each other. The wear on them shows that they were sliding to and fro, perhaps on a ship's deck. The pieces of wood 145 to 148 are of unknown purpose, all of the xiith dynasty from Kahun.

COMPASSES: PLS. LXXII, LXXVII

180. There is no sign of compasses being used in Egypt before Graeco-Roman influence. No compasses have been found, nor any trace of struck circles, or of intersecting circular patterns. Nor did such patterns take root in Egypt even in later times. The case was quite different in Asia, where the device of intersecting circles was used in Assyria, and in Palestine became a favourite decoration.

The long top handle of 212, lxxii, is very unusual; it has been revived in modern use, in order to turn the compasses more readily. The Roman form usually tightened the joint by a wedge through the pin, as in 213 to 217. This must have always worked loose by friction of the turning, not having a washer under it; hence it was probably kept loose, and only pushed home to fix the compasses to any set distance. The compass legs were always made overlapping, so that any small circles could not well be turned. This difficulty was avoided, by widening the legs apart in 217, so that the points could be brought opposite to each other. The upper part preserved here is of bronze; the legs were of iron.

In order to get over the difficulty of the legs being oblique when wide open, the plan of turning the points at right angles is excellent, as in 218, 219; but such a type is only good for measuring distances, and cannot well be used for drawing circles.

The type of crossing legs, 220, 221, was adopted in order to enable one hand to open or to close the compasses equally readily, by pressing above or below the crossing.

Proportional compasses are not uncommon; usually they are in the ratio of 1 to 2, as in that here from Oxyrhynkhos, 224, lxxvi (Brit. Mus. *Greek and Roman Life*, fig. 155). The pair drawn here, 222, have the ends respectively 2·3 and 3·3 inches from the middle. This is no simple ratio, but is that of the Roman foot to the Greek cubit. It would then enable a plan drawn in Greek cubits to be read off on a Roman foot rule as a scale. Calipers were well known; the pair of "egg calipers," 223, is of bronze, inlaid with silver vine pattern along both legs.

CHAINS

181. The earliest piece of chain known is from the tomb of Khosekhemui of the iind dynasty, 225 (li), with circular links of beaten copper wire. An iron chain of Roman age, 226, has twisted links. Large circular iron links were also made, as 227; and long links, such as those on a wedge, 228.

CASTING: PL. LXXVII

182. The tools used by the Egyptians in casting appear to have been very simple. Even where great castings are figured in process, they seem to have used only small crucibles, and many ducts in which the metal was poured (see Rekhmara, R.M.C. l). In this—as in all their handwork—the skill was the real means of success, and the means would be useless without that.

The crucibles were roughly made, mostly of ash in order to be infusible, and hence so weak that large sizes could not be attempted. Those here, 245 to 248, have all been used for copper; one has a tubular spout, 246, the others have only a rough lip. The crucible found at Serabit in Sinai, had a large spout near the bottom, so that it was tilted toward the back for melting, and then tilted forward to pour out. As it was a larger size than usual, this method of emptying was necessary in order to avoid lifting so weak a vessel at a white heat (P.S. fig. 161). Another form of melting-dish, with two handles, appears on a bronze model (244) in the foundation deposits of Tausert and Saptah (P.S.T. xvi, xviii). Two melting-dishes or crucibles of iron are in the Naples Museum, 241, 242, lxxii; whether intended for metals, resins or fats is unknown. The double bellows worked by the feet were used for the blast (Rekhmara, R.M.C. l).

183. Open moulds were used in early times in Egypt, the simple flat adzes of the prehistoric age being thus cast. In the xiith dynasty open moulds were cut in a thick piece of pottery, and lined with a smooth coat of clay and ash. The example from Kahun, 249, lxvii, was for casting chisels. Knives were similarly cast, about $\frac{1}{4}$ inch thick (250), and then hammered down to the thin blades required.

184. The earliest objects which would require a closed mould, and probably *cire perdue* casting, are the double spouts of vases of the end of the iind dynasty, found in the tomb of Khosekhemui (P.R. ii, ix, 13). The scarcity of copper objects of the Old or Middle Kingdoms, of a complicated form, does not allow us to follow the history of the process, but *cire perdue* was certainly used for the jewellery of the xiith dynasty. When we reach the xviiith dynasty we find that *cire perdue* bronze casting was in perfection. The skin of metal over the core is often only a fiftieth of an inch thick. The core is of blackened sand and ash, probably mixed with some gum to bind it, which has been charred by the heat. An absurd suggestion has been made that the thin castings were done in chilled moulds, and the liquid metal poured away from the inside. As all these castings are still on the burnt sand cores, like the hollow funeral axes of Britain, it would be totally impossible for them to be produced by chilling. Some hollow pewter pendants of Roman earrings, with a hole on each side and no core, appear to have been made in a chilled mould. See Catalogue of *Ornaments and Toilet objects*.

On many objects the tooling of the wax can be distinctly seen. The solid cast Osiris, 256, shows the slear of the finger on the back; the other Osiris, 257, shows the wax modelling of the flail and crook. On an ibis figure I have seen a long rolled pill of wax put in as a link between the beak and breast, intended to be cut away in finishing the work.

Many of the actual solid wax figures are found, ready prepared for the caster. 251 is a vulture. 252 is a figure of Isis, 253 is a hippopotamus, 254 a falcon, 255 a vulture. These had probably been set aside as damaged, to await retouching before being used for casting. The legs of a bronze Osiris, 258, are from Amarna, and therefore of xviiith dynasty; the metal is here a fiftieth of an inch thick, very regular around, with certainly not over a two-hundredth of an inch of displacement of the core to the exterior mould. 259 is a broken figure of Osiris with very thin bronze over the core, papery in parts. How such extremely thin castings could be run, we cannot understand; the mould must have been heated, and the difficulty would be to retain the core in place in a figure with bends, and without any cross connections between the core and the mould. We should expect the warping due to heating, and the flotation of the light porous core in the fluid metal, entirely to prevent such delicate casting.

The mode of preparing figures in wax is shown by the bronze casting, 261. The knees of the kneeling figure were completely modelled, and then a sheet of wax for the clothing was laid over them, and tooled in a pattern. Thus the Egyptian modelled like a modern artist, designing the bare figure first, and then the drapery. 260 is a remarkable piece of modelling, of a hollow bronze ring on a base, probably a ring on a platform for a rope to run through. The view is taken looking down one side of the ring through the hole from the ring into its base block; the top shell of the ring is broken away, and the back of the inner circle of the ring shows.

262 is a bull's head from a railing. The horizontal rails were of iron covered with a bronze facing, the upright standards that held the rails were of solid bronze, ending in a bull's head. A section of the rail is placed before this.

263 is a bronze foot of an ibis, showing the connecting bars between the claws.

264 is a hand from a figure in bronze, probably of the Magna Graecia school of Ptolemaic age. It

shows how poorly the core was worked, with thick wax over the palm of the hand and solid wax fingers. The Greek work did not approach the Egyptian in technical skill.

185. 265 is a stone mould for a bracelet; various other stone moulds will be treated in a volume on the moulds. 266 is one of a series of discs of pottery, each bearing moulds for six *minimi* of the latter part of the fourth century A.D. These discs were placed together in a rouleau, and one casting would make fifty or a hundred coins. The moulds were strongly heated to make the metal flow into the thin forms, and being overheated they stuck together by fusion and were useless. 267 is a similar clay mould for a Ptolemaic coin. It is probable that all these moulds were used by forgers. Another mould of iron, 243 (lxxii), looks as if it were for a coin; but it is not opened, nor any explanation of it provided, in the Kircherian Museum.

CHAPTER XIV

SOME HISTORICAL RESULTS

186. THE distribution of types of tools may be seen as a whole in the synopsis of the plates following this, on four pages of lithograph. In the synopsis the reference to the figures of each class is first given, then the name of the class; next the earliest age to which it can be traced, and the latest appearance of it; if continuing to the present time a long dash follows the earliest date. These dates are mostly approximations, and the starting may be really earlier. The Earlier Region stated, is the country in which the class can be first localised; probably fuller information would trace the form in some cases to a still earlier source, but at present these countries named may be accepted as an approximation. Where a dash is between two names it implies that the form passed on from one to the other; where a comma or & is used, the connection is less certain. The section and page list will make this synopsis serve for reference from the plates to the text.

The main matter to notice is the relation of Egypt to the rest of the world. In this the isolation of Egyptian types is extraordinary. The forms which were the commonest in Egypt were never adopted in other countries. We shall first notice the forms peculiar to Egypt, in historical order. Then, in geographical order, the forms of other countries, which were not accepted in Egypt. Lastly examples of the drift of forms, according to the direction of movement.

FORMS PECULIAR TO EGYPT

187. From the second prehistoric age, S.D. 50, the ivory crescent handle of the dagger appears (D 1), and can be traced onward down to the xviiith dynasty, the hollows within it being at last transformed into perforations in the blade of a dagger with a grasp handle (D 23). Yet this form of crescent, clutched into the palm of the hand to receive an end thrust from the arm, was never copied in other countries. All European handles are cylindrical, to be grasped across the hand.

The square axe (A 6–9, 101–4), without any curve or projection, is the regular type of the age of the earliest kings, and has not been found in any other country. There is some presumption, from its appearance with the large splay adze, that it came with that from Cyprus. It may have been made there for the Egyptian demand, as it was not accepted elsewhere.

The long narrow adze with parallel sides (Z 60–65) and little, or no, splay at the edge, is also characteristic of Egypt from 60 S.D. down to the 1st dynasty. The nearest approach to it are the Kythnos adzes (Z 19, 20), but these have more widening of the edge.

The round-top adze with parallel sides (Z 32, 69) began just before the first dynasty, and the straight sides are unknown elsewhere. With a slight splay, which arose later, it is similar to rare forms of Italy (Z 37) and Spain (Z 38).

The earliest small chisel, with an edge at each end of the bar (C 44–46), of the beginning of the second prehistoric civilisation, is unknown elsewhere.

The round axe was the favourite form in Egypt at least as early as the iiird dynasty, and continued to the xiith dynasty (A 55–70, 106–121). Not a single axe of this form has been noted outside of Egypt.

To the round axe succeeded the axe with lugs (A 71–81, 122–133), by which to lash it to the handle, from the xiith to the xxvith dynasty. This type had thus a long history and was universal in Egypt. None are known anywhere else in the Old World. The same form was evolved in Central America and Peru, owing to the same necessities of hafting a hammered copper axe without a socket hole.

The battleaxe was a lighter form of the same (A 82–94, 134–152), equally general in Egypt, but totally unknown elsewhere, except strangely a copy of a late form found in Wiltshire (A 96) which was probably imported like the Egyptian beads of the xixth dynasty. The very elongated axe of the xviiith dynasty (A 88–9) is also peculiar to Egypt.

The adze developed a necking and a rounded head, beginning in the iiird dynasty and most marked in the vith and xiith dynasties (Z 46–49). This is quite unknown elsewhere.

A favourite weapon of the Egyptian in the xiith dynasty was a stout stick with a long sharp edge of copper inserted in it (A 178–180). It was doubtless used for attacking the head. No such weapon has been met with in other lands.

The usual form of mortising chisel in Egypt was wide and thin, with two equal curves sloping to the edge (C 16–23), generally used from the iiird to the xixth dynasties. It is never found elsewhere.

The typical decoration of dagger blades in Egypt, about the xiith dynasty, was by fine parallel ribbing along the axis, with the lines very slightly diverging (D 37, 38, 42, 43). In all other countries the ribbing or grooving of daggers was parallel to the edge, never parallel to the axis.

The pole axe, a large wide blade figured in the xixth and xxth dynasties (A 181–3), is unknown elsewhere.

The semicircular halberd, A 187, seems also peculiar to Egypt, in all the Old World.

The broad knife with round end and double edge (U 24–31) is the most usual in the xviiith and xixth dynasties, and is only Egyptian. A dagger of similar form, D 108, 110, may be derived from a Cypriote type, D 140, which was traded to Tyre, D 139.

The cutting-out knife of the 1st dynasty is solely Egyptian ; as also is its later development with a notch, L 14–26, which is common in Egypt, but has never been found in any other country.

The forked spear-butt (H 182–9, 202–6) of the xxvith dynasty seems to be Egyptian by its decoration, and it has not been found elsewhere.

As late as Roman times there are two inventions peculiar to Egypt, both excellent, and yet never used elsewhere, the shears with a detachable leg (Q 13–16), and the sickle with a cutting edge of steel inserted, which could be renewed (F 26–30). This latter form may well have been derived from the wooden sickle with inserted saws of flint.

It appears thus that eighteen different tools, or forms of tools, which were usual in Egypt, were all of them unknown in other lands. Even if there were resemblances to one or two of them, that still leaves the great mass of the usual tools of Egypt standing apart from those of all other countries. This is the case from the prehistoric age, down to the Roman occupation. From the later instances we know that this isolation of types accompanied a considerable intercourse, and does not imply that one country was ignorant of another. What it does mean is that each country had its own independent civilisation, had developed its own modes of work, and had thus a barrier against the influence of a rival land.

FORMS UNKNOWN IN EGYPT

188. Next we turn to the converse cases, of types usual in various lands, but which are unknown in Egypt. As we know the Egyptian forms fairly completely from actual tools, models, and pictures, and have a full view of how they were working, it is improbable that any form was adopted by them of which we know nothing. The countries may be noted in the order of position, west and east, as showing what countries did not lend to Egypt. In Cyprus is the pillowy form of axes (A 1–5) and adzes (Z 1, 2), which result from hammering native copper. These are never found in Egypt, where the metal seems to have been melted and cast flat. From the identity of the Egyptian splay adze of the 1st dynasty with that of Cyprus, we may gather the date of the latter, which was probably the source of the Egyptian examples. This puts the full growth of straight-lined forms to the 1st dynasty, and therefore the pillow forms to an earlier age.

From Crete probably originated the double axe, found in the early Minoan age (T 15). Thence it spread far and wide ; but only one example is known from Egypt, of iron (T 41), and probably a Greek or Roman importation. From Crete also probably started the adze with lugs (Z 94–120), of which there are thirty-five examples outside of Egypt, but only two from Egypt, which are, very likely, importations.

Italy developed the socket for a handle, in the axe (O 1–14) and the adze (Z 136–142) ; yet no socket was adopted by the Egyptian, and it only appears on imported tools of Roman age. The adze-axe (T 45–67) was a common tool in Italy and Germany, but not one has appeared in Egypt. The tang chisel (C 105–127) and the socket chisel (C 128–160), were invented in the bronze age in Italy, and commonly used, but none were made by the Egyptians, and they only appear in iron, and as imported by Greeks at Naukratis, or by Assyrians at Thebes. Thus the most useful inventions of Italy, which seem to us essential, were entirely ignored in Egypt.

In North Europe the greatest inventions were the hammered flange to stiffen axes, the growth of flanges and of the stop ridge, and their finally leading to complete sockets. All of this was entirely unknown to the Egyptian, except a slight flangeing on a Syrian type of axe. Another northern form was the pike (H 111–121), of which only one or two Roman examples in iron occur in Egypt.

A western form of knife had a ring at the butt, in order to hang it at the girdle (K 57–64); this never appears in Egypt.

Of Eastern types there is the Oriental axe (O 132–45), the Mesopotamian sloping axe or adze (O 131, Z 144), and the Assyrian pickaxe (T 52), none of which were adopted in Egypt.

Thus just as eighteen familiar forms in Egyptian use were ignored elsewhere, so fourteen forms current in other lands, west and east, were ignored in Egypt. The evidence of the independence of the ancient civilisations, and of their separate growth would hardly be more strongly attested. Had Egypt been the motherland of the use of copper tools, as some writers have recently supposed, it would be incredible that all the commonest forms of tools which would naturally be prototypes, should have been ignored, and entirely new forms started. It seems evident that Egypt neither gave to, nor borrowed from, other lands, but that each country developed its own civilisation.

FORMS WIDELY SPREAD

189. After seeing the many cases of separation between Egypt and other countries, we may now notice about an equal number of cases suggesting connections between countries. These will be noted in their historical order, and the direction of movement which they suggest. In some cases a movement may be only in one direction, as by migration; in other cases it is more commonly reciprocal, as by trade.

In the beginning of the Ist dynasty there is the splayed adze of large size, suddenly appearing in Egypt (Z 8), and identical with the Cyprus adze (Z 7). As copperless Egypt would not be supposed to supply the land of copper with tools, and the form and size were new features in Egypt, it appears that Cyprus was then supplying the great adze to Egypt. This, as we have mentioned, puts the pillowy forms in Cyprus to an earlier date. As the adze is a tool and not a weapon, it points to a trade movement from Cyprus to Egypt at the rise of the dynasties.

In the vth dynasty the scolloped axe appears in Egypt; and as in the xiith dynasty it is far more advanced in the hands of Syrians (A 173) than of Egyptians, it probably came from Syria (A 168–9), very likely originating in Mesopotamia (see A 172). This movement from the east into Egypt seems connected with the invaders who used button seals; they were arriving in the vith dynasty, and the designs of their seals are paralleled from Aleppo and Bismiya in Mesopotamia.

In the xiith dynasty a movement is indicated from Switzerland to Cyprus and Egypt. The close resemblance of a Swiss sickle, F 12, to an Egyptian drawing of the xiith dynasty, F 11, which is unlike any other Egyptian form, does not stand alone. A group of small daggers with notched tangs, copied from a flint form, appear in Switzerland, D 112–114, the Terremare, 115–117, and then in Cyprus, 119. These two lines of movement of about the same period, corroborate each other. There is nothing impossible in trade of the copper age reaching from Italy to Cyprus, as, long before that, the Egyptians were importing emery and obsidian from the Aegean. It suggests that the drift from the east into Egypt which overthrew the Old Kingdom, was repelled by a drift from the west or north, which raised up the Middle Kingdom.

In the xviiith dynasty we know of great influence from Syria upon Egypt, which agrees with the introduction of the toggle-pin known in the Caspian region, N 14, to Egypt, N 15–17. Thence it passed on to Mykenae. Another importation, apparently from Mesopotamia, was the falchion or *khopesh*, K 190–202. Rather before that, there is a suggestion of intercourse along the southern Mediterranean in the form of the spear head of Kames, H 57, like those of Cuma H 46, Sardinia 47, and Spain 48.

In the xixth dynasty there sets in a drift from

the north-west. The pruning-hook of Noricum P 20 is the nearest analogy to the Ramesside hook P 17, and, probably later, the hook P 60 from Nebesheh. The rhombic type of arrow head, R 124-132, 196–203, is found spread in Epirus, Mykenae and Bologna, and therefore probably belonging to the Adriatic centre; if so, the Egyptian examples of the xixth or xxth dynasties are due to importation. Another instance of movement is the bronze hoe from Cyprus (J 4, 5) imported into Egypt so commonly. The thin type 33 being found of iron in Noricum, like the copper forms 50, 51 in Egypt, suggests the previous connection with Adriatic imports. Rather later, about 800 B.C. the leaf sword of Norican form, E 2, 3, is found in Egypt of bronze, E 4, and of iron, K 248. All of these agree with a trade with the Adriatic 1200 to 800 B.C. The bronze swords of the Hallstatt type found in Egypt are dated by E 7 of Sety II to 1200 B.C.

An important connection of types in the historical aspect is that of the narrow straight knife with the tip turned back, K 130–140, 231. This is mainly Sicilian, and evidently native there; while at the same time it is represented among arms in Egypt, and one specimen is in the Cairo Museum. This strongly shows the connection between Eastern Sicily and Egypt about 1200 B.C., just at the time that the Shakalsha are mentioned as attacking Egypt. According to Hellenicos, the Sikels were moving into Sicily about 1250 B.C., they might readily be in a migratory state at 1230 to 1200 B.C. when the Shakalsha are named, and the type being found in Sicily and in Egypt is thus explained. Next there is evidence of strong trade lines from Sicily, by the remarkable drift of the Sicilian razor (X 43–7), already described, along three different lines of descent, to Italy (X 59–63), to Germany (X 57–8), and to Britain (X 51–6). This implies different trade routes to the three countries, as none of the three forms could be derived from either of the others. The route of the Italian form is obvious; the German form probably went by the Adriatic trade; and the Flemish and British form by the Rhone route. The date is probably between 1000 and 800 B.C.

The spread of the South Russian, or Asiatic, triangular arrow in Egypt may be fairly connected with the Scythian invasion of Syria, 600 B.C., and attack on Egyptian power at the time. The importance of Scythia at that period is shown by the extension of the type to Central Europe and Central Asia, which accords with the prominence of Scythia in the Herodotean view of the world.

On Central Europe two different influences were continually working. From the East the oriental axe and other types were passing into Hungary, which land shows more affinity with Asiatic than with Western design. From the south the mechanical genius of Italy was pressing into Germany, most clearly shown by the flamboyant knife, K 150–167, which appears with a tang in Germany, 162–64.

The Adriatic line of northern influence continued after the examples of the xixth dynasty. The Norican produce was still exported, as shown by the peculiar knife and sword of Carniola, K 188, E 29, 30, which appear at Pesaro and Ancona; K 185, 186, E 28. Down to Roman times the swords of Noricum continued in repute.

Thus many lines of trade and connection are indicated by the transfer of the forms of tools, in accord with what is known from other sources, while the remarkable resisting power of each country against the introduction of some of the commonest types, shows how strong and independent were the separate civilisations.

INDEX

Abbreviations employed, 3
Adriatic trade, 65
Adze, distinguished from axe, 5
earlier than axe in Egypt, 5, 62, 63
hafting of, 18
varieties of, 16–18
with lugs, 17–18
for stone facing, 42
Adze-axe, 15
Adze-hammer, 15, 18
Aebutius, stele of, 42, 43
Agricultural tools, 54
Ambu, chisel of, 20
Amenemhot III, late knife, 23
razor, 49
Amenhetep II, adze of, 16
chisel, 20
knife, 23
scale armour, 38
Amenhetep III, axe of, 9
chisel, 20
American copper tools hammered, 6, 23, 24
harpoons, 37
Amulet axe, 11, 12
Anhur, priest of, 51
Animal-head handles, 23, 24
Antiochos IV, 36
Anvil, 40
Aoh-hetep daggers, 29
Aohmes I, chisel, 20
stamp, 57
Armour, scale, 38
Arrangement of plates, 2
Arrow-head, 33–36, 65
triple, 36
prehistoric, 36
ivory or bone, 36
flint, 36
Auger, 39
Authors referred to, 3
Axe, curved blade, 13
double, 13–15
hafting of, 7
heavy form beginning, 5
plain blade, 5, 62
round, 7, 62
scolloped, 9, 64
socketted, 11
splayed, 7
with lugs, 8, 62
with square tang, 9
Axe-hammer, 41

Barking axe, 12
Bat for flax, 54
Baton with edge, 10, 63
Battle-axes, Egyptian, 9, 63
Bellows, 61
Bick irons, 40
Bill-hook, 47
Bits for cutting wood, 39
Bobbins, 53
Bodkin, 53
Bolt, 59
Borers for skins, 52
for stone vases, 45
Bow, prehistoric, 36
Egyptian, 36
compound, 36
Bow drill, 39
Bowls cut in stone, 46
Brace and bits, 38, 39
Brand, 56
Brick-dresser, 21
Brick-mould, 42
British development of spear, 31
importations, 9, 30
types formed independently, 22, 27, 31
Bronze axes, types of, 7
use of, 7

Builders' tools, 41–43
Bullets for sling, 36
Butts of spears, 33
  forked, 33, 63
Byblos temple weights, 14

Carpenter's hammer, 40
Casting arrowheads, 34
  chilled, 61
  duct on axes, 11
  methods, 12, 60, 61
  thin spear-heads, 31
Castings, earliest are flat, 6, 61
  in closed moulds, 12
Caulking tool, 16, 20
Centre-bit, 39
Ceremonial adzes, 18
  double axe, 13–15
  harpoons, 37
  scimetar, 32
  spears, 31, 32
  sticks, 36
  swords, 32
Chains, 60
Childeric I, *francisca*, 11
Chisel, bare metal, 19, 20
  tang in handle, 20, 21, 64
  handle in socket, 21, 22, 64
  sharp at both ends, 19, 62
  wooden, 41
Chopper, 47
Cire perdue casting, 61
Claw-hammer, 40
Claw-tool for dressing stone, 42
Clothing influencing weapon types, 31, 34, 35
Club, 54
Coin moulds, 62
Comb for weaving, 54
Comb-pick, 42
Compasses, 60
Cooper's hammer, 16, 41
Copper, hammered forms of, 6, 8
  native, used, 6
  use of hammered, 6, 16, 34
  spear-heads, 31
Cores from stone drilling, 44, 45
Corn cut at ear, 46
  grinders, 58
Cradle for large stones, 41
Cross for benediction, 59
Crowbar, 41

Crucibles, 61
Culter, 47
Curlers for wigs, 48, 49
Cutting-out tool, 51, 63

Dagger, Egyptian, 28, 29, 62
  European, 30, 64
Den, fish-hook, 37
Divination by spears, 31, 32
Double axe, 13–15, 63
  types local, 14
  weights, 14
Drawing knife, 39
Dressing stones, 42
Drill for fire, 58
  for hard stone, 44, 45
Drills, 39
Duck's head handle, 23, 24

Egypt, forms peculiar to, 62
  forms unknown in, 63

Emery in saw cut, 45
Emsaht, axes of, 8
  chisel, 20

Facing plate to test flatness, 42
Falx, Etruscan, 27
Feathers for wedges, 41
Ferrules, 8
Fifehead, Egyptian axe from, 9
File, 44
Fire-drill, 58
Fire-hook, 57
Fish design on axes, 8
  on halberd, 11
Fish-hook, 37
Fish-spear, 32, 57
Flamboyant knife, 25, 27, 65
Flanged edges, 10, 64
Flaying knife, 22
Flesh-hook, 57
Flint sickles, 46
Float for plastering, 42
Flower design on axes, 8
Fonderia deposit of tools, 21
Fork for agriculture, 55
Forked arrow, 35
Francisca, 12
  wrongly called, 15

Frankish shield boss, 38

Gazelle-leg handle, 24, 25
Girdle-knife, 23, 64
Goldsmith's tools from Ireland, 20, 40
Gouge, 22
Gouging-adze, 18
Granite drilling and sawing, 44, 45
Grinders for corn, 58

Hair-curlers, 48, 49
Halberd, 10, 63
Hammer dressing, 46
  stone, 40
  with handle, 40
Handles, inlayed, 29
Harpoon, 37
Headsman's axe, 12
Hen-nekht, chisel, 20
Historical results, 62–65
  forms peculiar to Egypt, 62
  forms unknown in Egypt, 63
  forms widely spread, 64
Hoe and pick, 55
  compound, 54
  metal, 18, 19, 65
  narrow, 55
  natural, 54
  Roman, 54
Horse-bit, 55, 56
Hotshepsut, axe of, 9
  razor, 49
Hungarian like Oriental types, 11

Independent invention, 8, 10, 10, 10, 25, 33, 62–65
Inlayed handles, 29
Iron axes, 8
  early knives, 25
  halberd, xxth dynasty, 10
  united with bronze, 10, 25, 26, 61

Kames spear-head, 32, 64
Kash, axe of, 6
Key, 59, 60
Khabbash, sling bullet, 36
Khofra, statue drill-cut, 45, 46
Khopesh, 26, 64
Khosekhemui, 20, 23, 37
Khufu, plumb bob of, 42
  hammer-dressing, 46
  sarcophagus drilled, 45

Knife, flaying, 22
  straight back, 23
  straight edge, 23
  hollow back, 24
  hollow edge, 24
  recurved, 25
  flamboyant, 25
  crook-back, 25
  Khopesh, 26
  double convex, 26
  double-edged, 26, 63
  leaf-shaped, 26
  for papyrus, 52
Kukri, 28

Ladle, 58
Lamp-trimmers, 48, 52
Lance, *see* Spear
Last for shoemakers, 40
Lath-hammer, 41
Leather-cutter, 50
Leather lashing for tools, 9
Level for masons, 42
Lewis, 42
Limits of the present work, 1
Lock, lifting, 59
  turning, 60
Loom parts, 53
Lotus flower pattern of axe, 8
Lug adze, 17, 18

Maize-cutter, 50
Maket harpoon, 37
Mallet, 40
Manacles, 57
Mason's chisel, 20
  pick and chopper, 23
  hammer, 40
Mattock, 15
Mauls for dressing stone, 46
Meydum, saw, 43
Miner's pick, 16
Mitre square, 43
Mortar and pestle, 58
  rake, 41
Mortising chisel, 20, 21, 21, 63
Moulds, open for flat casting, 6
  for bricks, 42
Museums, material from, 1

Nails driven in temples, 32

Needle, 53
Nefermaot, 20
Neterhen, 20
Netting bones, 53
needle, 53
Northern soldiers in Egypt, 38
Nubian forms, 23, 25, 29, 33

Omens from spears, 31, 32
Oriental cast ornament, 12
flamboyant curves, 13
types in Hungary, 11, 65
types not in Egypt, 64
Ornament, Western and Oriental, 12
Osier hook, 48

Pamoun, Apa, 48
Papyrus knife, 52
Pasar, razor of, 50
Pegs for ground loom, 54
Perabsen fish-hook, 37
Pestle, 58
Pickaxe, 15, 16
Pick-hoe, 55
Pike, 33, 64
Pillowy forms of adzes, 16
of beaten copper, 6, 63
older than flat, 6
Pin, 52
Pincers, 41
surgical, 52
Pintadera, 56
Pivot block, 46
Plane, 39, 40
for moulding, 40
Plasterer's moulding tool, 41
Plough derived from hoe, 54
Italian, 55
Plough-share, 55
Plumb bob, 42
Poleaxe, 10, 63
Pollo, Apa, 48
Pruning hook for vines, 47, 48, 65
Ptolemaic coinage cast, 39
Ptolemy II, model tools, 41
Pulley, 60
Pump-drill, 39
Purpose of tools considered, 1

Quarryman's pick, 15
Quern, 58

Rake, 54, 55
Rameses II, hoe, 19
chisel, 20
sword, 27
spear, 32
arrowhead, 35
bill-hook, 47
Rameses III, halberd, 11
scale armour, 38
Ramesseum tools, 9, 19, 20, 25, 26, 41, 53
Rapier, 27, 30
Rasp, 38
Razor, 49, 50, 65
Record of tools very imperfect, 21
Reeds for tanged arrow-heads, 33
Reels, 53
Rekhmara tomb, 42, 43, 50, 61
Ribbing of daggers, 29, 30, 63
Rimer, 39
Rods of wood for stone-dressing, 42
Rollers, 41

S, letter, earliest, 6
Sabre, 28
Sacred weapons, 31, 32
Sa-neit, axe of, 6
Sa-ptah, adze of, 16
hoe of, 19
chisel, 20
knife, 27
falx, 27
mortar, 58
melting-dish, 61
Saw, 43, 44
in frame, 44
for hard stone, 44, 45
Scale armour, 38
Scimetar, sacred, 32
Scissors, 48
Scolloped axe, 9, 64
Scoop, 58
Scramasax, 27
Scraper, 38
Scythe differs from sickle, 46
Scythian invasion, 34
Sekhenu, axe of, 8
Semerkhet, harpoons of, 37
tweezers of, 51
Sen-nehem, 42, 43
Senusert I, axe of, 9
Senusert III, dagger, 29

Sety II, sword, 27, 65
Shakalsha and Siculi, 25, 65
Shardana sword, 27
Shears, 48, 63
Sheshenq I, scale armour, 38
Shield boss, 38
Shovel, 55, 57
Shuttle, 53
Sickle, 46, 47, 64
    with inserted flints, 46
    ,, ,, teeth, 47, 63
Siculi, knives of, 25, 65
Skew form of axe, 9
Sling, 36
    bullet, 36
Socketted arrows, for wood shafts, 33
    axe, 11–13
Socketting first in Syria, 9, 11
    not Egyptian, 11, 63
    tubular, 12
    varies by use and climate, 11, 12
Spade, 55
Spear, copper, 31
    cast, 31
    British, 31
    uses of forms, 31
    ceremonial, 31
    ribbed, 32
    flat, 33
    butt, 33
Specialising of tools, 2
Spindle whorls, 53
Spoon, 58
Spoon-bit, 39
Spur, 56
Squares for masons, 42, 43
Staff-head, 57
Standard weights in temples, 14
Stone-cutter's chisel, 20
Stone cutting by saw and drill, 44
    dressing rods, 42
    implements, ceremonial copies, 8
    ,, imitated by pillowy forms, 6
    ,, influenced by metal, 1
    ,, not included, 1
Straw preserved whole, 46
Strigil, 59
Surgeon's knife, 23
    tweezers, 52
Sword, 27, 28, 65
    sacred, 32
Syrian group of weapons, 9, 10, 12, 59
    use of socketting, 9

T hieroglyph, 39
Tehutmes III, adze of, 16
    axe of, 9
    chisel of, 20
    knife, 23, 26
Thimble, 53
Thorn extractors, 51
Thread balls, 53
Throw stick, 36
Toggle for dress, 60
    for ropes, 60
    pin, 53, 64
Tongs, 41
Tools hitherto neglected, 1, 2
Trade routes, 50
Trident, 57
Trowel, 41
Tubular socket, 12, 15, 18, 55
Tweezers, 51

University College, 1

Vine pattern on halberd, 11

Wax figures for casting, 61
Weapons seldom worn down, 30
Weavers' combs, 54
Weaving, 53
Wedges, 41
Weights of double axes, 14
Wig curlers, 49
Winnowing fans, 54
Wisconsin tools of copper, 6, 23, 24, 33
Wood, hardness of, determines socket, 11
Wooden chisels, 41

Yoke, 54

Zer, harpoons of, 37

A. PLAIN BLADE AXE; STRAIGHT AND SPLAYED.

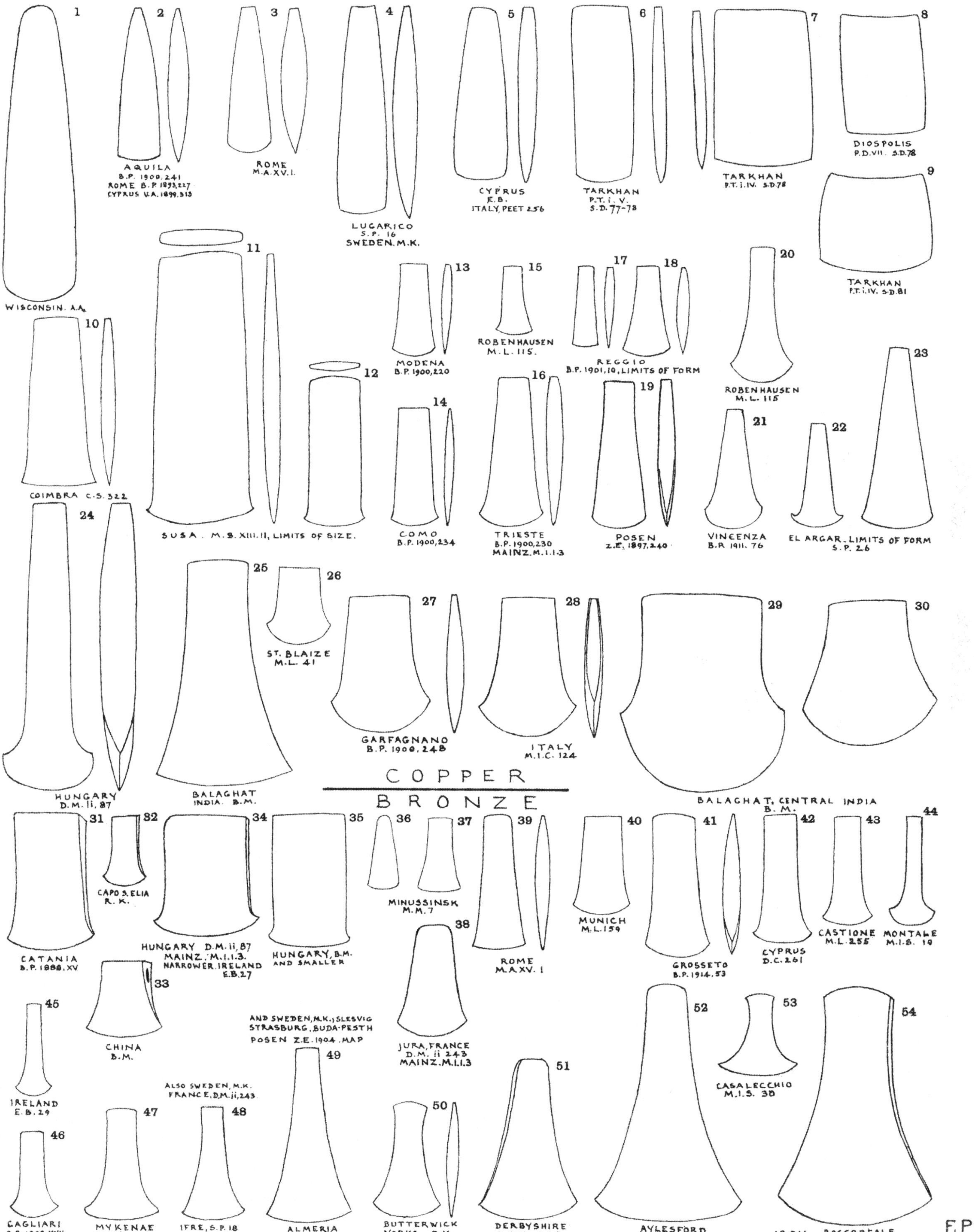

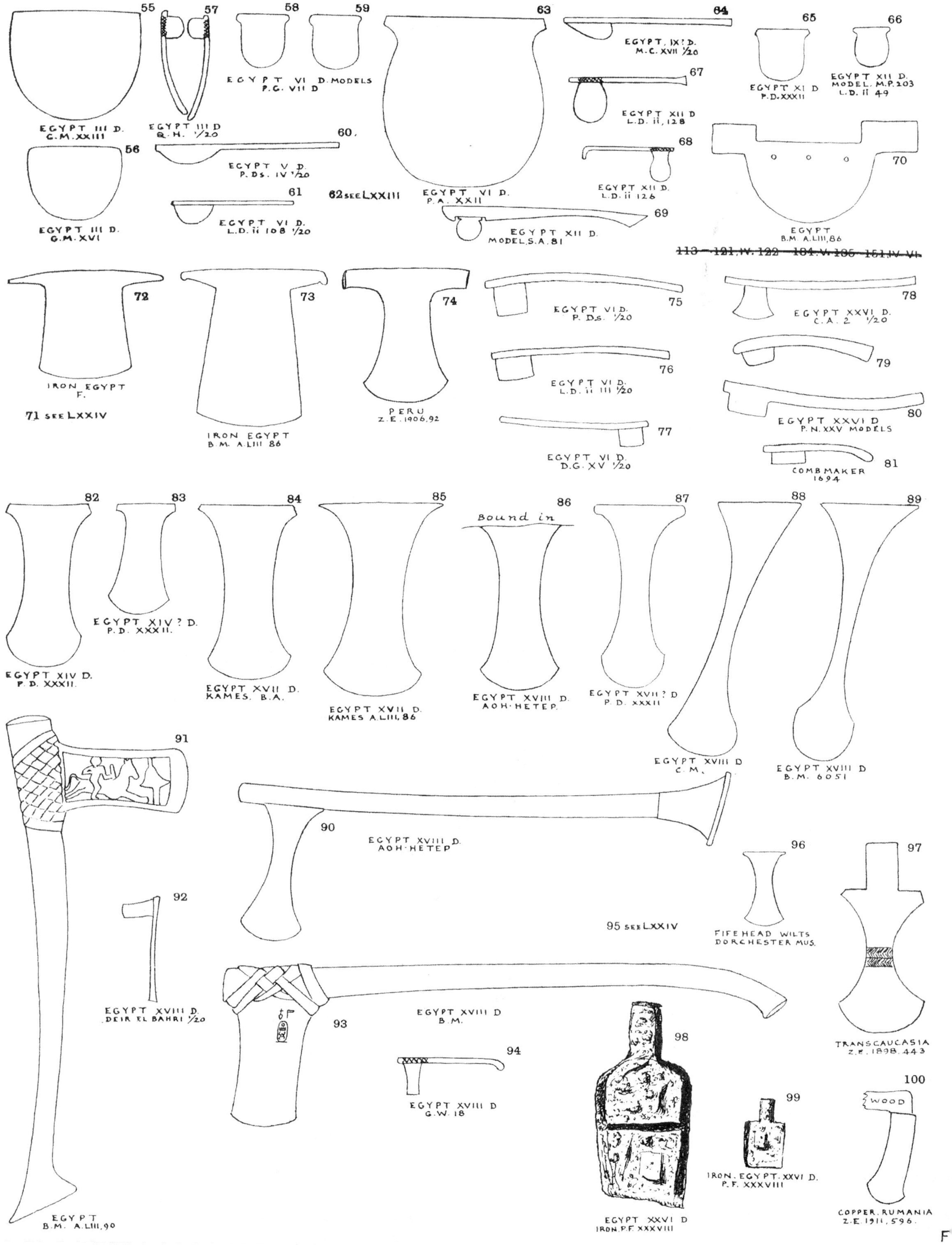
55
EGYPT III D.
G.M. XXIII
57
EGYPT III D
Q.H. 1/20
58
59
EGYPT VI D. MODELS
P.G. VII D
56
EGYPT III D.
G.M. XVI
60.
EGYPT V D.
P. Ds. IV 1/20
61
EGYPT VI D.
L.D. ii 108 1/20
62 see LXXIII
63
EGYPT VI D.
P.A. XXII
64
EGYPT. IX? D.
M.C. XVII 1/20
67
EGYPT XII D
L.D. ii, 128
68
EGYPT XII D.
L.D. ii 126
69
EGYPT XII D.
MODEL. S.A. 81
65
EGYPT XI D
P.D. XXXII
66
EGYPT XII D.
MODEL. M.P. 203
L.D. ii 49
70
EGYPT
B.M. A.LIII, 86
113 – 121. IV. 122 – 184. V. 185 – 151. IV. VI.
72
IRON EGYPT
F.
71 see LXXIV
73
IRON EGYPT
B.M. A.LIII 86
74
PERU
Z.E. 1906, 92
75
EGYPT VI D.
P. Ds. 1/20
76
EGYPT VI D.
L.D. ii III 1/20
77
EGYPT VI D.
D.G. XV 1/20
78
EGYPT XXVI D.
C.A. 2 1/20
79
80
EGYPT XXVI D
P.N. XXV MODELS
81
COMB MAKER
1694
82
EGYPT XIV D.
P.D. XXXII.
83
EGYPT XIV? D.
P.D. XXXII.
84
EGYPT XVII D.
KAMES. B.A.
85
EGYPT XVII D.
KAMES A.LIII, 86
86
Bound in
EGYPT XVIII D.
AOH-HETEP.
87
EGYPT XVII? D
P.D. XXXII
88
EGYPT XVIII D
C.M.
89
EGYPT XVIII D
B.M. 6051
91
EGYPT
B.M. A.LIII, 90
90
EGYPT XVIII D.
AOH-HETEP
92
EGYPT XVIII D.
DEIR EL BAHRI 1/20
95 see LXXIV
96
FIFEHEAD WILTS
DORCHESTER MUS.
97
TRANSCAUCASIA
Z.E. 1898, 443
93
EGYPT XVIII D
B.M.
94
EGYPT XVIII D
G.W. 18
98
EGYPT XXVI D
IRON. P.F. XXXVIII
99
IRON. EGYPT. XXVI D.
P.F. XXXVIII
100
WOOD
COPPER. RUMANIA
Z.E. 1911, 596.

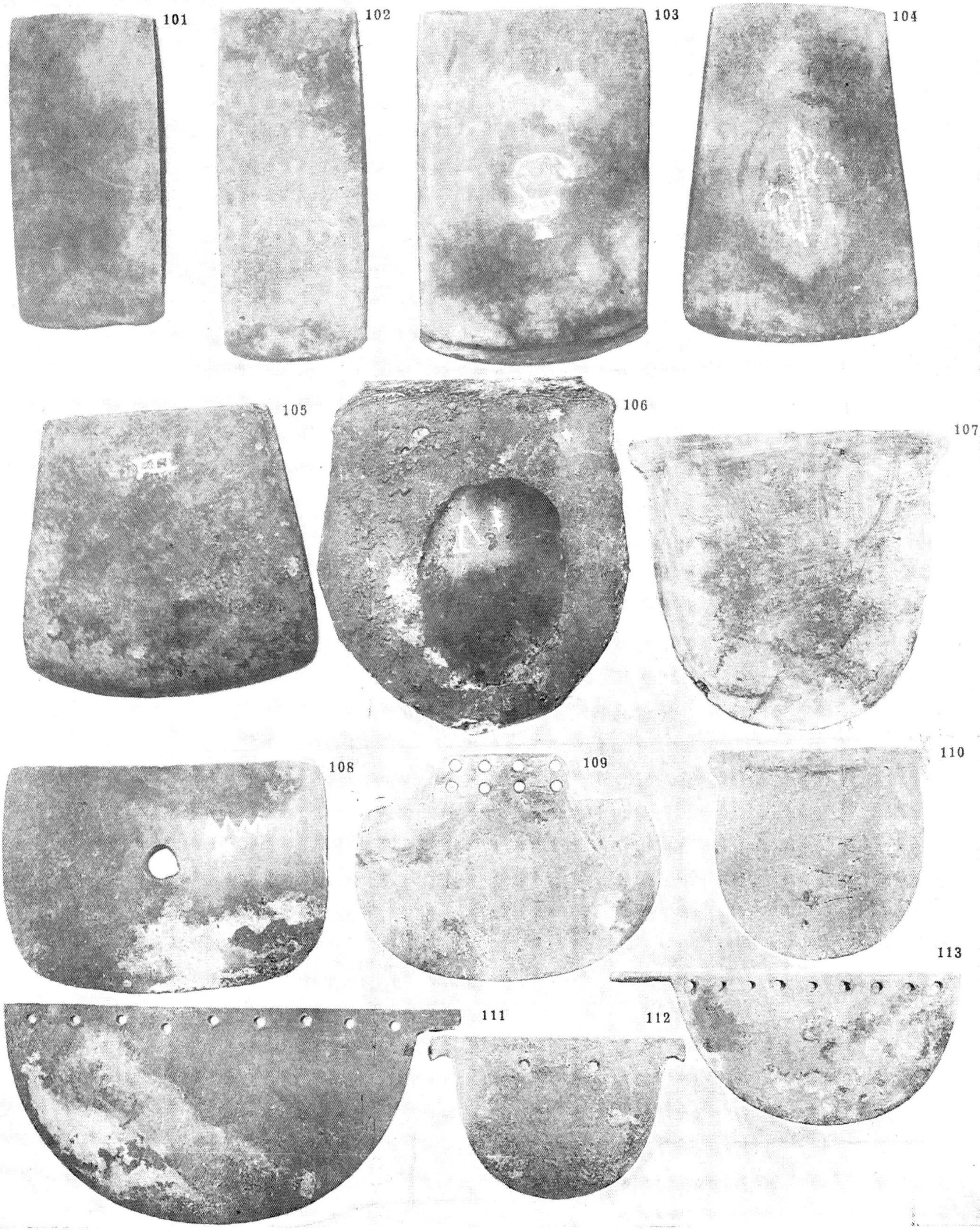
101
102
103
104
105
106
107
108
109
110
111
112
113

114
115
116
117
118
119
120
121
122
123
124
125
126
127

128
129
130
131
132
133
134
135
136
137
138
139

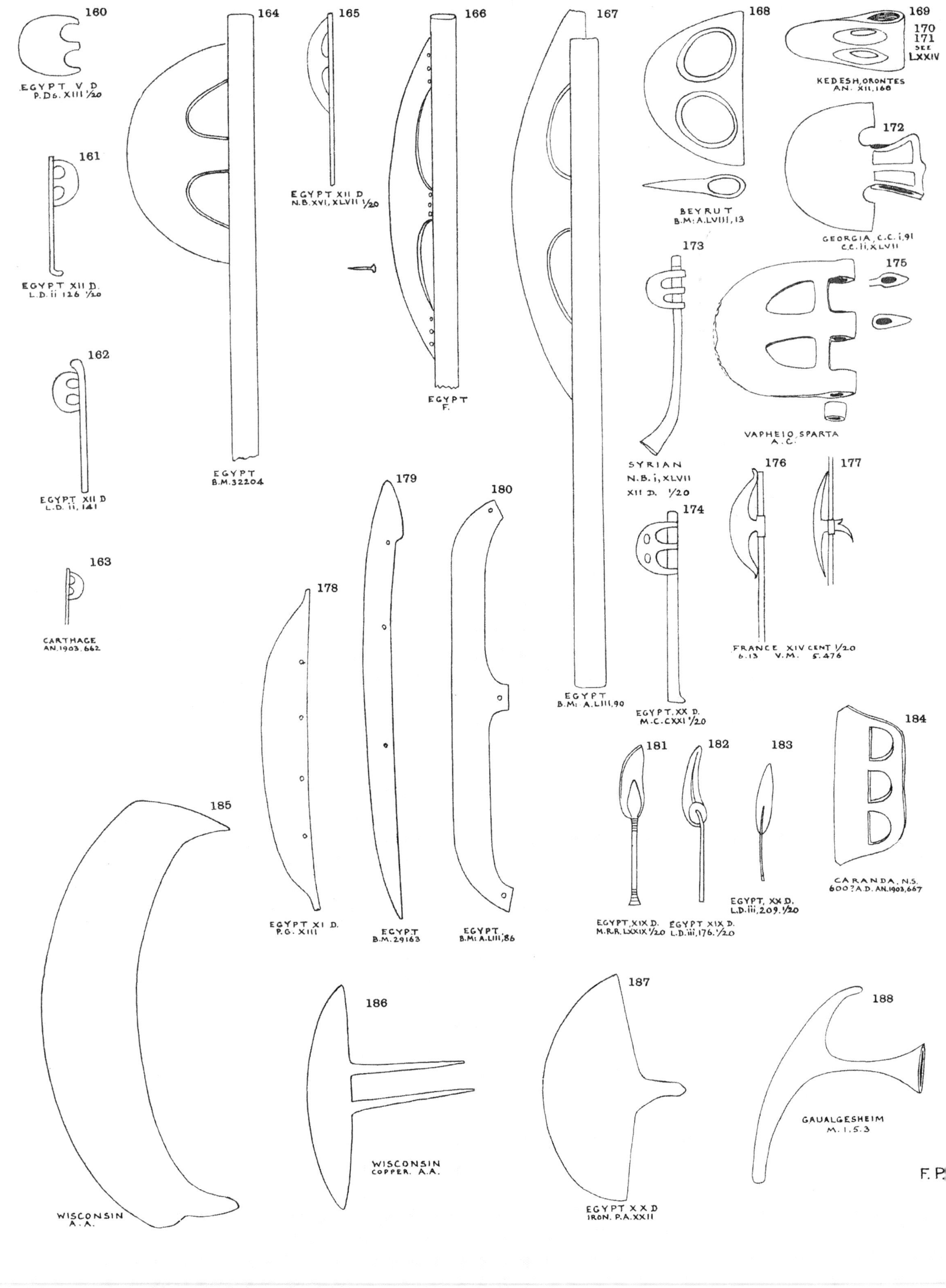
160
EGYPT V D
P. Ds. XIII 1/20
161
EGYPT XII D.
L.D. ii 126 1/20
162
EGYPT XII D
L.D. ii, 141
163
CARTHAGE
AN. 1903. 662
164
EGYPT
B.M. 32204
165
EGYPT XII D
N.B. XVI, XLVII 1/20
166
EGYPT
F.
167
EGYPT
B.M. A.LIII, 90
168
BEYRUT
B.M: A.LVIII, 13
169
170
171
SEE
LXXIV
KEDESH, ORONTES
AN. XII, 168
172
GEORGIA, C.C. i, 91
C.C. ii, XLVII
173
SYRIAN
N.B. i, XLVII
XII D. 1/20
174
EGYPT. XX D.
M.C. CXXI 1/20
175
VAPHEIO, SPARTA
A.C.
176
177
FRANCE XIV CENT 1/20
6.13 V.M. 5.476
178
EGYPT XI D.
P.G. XIII
179
EGYPT
B.M. 29163
180
EGYPT
B.M: A.LIII, 86
181
182
183
EGYPT, XX D.
L.D. iii, 209. 1/20
EGYPT, XIX D.
M.R.R. LXXIX 1/20
EGYPT XIX D.
L.D. iii, 176. 1/20
184
CARANDA, N.S.
600 ? A.D. AN. 1903, 667
185
WISCONSIN
A.A.
186
WISCONSIN
COPPER. A.A.
187
EGYPT X X D
IRON. P.A. XXII
188
GAUALGESHEIM
M. 1.5.3
F. P.

A. PLAIN BLADE AXE; BATTLE AXE, EDGED BATON.

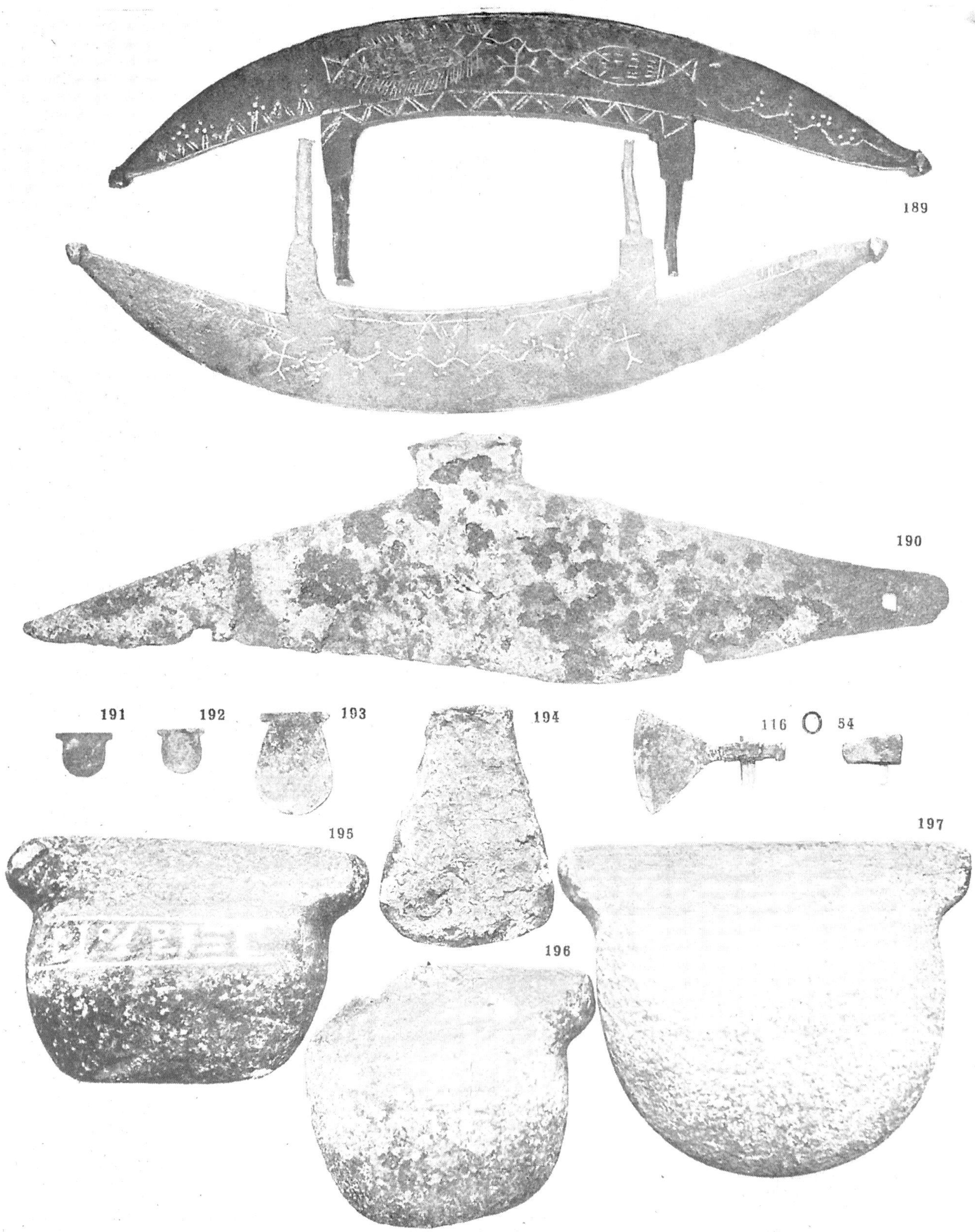

REVERSE O 116 AND 54.

1:4 O. SOCKETTED AXE; SIMPLE AND WIDE BLADES. IX.

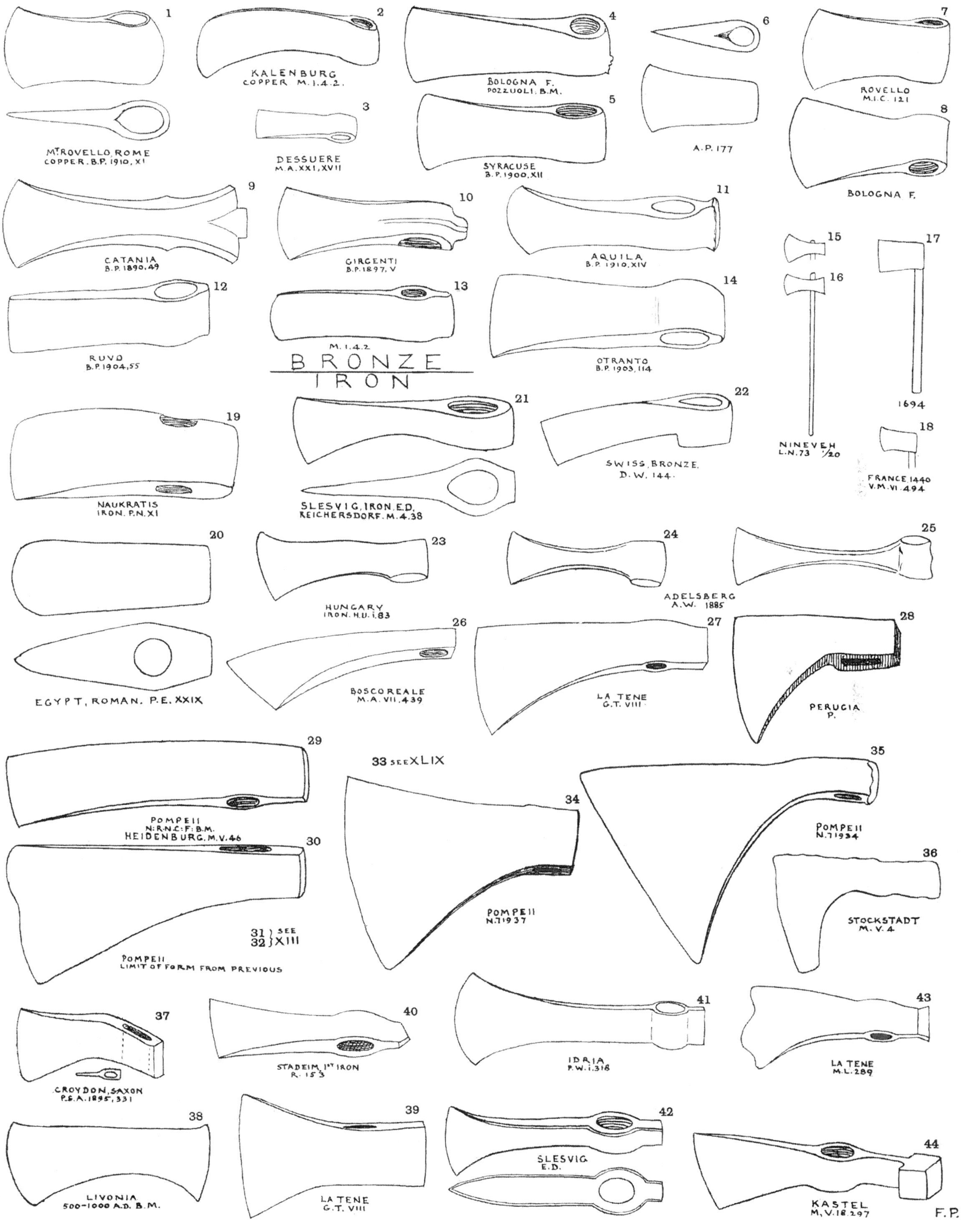

1:4 **O. SOCKETTED AXE; DEEPENED AND ROUND SOCKETS.** X.

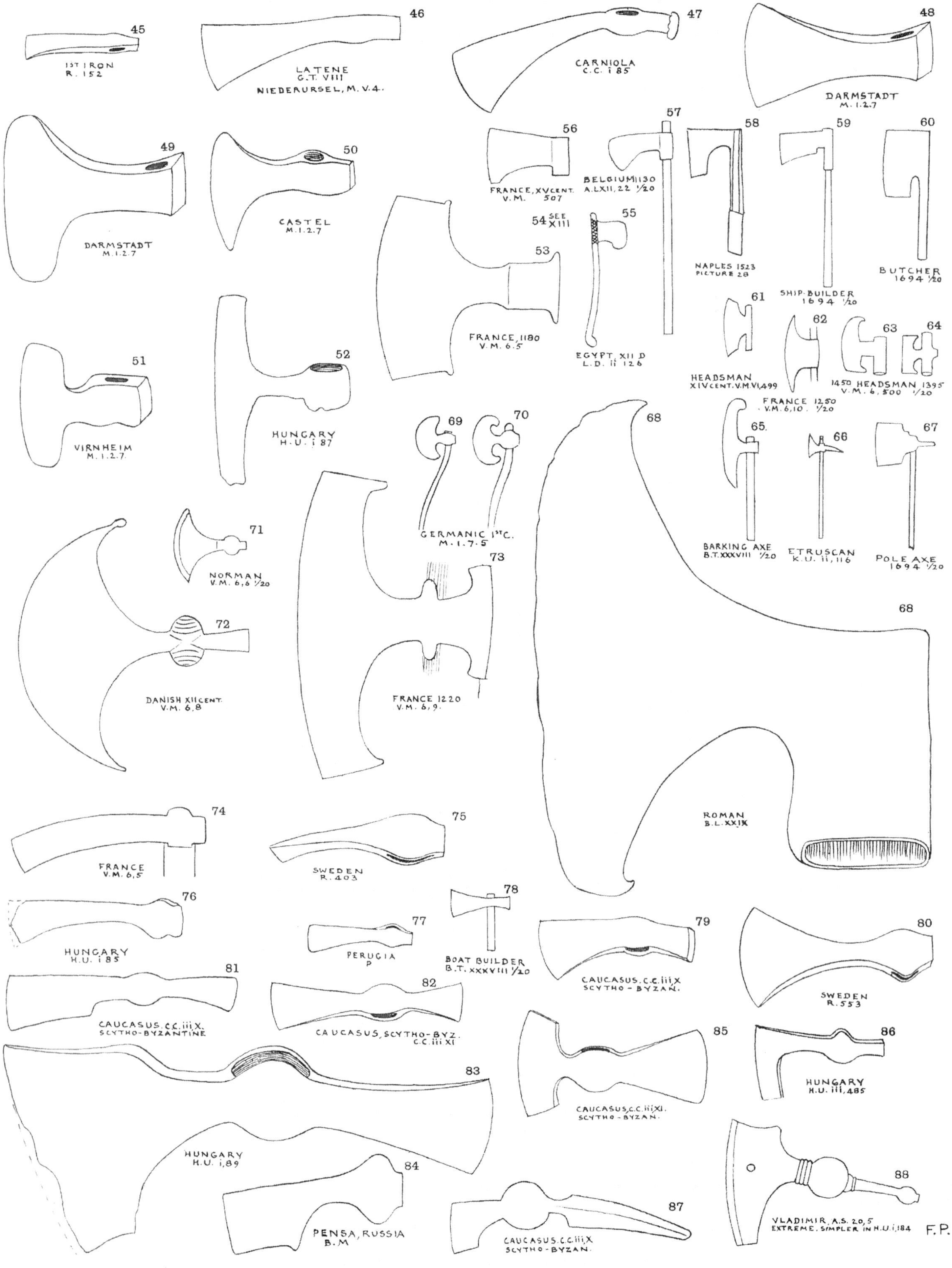

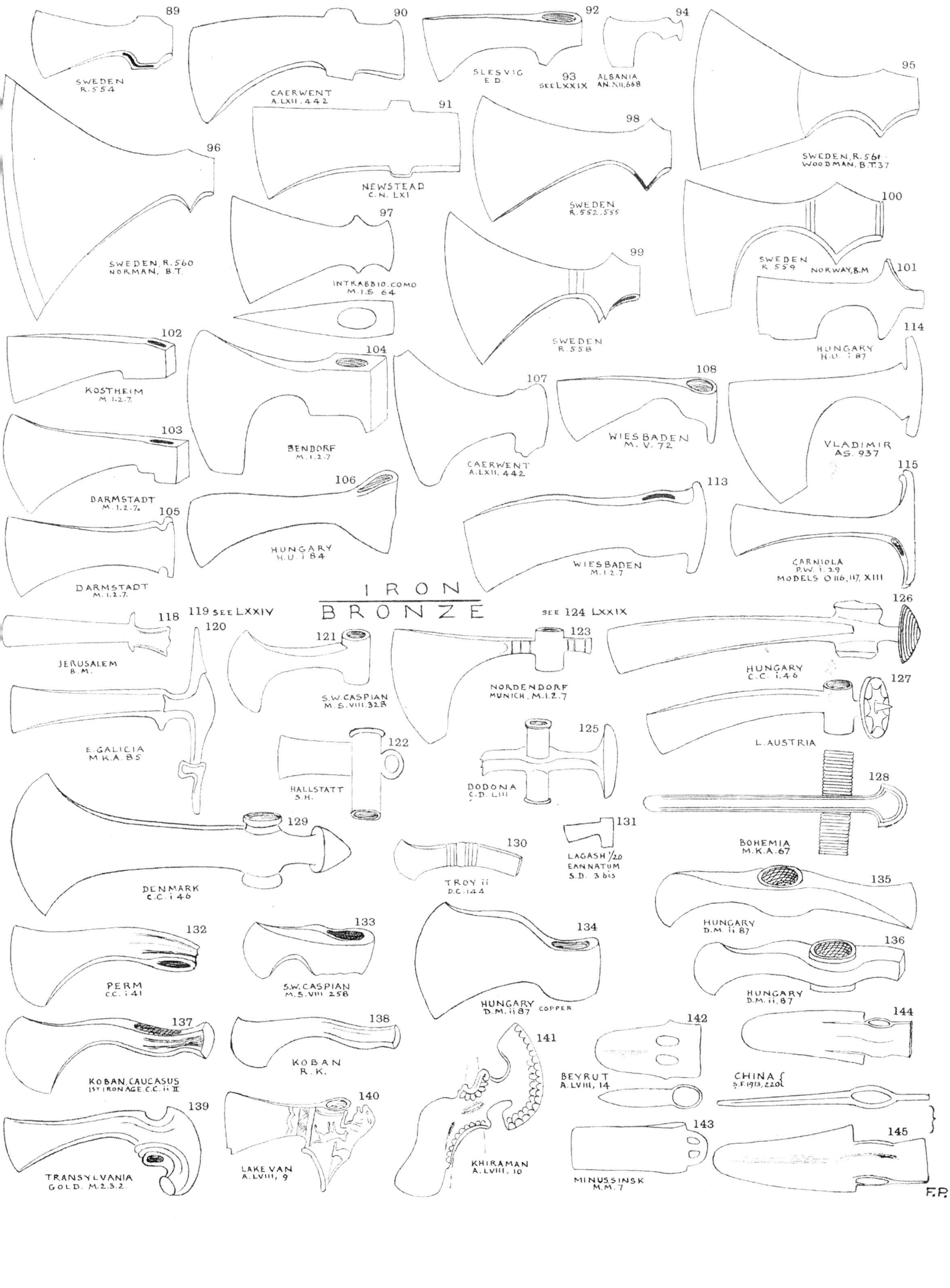
89 SWEDEN R.554
90 CAERWENT A.LXII.442
92 SLESVIG E.D.
93 SEE LXXIX
94 ALBANIA AN.XII.668
95 SWEDEN, R.561 WOODMAN, B.T.37
91 NEWSTEAD C.N. LXI
96 SWEDEN, R.560 NORMAN, B.T.
98 SWEDEN R.552.555
97 INTRABBIO.COMO M.I.S. 64
100 SWEDEN R.559 NORWAY, B.M
99 SWEDEN R.558
101 HUNGARY H.U. i 87
102 KOSTHEIM M.1.2.7.
104 BENDORF M.1.2.7
107 CAERWENT A.LXII.442
108 WIESBADEN M.V.72
114 VLADIMIR AS.937
103 DARMSTADT M.1.2.7.
105 DARMSTADT M.1.2.7.
106 HUNGARY H.U. i 84
113 WIESBADEN M.1.2.7
115 CARNIOLA P.W. i.29 MODELS O 116, 117, XIII
IRON
BRONZE
118 JERUSALEM B.M.
119 SEE LXXIV
120 E.GALICIA M.K.A.85
121 S.W.CASPIAN M.S.VIII.328
122 HALLSTATT S.H.
SEE 124 LXXIX
123 NORDENDORF MUNICH, M.1.2.7
125 DODONA C.D. LIII
126 HUNGARY C.C. i.46
127 L.AUSTRIA
128 BOHEMIA M.K.A.67
129 DENMARK C.C. i 46
130 TROY ii D.C.144
131 LAGASH 1/20 EANNATUM S.D. 3 bis
135 HUNGARY D.M. ii 87
132 PERM C.C. i 41
133 S.W.CASPIAN M.S.VIII 258
134 HUNGARY D.M. ii 87 COPPER
136 HUNGARY D.M. ii 87
137 KOBAN, CAUCASUS 1ST IRON AGE C.C. ii II
138 KOBAN R.K.
141 KHIRAMAN A.LVIII, 10
142 BEYRUT A.LVIII, 14
144 CHINA S.F.1913, 220
139 TRANSYLVANIA GOLD. M.2.3.2.
140 LAKE VAN A.LVIII, 9
143 MINUSSINSK M.M.7
145
F.P.

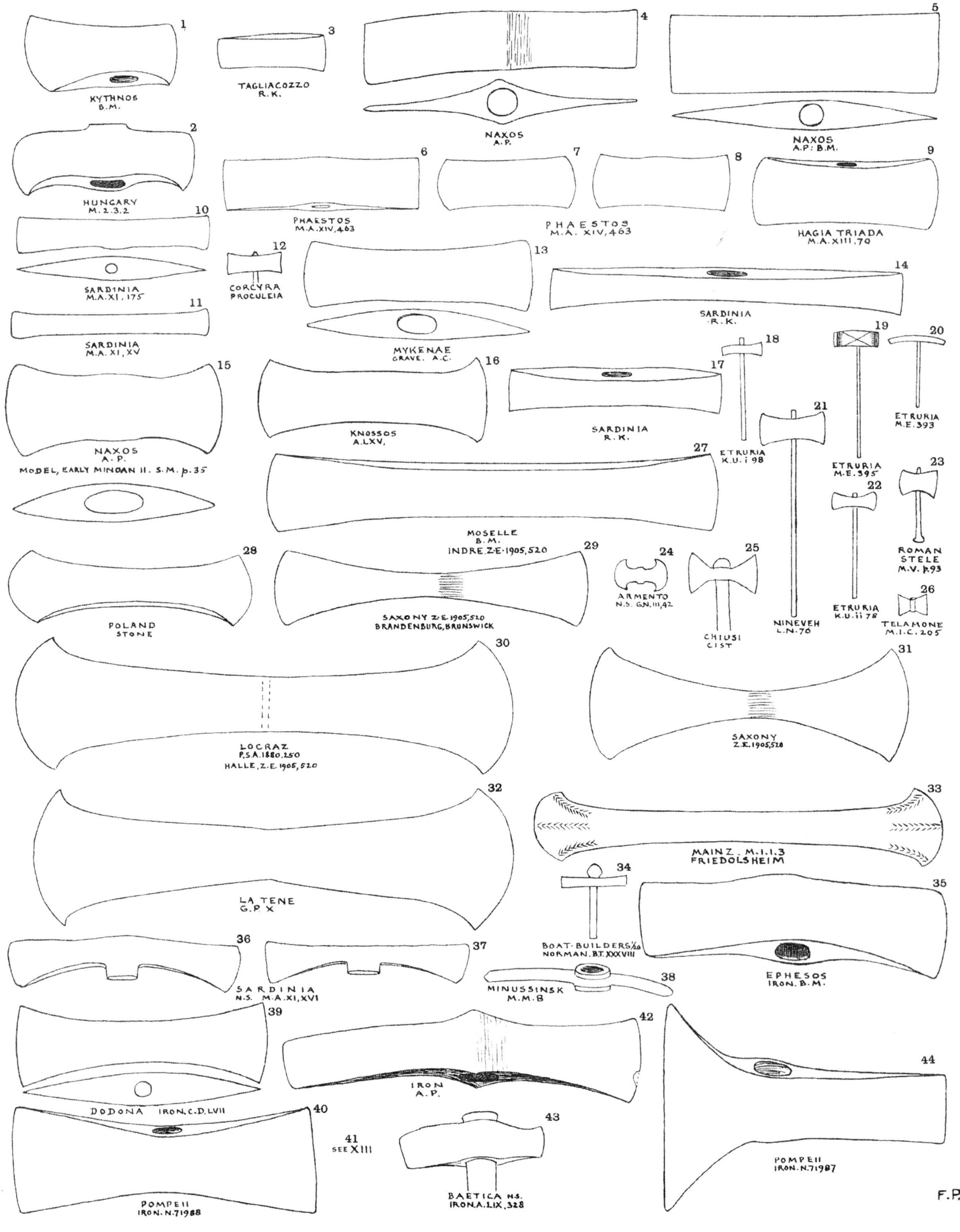
1 KYTHNOS B.M.
2 HUNGARY M.2.3.2
3 TAGLIACOZZO R.K.
4 NAXOS A.P.
5 NAXOS A.P: B.M.
6 PHAESTOS M.A.XIV,463
7
8 PHAESTOS M.A. XIV,463
9 HAGIA TRIADA M.A.XIII,70
10 SARDINIA M.A.XI,175
11 SARDINIA M.A.XI,XV
12 CORCYRA PROCULEIA
13 MYKENAE GRAVE. A.C.
14 SARDINIA R.K.
15 NAXOS A.P. MODEL, EARLY MINOAN II. S.M. p.35
16 KNOSSOS A.LXV.
17 SARDINIA R.K.
18 ETRURIA K.U.i 98
19 ETRURIA M.E.395
20 ETRURIA M.E.393
21 NINEVEH L.N.76
22 ETRURIA K.U.ii 78
23 ROMAN STELE M.V. p.93
24 ARMENTO N.S. G.N.III,42
25 CHIUSI CIST
26 TELAMONE M.I.C.205
27 MOSELLE B.M. INDRE.Z.E.1905,520
28 POLAND STONE
29 SAXONY Z.E.1905,520 BRANDENBURG,BRUNSWICK
30 LOCRAZ P.S.A.1880.250 HALLE,Z.E.1905,520
31 SAXONY Z.E.1905,520
32 LA TENE G.P. X
33 MAINZ. M.I.1.3 FRIEDOLSHEIM
34 BOAT-BUILDERS 1/20 NORMAN.B.T.XXVIII
35 EPHESOS IRON. B.M.
36
37 SARDINIA N.S. M.A.XI,XVI
38 MINUSSINSK M.M.B
39 DODONA IRON.C.D.LVII
40 POMPEII IRON.N.71988
41 SEE XIII
42 IRON A.P.
43 BAETICA N.S. IRON.A.LIX,328
44 POMPEII IRON.N.71987
F.P.

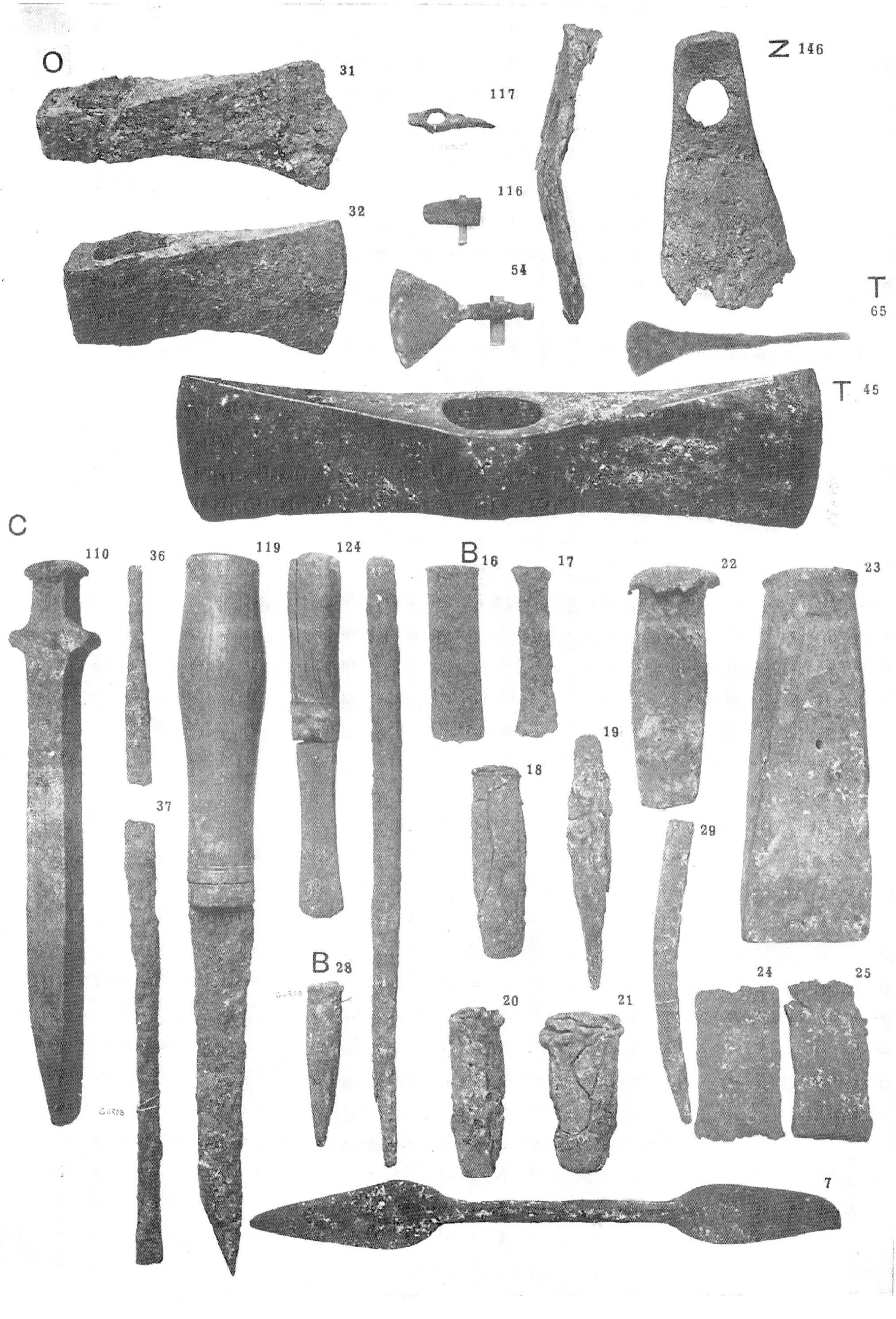

FOR T 45 READ 41.

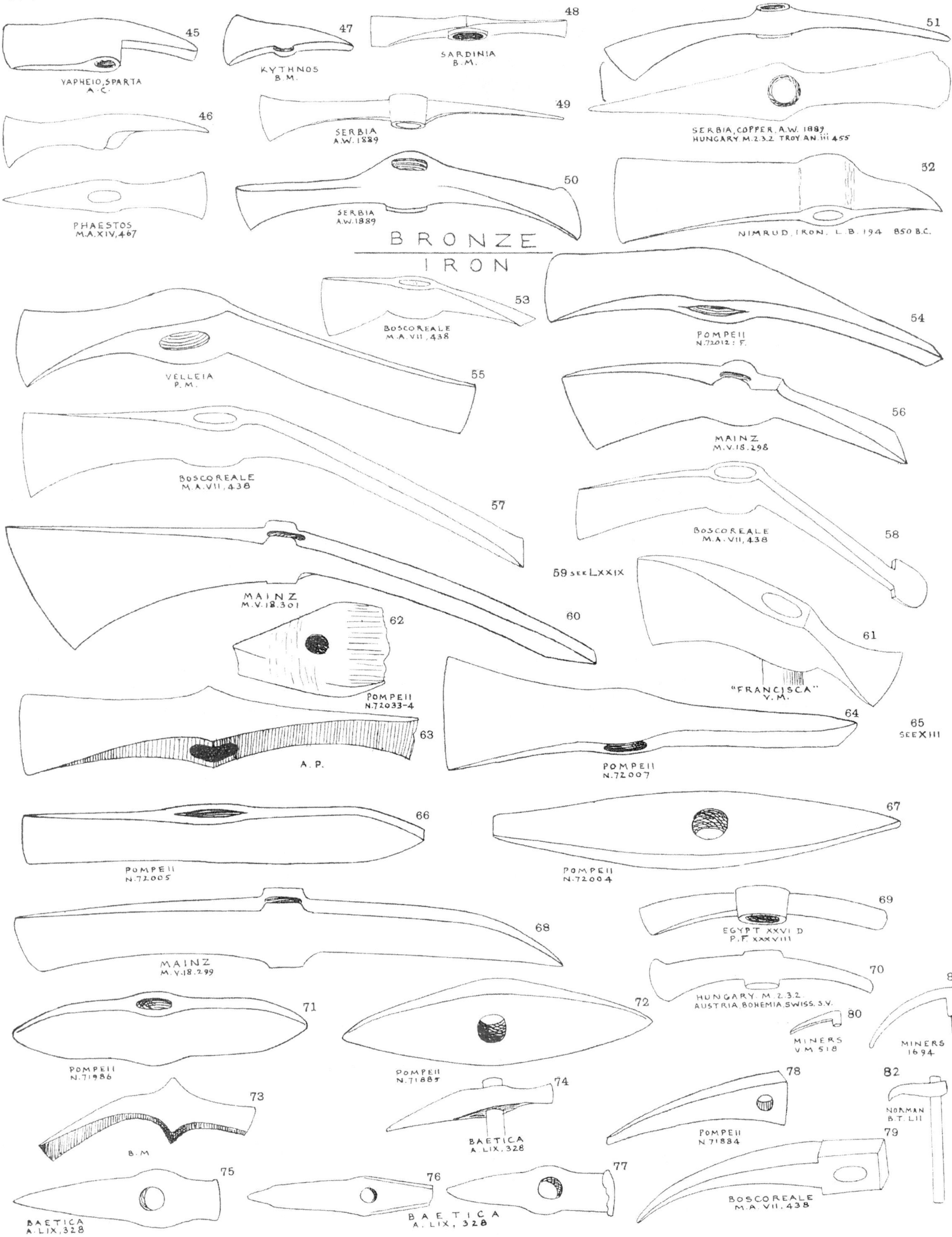
45
YAPHEIO, SPARTA
A.C.
47
KYTHNOS
B.M.
48
SARDINIA
B.M.
51
SERBIA, COPPER, A.W. 1889.
HUNGARY M.2.3.2 TROY AN. iii 455
46
49
SERBIA
A.W. 1889
PHAESTOS
M.A. XIV, 467
50
SERBIA
A.W. 1889
52
NIMRUD, IRON, L.B. 194 850 B.C.
BRONZE
IRON
53
BOSCOREALE
M.A. VII, 438
54
POMPEII
N.72012: F.
55
VELLEIA
P.M.
56
MAINZ
M.V.18.298
57
BOSCOREALE
M.A. VII, 438
58
BOSCOREALE
M.A. VII, 438
59 SEE LXXIX
60
MAINZ
M.V.18.301
61
"FRANCISCA"
V.M.
62
POMPEII
N.72033-4
63
A.P.
64
POMPEII
N.72007
65
SEE XIII
66
POMPEII
N.72005
67
POMPEII
N.72004
68
MAINZ
M.V.18.299
69
EGYPT XXVI D
P.F. XXXVIII
70
HUNGARY M.2.3.2.
AUSTRIA, BOHEMIA, SWISS. S.V.
71
POMPEII
N.71986
72
POMPEII
N.71885
80
MINERS
V M 518
81
MINERS
1694
73
B.M
74
BAETICA
A. LIX, 328
78
POMPEII
N 71884
82
NORMAN
B.T. LII
79
BOSCOREALE
M.A. VII, 438
75
BAETICA
A. LIX, 328
76
77
BAETICA
A. LIX, 328

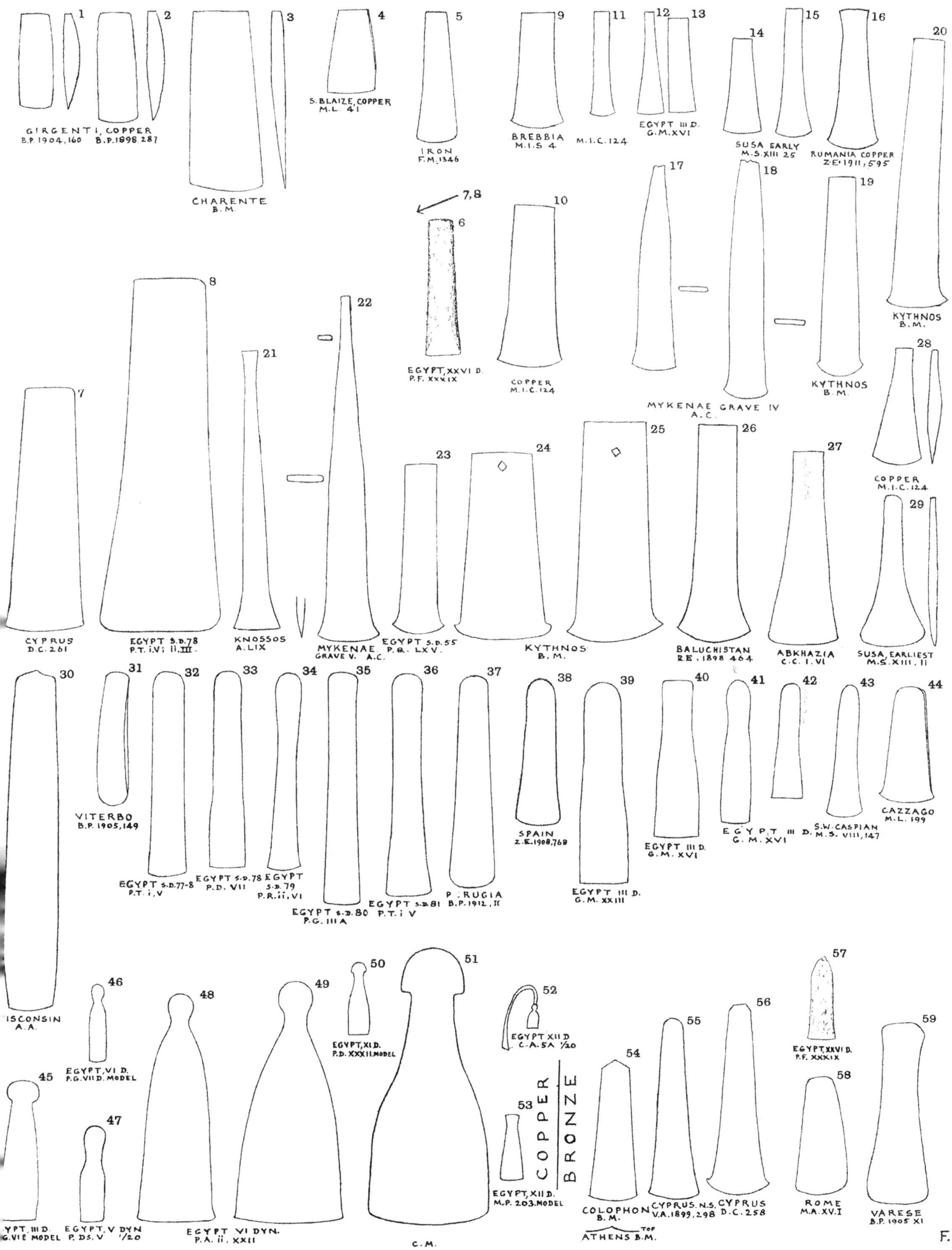

GIRGENTI, COPPER
B.P. 1904, 160 B.P. 1898, 287
CHARENTE B.M.
S. BLAIZE, COPPER M.L. 41
IRON F.M. 1346
BREBBIA M.I.S 4
M.I.C. 124
EGYPT III D. G.M. XVI
SUSA EARLY M.S. XIII 25
RUMANIA COPPER Z.E. 1911, 595
EGYPT, XXVI D. P.F. XXXIX
COPPER M.I.C. 124
MYKENAE GRAVE IV A.C.
KYTHNOS B.M.
KYTHNOS B.M.
COPPER M.I.C. 124
CYPRUS D.C. 261
EGYPT S.D. 78 P.T. i.V; II.III.
KNOSSOS A.LIX
MYKENAE GRAVE V. A.C.
EGYPT S.D. 55 P.Q. LXV.
KYTHNOS B.M.
BALUCHISTAN R.E. 1898 464
ABKHAZIA C.C. I. VI
SUSA, EARLIEST M.S. XIII, II
VITERBO B.P. 1905, 149
EGYPT S.D. 77-8 P.T. i, V
EGYPT S.D. 78 P.D. VII
EGYPT S.D. 79 P.R. ii, VI
EGYPT S.D. 80 P.G. III A
EGYPT S.D. 81 P.T. i V
PERUGIA B.P. 1912, II
SPAIN Z.E. 1908, 768
EGYPT III D. G.M. XXIII
EGYPT III D. G.M. XVI
EGYPT III D. G.M. XVI
S.W. CASPIAN M.S. VIII, 147
CAZZAGO M.L. 199
WISCONSIN A.A.
EGYPT, VI D. P.G. VII D. MODEL
EGYPT, XI D. P.D. XXXII. MODEL
EGYPT XII D. C.A. 5A 1/20
EGYPT, XXVI D. P.F. XXXIX
COPPER
BRONZE
EGYPT, XII D. M.P. 203. MODEL
EGYPT III D. G. VIE MODEL
EGYPT, V DYN P. DS. V 1/20
EGYPT VI DYN. P.A. ii, XXII
C.M.
COLOPHON B.M.
ATHENS B.M. TOP
CYPRUS. N.S. V.A. 1899, 298
CYPRUS D.C. 258
ROME M.A. XV. I
VARESE B.P. 1905 XI
F.P.

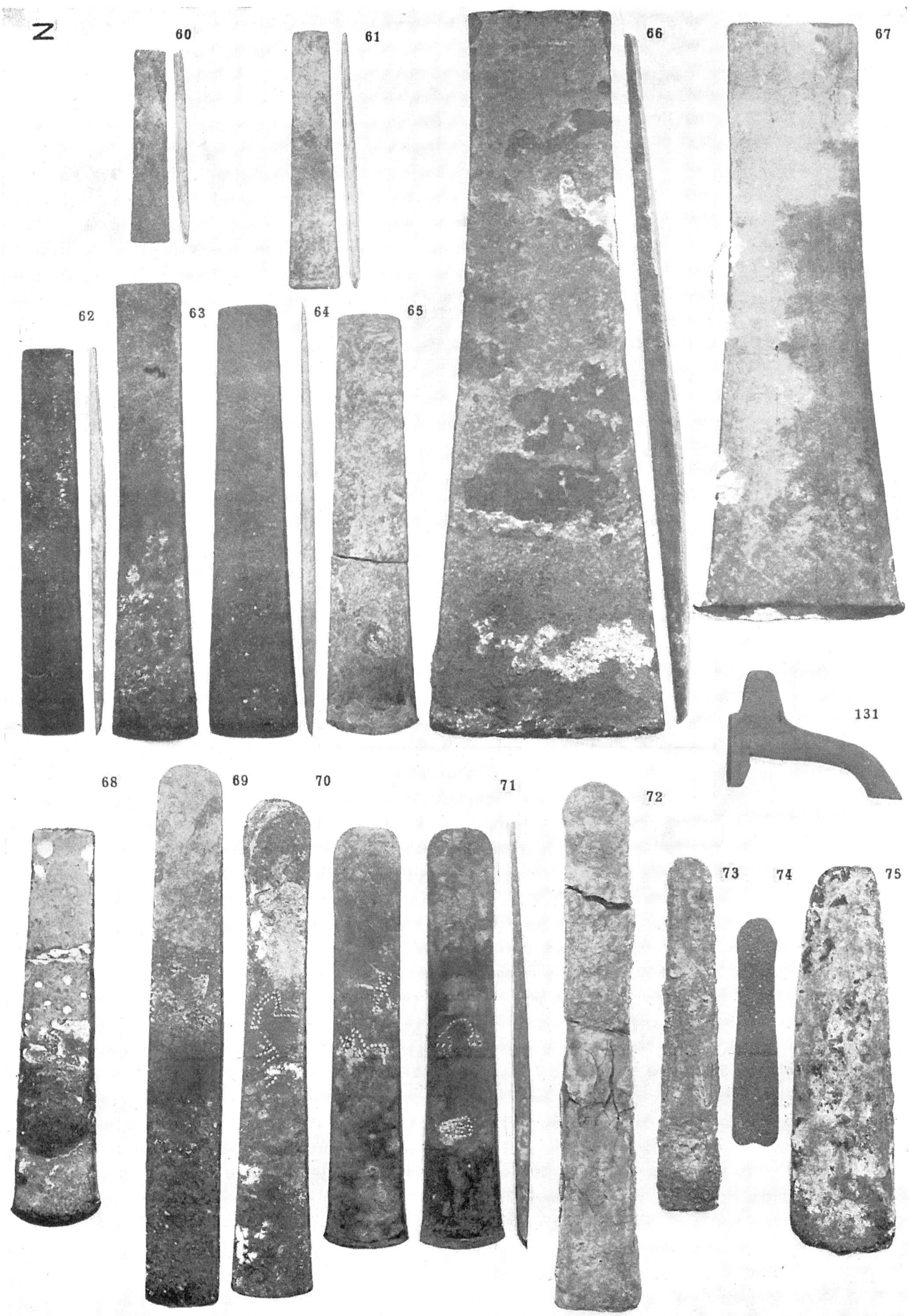
Z
60
61
66
67
62
63
64
65
131
68
69
70
71
72
73
74
75

76
77
78
79
80
81
82
83
84
85
86
87
88
89
90
91
92
93

Z. ADZE WITH LUGS; HAFTING; SOCKETTED ADZE.

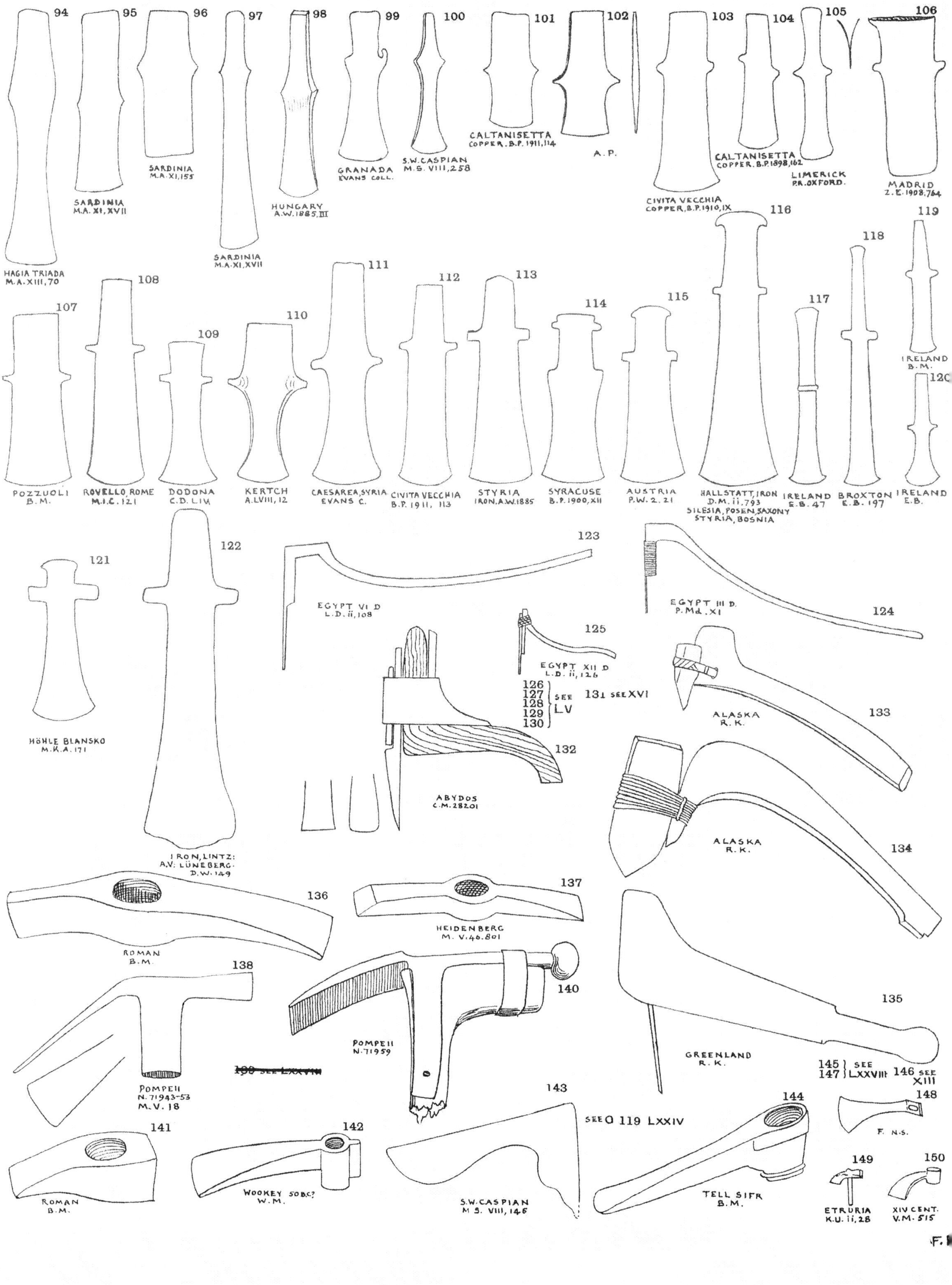

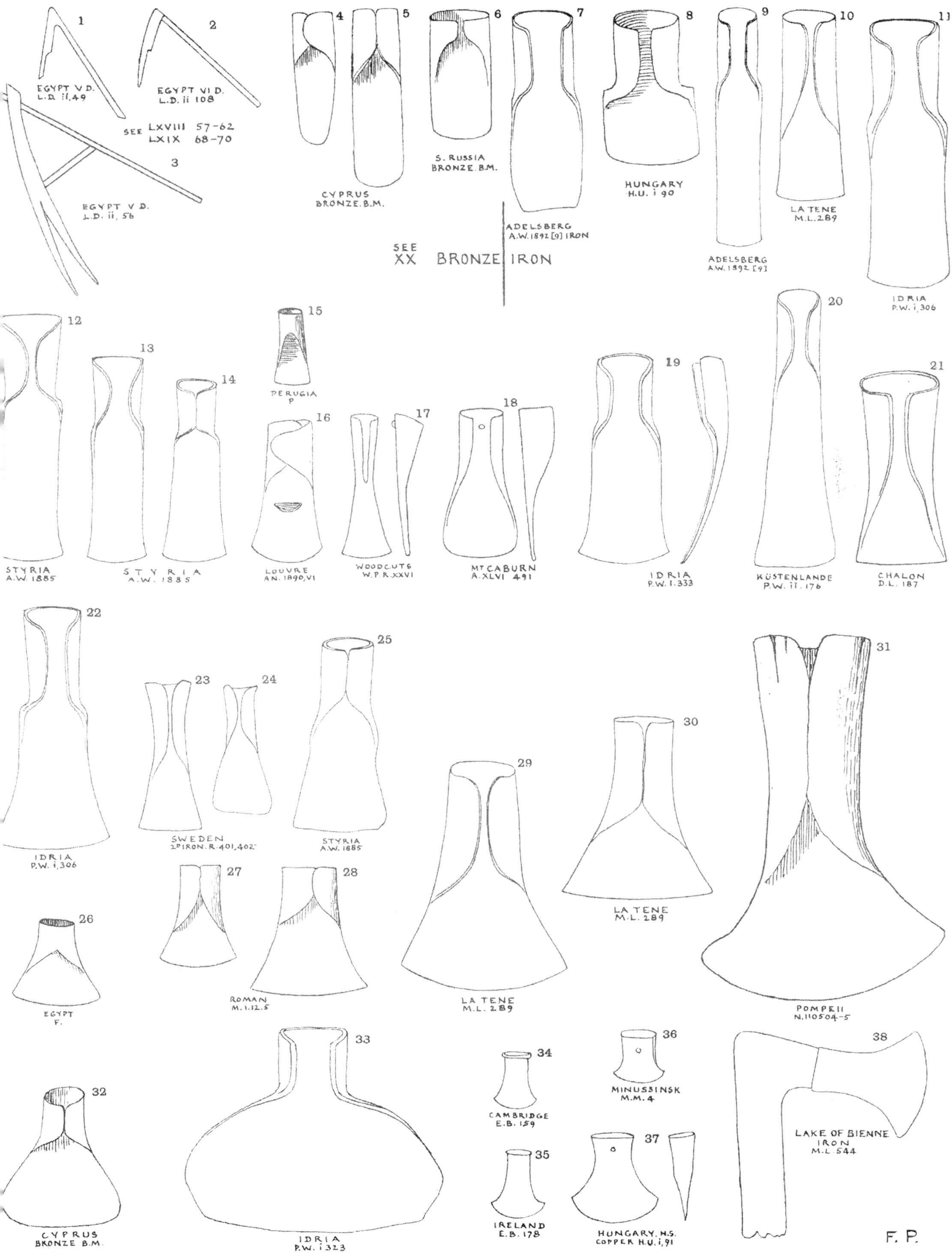
EGYPT V D.
L.D. ii, 49
EGYPT VI D.
L.D. ii 108
SEE LXVIII 57-62
LXIX 68-70
EGYPT V D.
L.D. ii, 56
CYPRUS
BRONZE. B.M.
S. RUSSIA
BRONZE. B.M.
ADELSBERG
A.W. 1892 [9] IRON
SEE
XX BRONZE IRON
HUNGARY
H.U. i 90
ADELSBERG
A.W. 1892 [9]
LA TENE
M.L. 289
IDRIA
P.W. i, 306
STYRIA
A.W. 1885
STYRIA
A.W. 1885
PERUGIA
P
LOUVRE
AN. 1890, VI
WOODCUTS
W.P.R. XXVI
MT CABURN
A. XLVI 491
IDRIA
P.W. I. 333
KÜSTENLANDE
P.W. ii. 176
CHALON
D.L. 187
IDRIA
P.W. i, 306
SWEDEN
2nd IRON. R. 401, 402
STYRIA
A.W. 1885
LA TENE
M.L. 289
EGYPT
F.
ROMAN
M. i. 12. 5
LA TENE
M.L. 289
POMPEII
N. 110504-5
CYPRUS
BRONZE B.M.
IDRIA
P.W. i 323
CAMBRIDGE
E.B. 159
MINUSSINSK
M.M. 4
IRELAND
E.B. 178
HUNGARY, N.S.
COPPER H.U. i, 91
LAKE OF BIENNE
IRON
M.L. 544
F. P.

39
40
41
42
44
45
46
43
47
48
49
50
51
52
53
54
55
56
57
58
RAMESSEUM
59

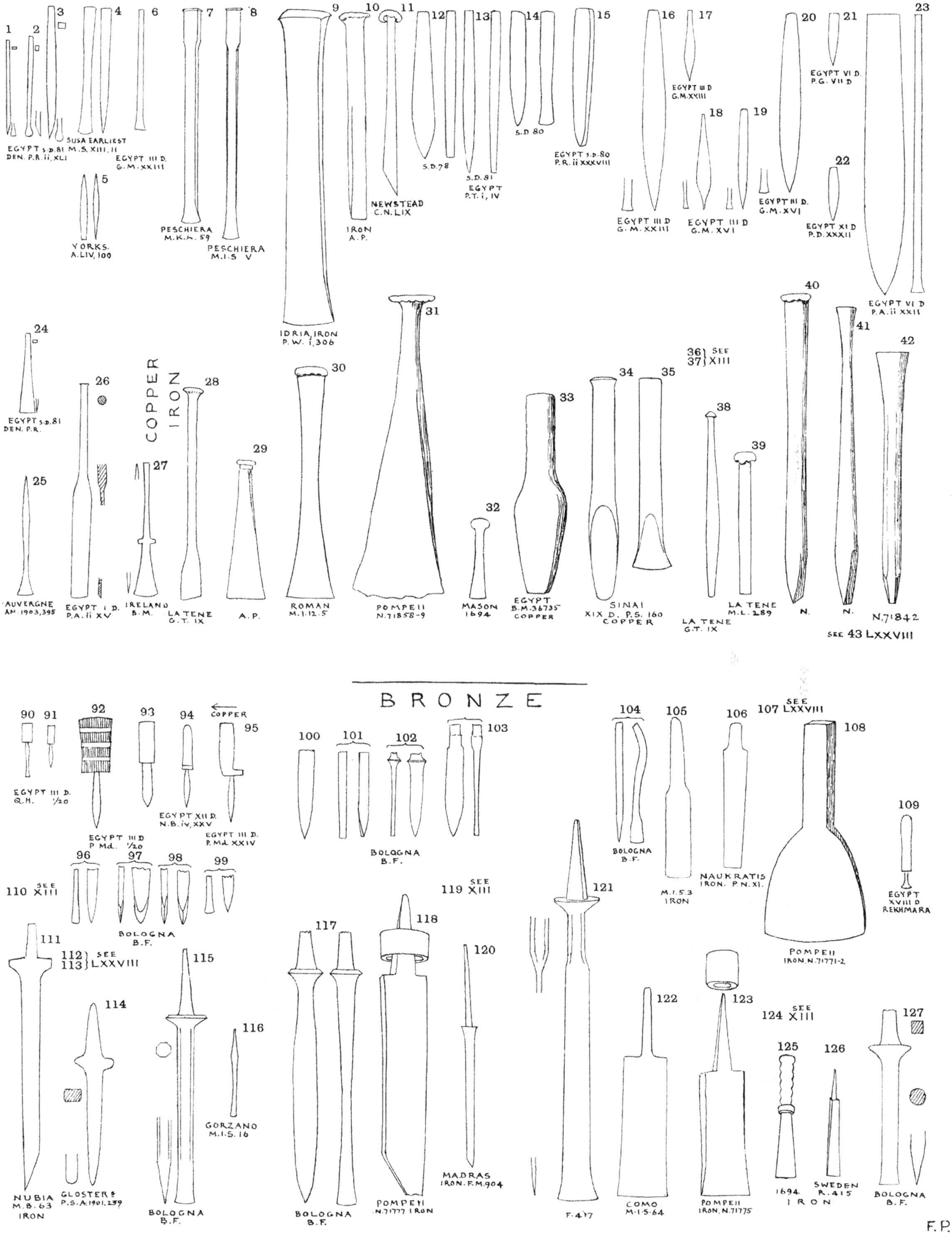
EGYPT S.D.81 DEN. P.R. ii, XLI
SUSA EARLIEST M.S. XIII, 11
EGYPT III D. G.M. XXIII
YORKS. A. LIV, 100
PESCHIERA M.K.A. 59
PESCHIERA M.I.S. V
IDRIA, IRON P.W. i, 306
IRON A.P.
NEWSTEAD C.N. LIX
S.D. 78
S.D. 81 EGYPT P.T. i, IV
S.D. 80
EGYPT S.D. 80 P.R. ii XXXVIII
EGYPT III D G.M. XXIII
EGYPT III D G.M. XVI
EGYPT III D. G.M. XVI
EGYPT VI D. P.G. VII D
EGYPT XI D P.D. XXXII
EGYPT VI D P.A. ii XXII
EGYPT S.D.81 DEN. P.R.
COPPER
IRON
AUVERGNE AN. 1903, 395
EGYPT I D. P.A. ii XV
IRELAND B.M.
LA TENE G.T. IX
A.P.
ROMAN M.1.12.5
POMPEII N.71858-9
MASON 1694
EGYPT B.M. 36735 COPPER
36} SEE 37} XIII
SINAI XIX D. P.S. 160 COPPER
LA TENE G.T. IX
LA TENE M.L. 289
N.
N.
N.71842
SEE 43 LXXVIII
BRONZE
EGYPT III D. Q.H. 1/20
EGYPT III D P Md. 1/20
EGYPT XII D. N.B. iv, XXV
COPPER
EGYPT III D. P. Md. XXIV
BOLOGNA B.F.
BOLOGNA B.F.
SEE 107 LXXVIII
NAUKRATIS IRON. P.N. XI.
M.I.S.3 IRON
EGYPT XVIII D REKHMARA
POMPEII IRON, N.71771-2.
SEE 110 XIII
BOLOGNA B.F.
SEE 119 XIII
112} SEE 113} LXXVIII
NUBIA M.B. 63 IRON
GLOSTER P.S.A. 1901, 239
BOLOGNA B.F.
GORZANO M.I.S. 16
BOLOGNA B.F.
POMPEII N.71777 IRON
MADRAS IRON. F.M. 904
F. 417
COMO M.I.S. 64
POMPEII IRON, N.71775
SEE 124 XIII
1694 IRON
SWEDEN R. 415
BOLOGNA B.F.
F.P.

44 45 46 47 48 52 56 58 60 63 65 68 69 71 73
55
61
66
70
49
53
64
50 51 54 57 59 62 67 72 74 75
76 77 78 79 80 81 82 83 84
85
87 88
89
86

1:4 **C.** CHISEL, SOCKETTED GOUGE. **K.** FLAYING KNIFE. XXIII.

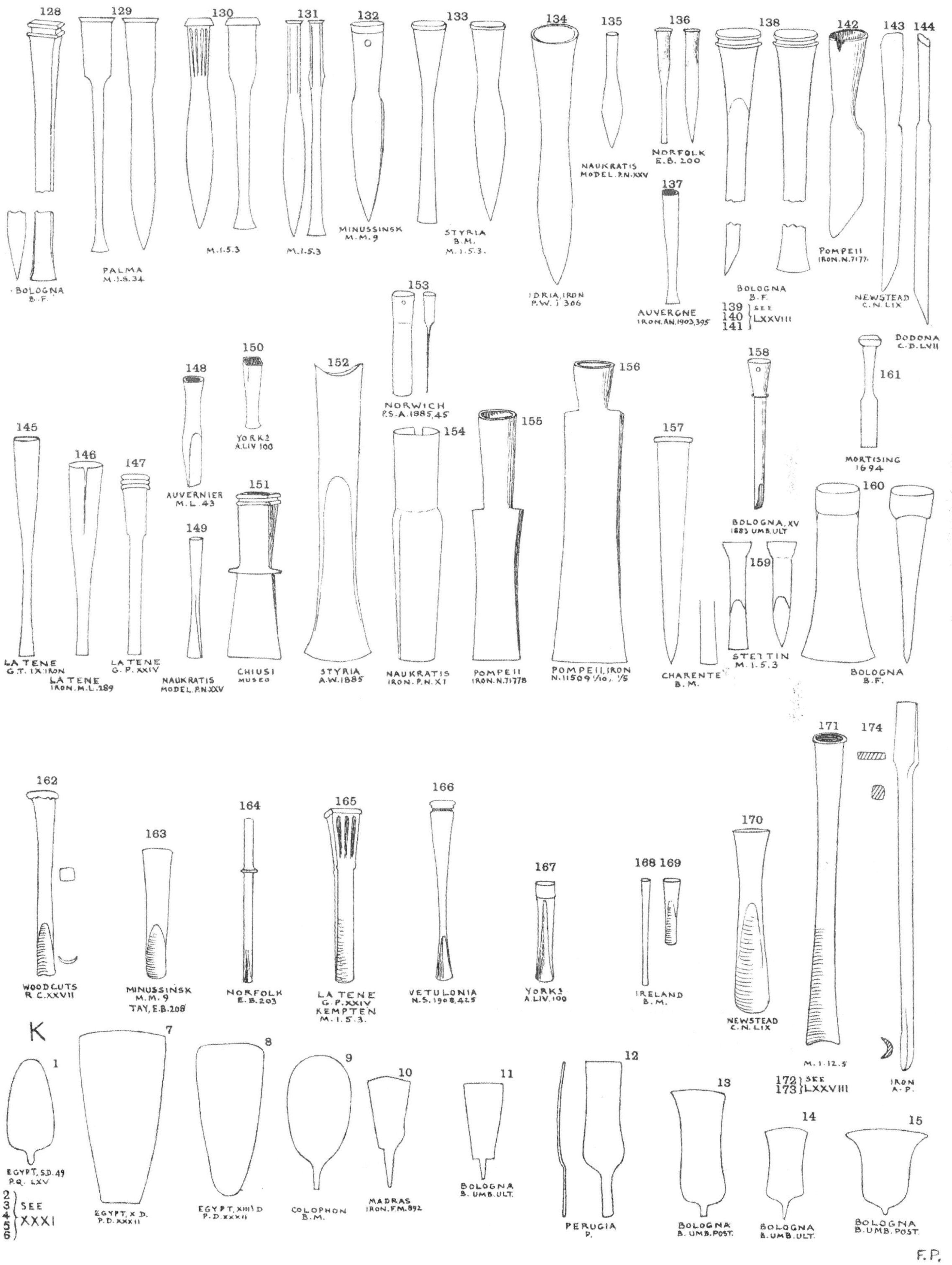

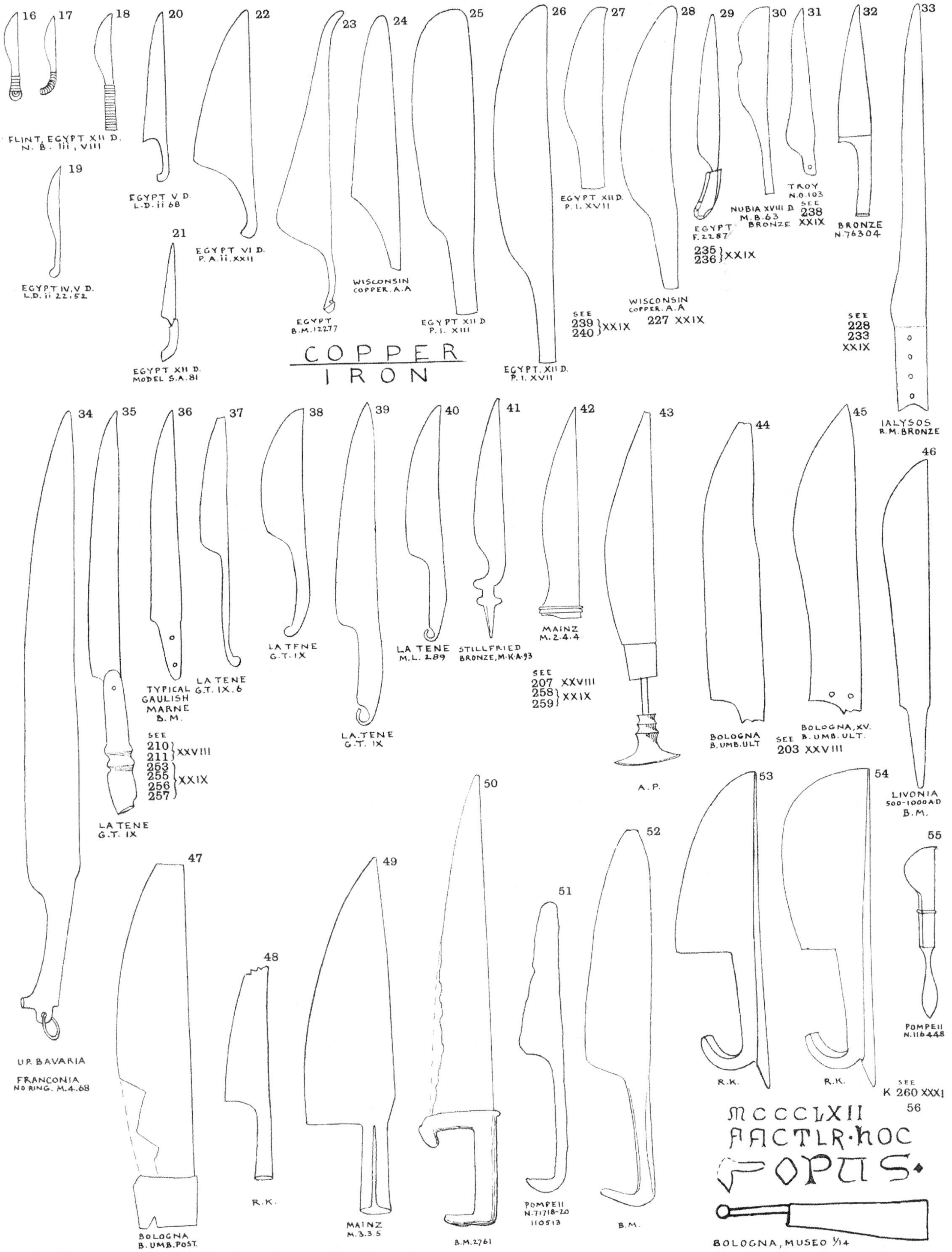
16 17 18
FLINT, EGYPT XII D. N. B. iii, VIII
19
EGYPT IV, V D. L.D. ii 22. 52
20
EGYPT V D. L.D. ii 68
21
EGYPT XII D. MODEL S.A. 81
22
EGYPT VI D. P. A. ii. XXII
23
EGYPT B.M. 12277
24
WISCONSIN COPPER. A.A
25
EGYPT XII D P. I. XIII
26
EGYPT. XII D. P. I. XVII
27
EGYPT XII D. P. I. XVII
SEE 239 240 } XXIX
28
WISCONSIN COPPER. A.A
227 XXIX
29
EGYPT F. 2287
235 236 } XXIX
30
NUBIA XVIII D. M.B. 63 BRONZE
31
TROY N.O. 103
SEE 238 XXIX
32
BRONZE N. 76304
33
SEE 228 233 XXIX
IALYSOS R.M. BRONZE
COPPER
IRON
34
UP. BAVARIA
FRANCONIA NO RING. M. 4. 68
35
LA TENE G.T. IX
SEE 210 211 } XXVIII
253 255 256 257 } XXIX
36
TYPICAL GAULISH MARNE B. M.
37
LA TENE G.T. IX. 6
38
LA TENE G.T. IX
39
LA TENE G.T. IX
40
LA TENE M.L. 289
41
STILLFRIED BRONZE, M.K.A. 93
42
MAINZ M. 2. 4. 4
SEE 207 XXVIII
258 259 } XXIX
43
A. P.
44
BOLOGNA B. UMB. ULT
45
BOLOGNA, XV. B. UMB. ULT.
SEE 203 XXVIII
46
LIVONIA 500-1000 A.D B. M.
47
BOLOGNA B. UMB. POST.
48
R. K.
49
MAINZ M. 3. 3. 5
50
B.M. 2761
51
POMPEII N. 71718-20 110513
52
B. M.
53
R. K.
54
R. K.
55
POMPEII N. 116448
SEE K 260 XXXI
56
MCCCLXII
FACTLR·HOC
OPUS
BOLOGNA, MUSEO 1/14

F.P.

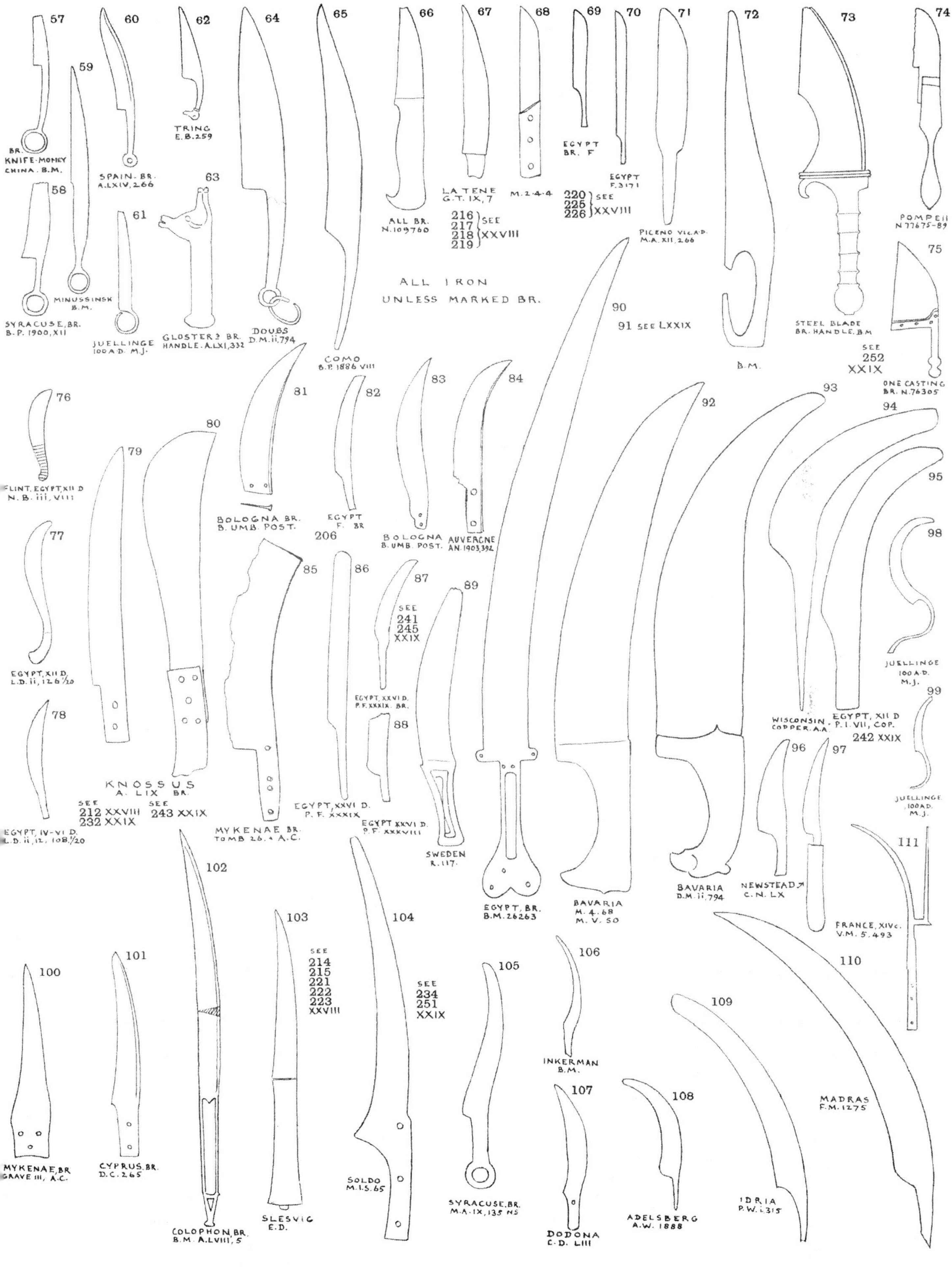
57
BR. KNIFE-MONEY CHINA. B.M.
58
SYRACUSE. BR. B.P. 1900, XII
59
MINUSSINSK B.M.
60
SPAIN. BR. A.LXIV, 266
61
JUELLINGE 100 A.D. M.J.
62
TRING E.B. 259
63
GLOSTER? BR. HANDLE. A.LXI, 332
64
DOUBS D.M. ii, 794
65
COMO B.P. 1886 VIII
66
ALL BR. N.109760
67
LA TENE G.T. IX, 7
216 217 218 219 SEE XXVIII
68
M. 2.4.4
69
EGYPT BR. F
70
EGYPT F. 3171
220 225 226 SEE XXVIII
71
PICENO VI c. A.D. M.A. XII, 266
ALL IRON UNLESS MARKED BR.
72
B.M.
73
STEEL BLADE BR. HANDLE. B.M
74
POMPEII N 77675-89
75
ONE CASTING BR. N. 76305
SEE 252 XXIX
76
FLINT, EGYPT, XII D N. B. iii, VIII
77
EGYPT, XII D. L.D. ii, 126 1/20
78
EGYPT, IV-VI D. L.D. ii, 12, 108 1/20
79
80
KNOSSUS A. LIX BR.
SEE 212 XXVIII 232 XXIX
SEE 243 XXIX
81
BOLOGNA BR. B. UMB. POST.
82
EGYPT F. BR
206
83
BOLOGNA BR. B. UMB. POST.
84
AUVERGNE AN. 1903, 392
85
MYKENAE BR. TOMB 26. A.C.
86
EGYPT, XXVI D. P. F. XXXIX
87
SEE 241 245 XXIX
EGYPT, XXVI D. P.F. XXXIX. BR.
88
EGYPT XXVI D. P.F. XXXVIII
89
SWEDEN R. 117.
90
91 SEE LXXIX
EGYPT, BR. B.M. 26263
92
BAVARIA M. 4. 68 M. V. 50
93
BAVARIA D.M. ii, 794
94
WISCONSIN COPPER. A.A.
95
EGYPT, XII D. P. I. VII, COP.
242 XXIX
96
NEWSTEAD C. N. LX
97
98
JUELLINGE 100 A.D. M.J.
99
JUELLINGE 100 A.D. M.J.
100
MYKENAE, BR GRAVE III, A.C.
101
CYPRUS, BR. D.C. 265
102
COLOPHON, BR. B.M. A.LVIII, 5
103
SEE 214 215 221 222 223 XXVIII
SLESVIG E.D.
104
SEE 234 251 XXIX
SOLDO M.I.S. 65
105
SYRACUSE, BR. M.A. IX, 135 NS
106
INKERMAN B.M.
107
DODONA C.D. LIII
108
ADELSBERG A.W. 1888
109
IDRIA P.W. i, 315
110
MADRAS F.M. 1275
111
FRANCE, XIV c. V.M. 5. 493

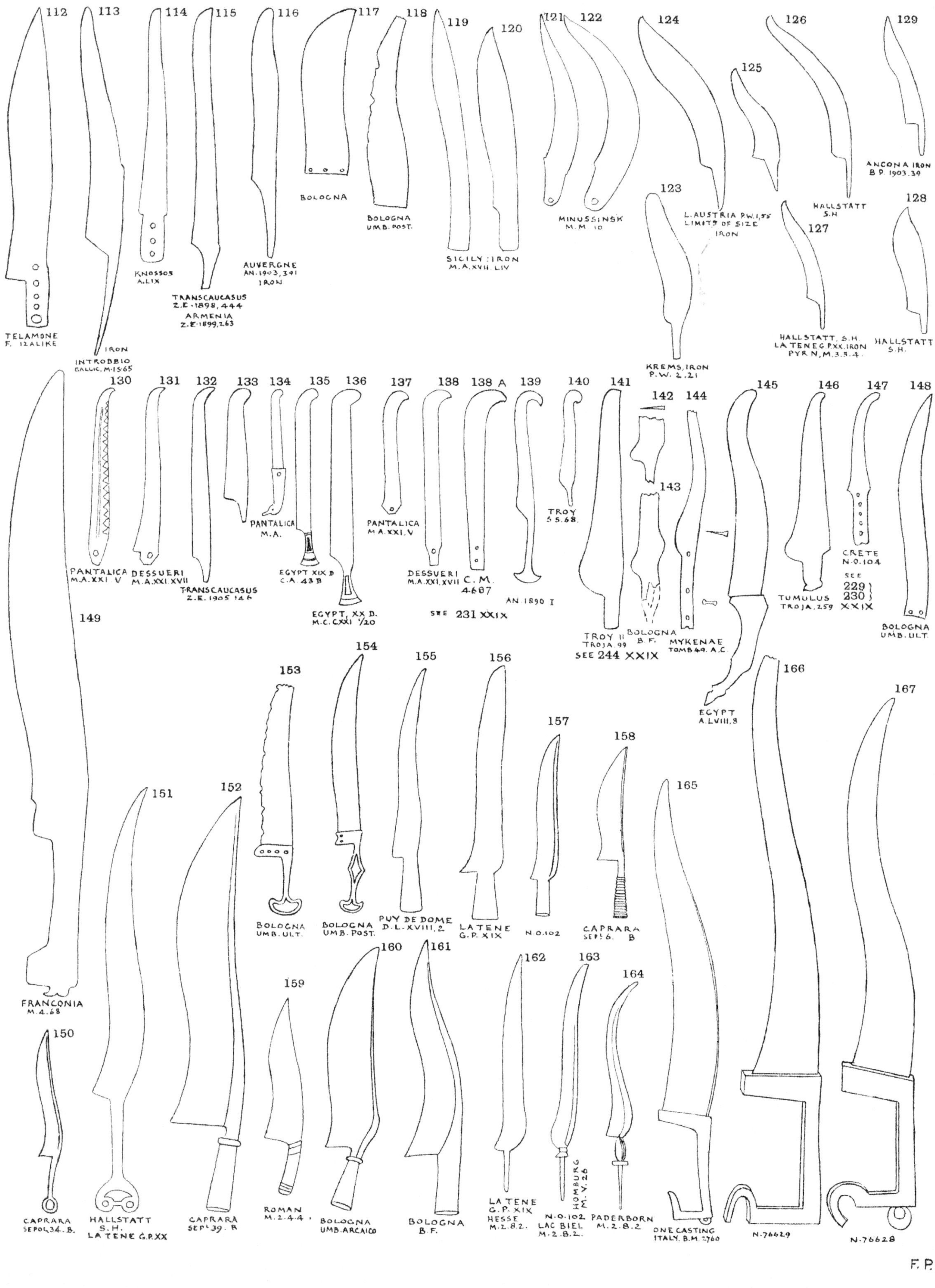
112
113
114
115
116
117
118
119
120
121
122
124
125
126
129
TELAMONE F. 12 ALIKE
IRON
INTROBBIO GALLIC. M.15.65
KNOSSOS A.LIX
TRANSCAUCASUS Z.E.1898,444
ARMENIA Z.E.1899,263
AUVERGNE AN.1903,341 IRON
BOLOGNA
BOLOGNA UMB. POST.
SICILY: IRON M.A.XVII. LIV
MINUSSINSK M.M. 10
123
L. AUSTRIA P.W.1,55 LIMITS OF SIZE IRON
127
HALLSTATT S.H
ANCONA IRON B.P. 1903.39
128
HALLSTATT, S.H LA TENE G.P.XX.IRON PYR.N, M.3.3.4.
HALLSTATT S.H.
KREMS, IRON P.W. 2.21
130
131
132
133
134
135
136
137
138
138 A
139
140
141
142
144
145
146
147
148
143
PANTALICA M.A.
PANTALICA M.A.XXI.V
TROY 55.68.
CRETE N.O.104
SEE 229 230 XXIX
PANTALICA M.A.XXI V
DESSUERI M.A.XXI.XVII
TRANSCAUCASUS Z.E.1905 146
EGYPT XIX D C.A. 43 B
DESSUERI M.A.XXI.XVII
C. M. 4687
AN.1890 I
TUMULUS TROJA.259
149
EGYPT, XX D. M.C.CXXI 1/20
SEE 231 XXIX
TROY II TROJA.99
BOLOGNA B.F.
MYKENAE TOMB 49. A.C
BOLOGNA UMB. ULT.
SEE 244 XXIX
EGYPT A.LVIII.8
153
154
155
156
157
158
165
166
167
151
152
BOLOGNA UMB. ULT.
BOLOGNA UMB. POST.
PUY DE DOME D.L.XVIII.2
LA TENE G.P. XIX
N.O.102
CAPRARA SEPt 6. B
FRANCONIA M.4.68
150
159
160
161
162
163
164
CAPRARA SEPOL.34. B.
HALLSTATT S.H. LA TENE G.P.XX
CAPRARA SEPt 39. B
ROMAN M.2.4.4
BOLOGNA UMB. ARCAICO
BOLOGNA B.F.
LA TENE G.P. XIX HESSE M.2.8.2.
N.O.102 LAC BIEL M.2.B.2.
HOMBURG M.V.26
PADERBORN M.2.B.2
ONE CASTING ITALY. B.M. 2760
N.76629
N.76628

F. P.

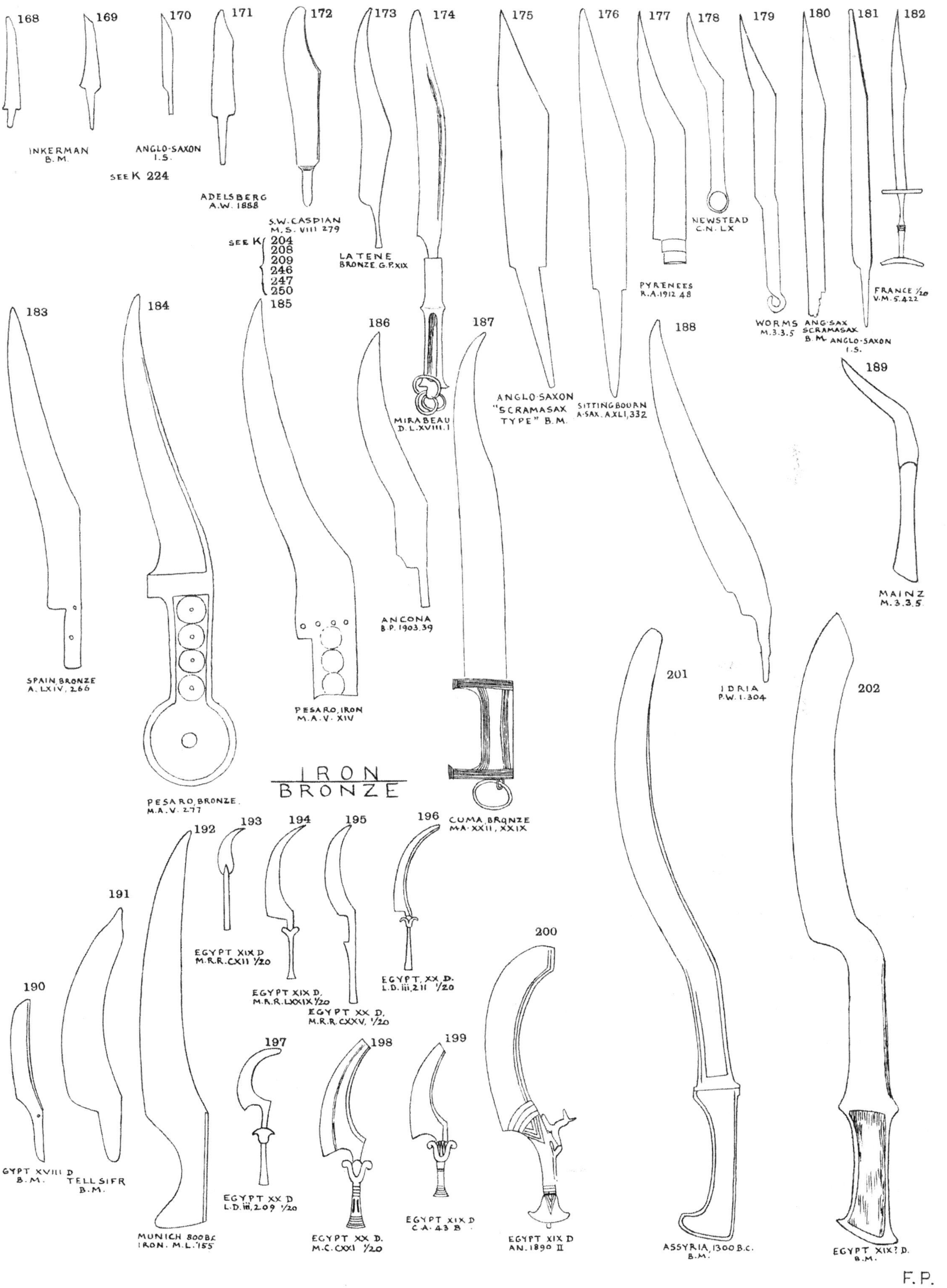
168
169
INKERMAN B.M.
170
ANGLO-SAXON I.S.
SEE K 224
171
ADELSBERG A.W. 1888
172
S.W. CASPIAN M.S. VIII 279
SEE K 204 208 209 246 247 250
173
LA TENE BRONZE G.P. XIX
174
MIRABEAU D.L. XVIII. 1
175
ANGLO-SAXON "SCRAMASAX TYPE" B.M.
176
SITTINGBOURN A.SAX. A.XLI, 332
177
PYRENEES R.A. 1912 48
178
NEWSTEAD C.N. LX
179
WORMS M.3.3.5
180
ANG-SAX SCRAMASAX B.M.
181
ANGLO-SAXON I.S.
182
FRANCE 1/20 V.M. 5.422
183
SPAIN BRONZE A. LXIV. 266
184
PESARO, BRONZE. M.A.V. 277
185
PESARO, IRON M.A.V. XIV
186
ANCONA B.P. 1903.39
187
CUMA BRONZE M.A. XXII, XXIX
188
IDRIA P.W. I. 304
189
MAINZ M.3.3.5.
IRON
BRONZE
190
GYPT XVIII D B.M.
191
TELL SIFR B.M.
192
MUNICH 800 BC IRON. M.L. 155
193
EGYPT XIX D M.R.R. CXII 1/20
194
EGYPT XIX D. M.R.R. LXXIX 1/20
195
EGYPT XX D. M.R.R. CXXV. 1/20
196
EGYPT XX D. L.D. iii, 211 1/20
197
EGYPT XX D L.D. iii, 209 1/20
198
EGYPT XX D. M.C. CXXI 1/20
199
EGYPT XIX D C.A. 43 B
200
EGYPT XIX D AN. 1890 II
201
ASSYRIA, 1300 B.C. B.M.
202
EGYPT XIX? D. B.M.
F. P.

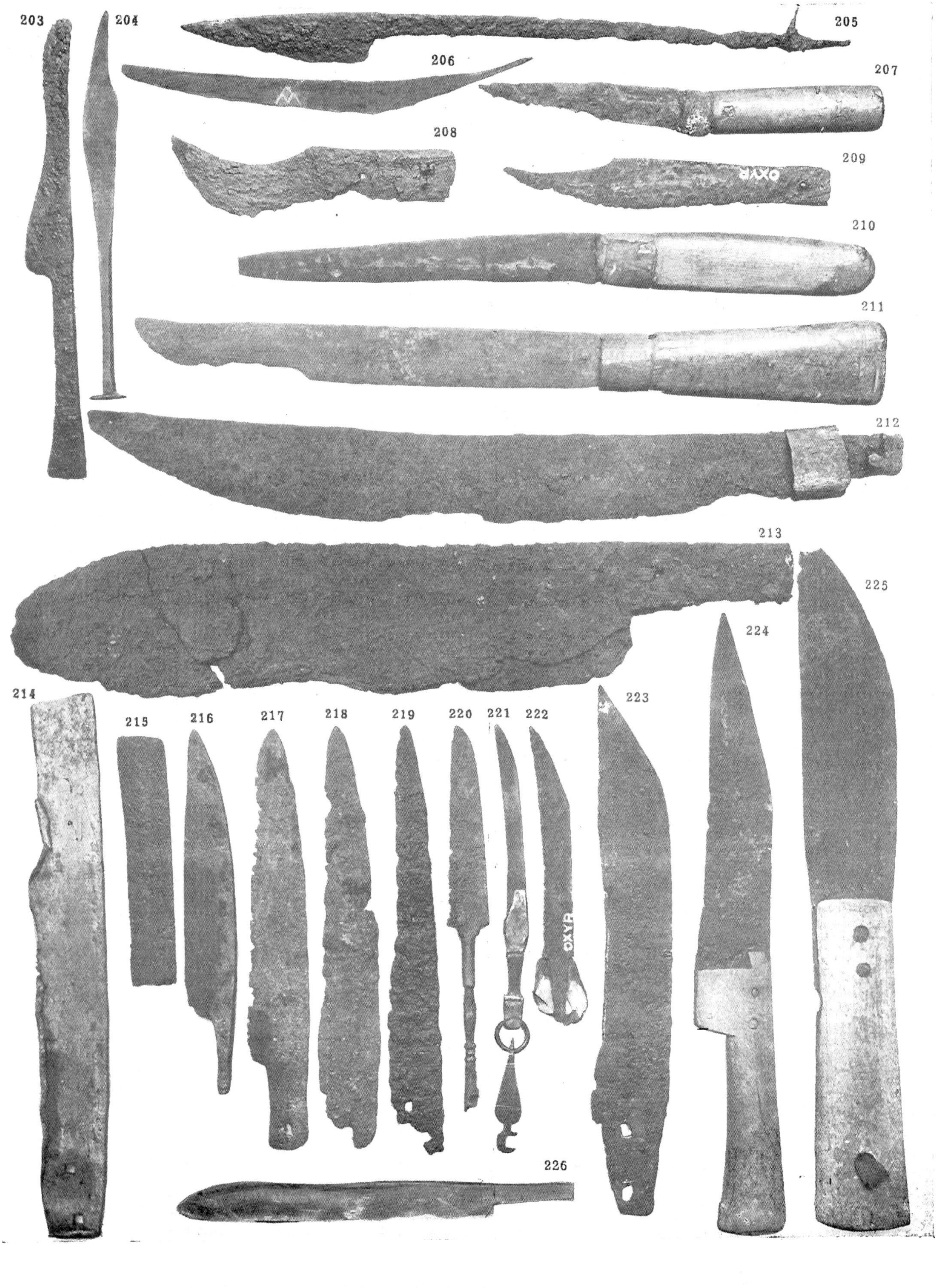
203
204
205
206
207
208
209
210
211
212
213
214
215
216
217
218
219
220
221
222
223
224
225
226

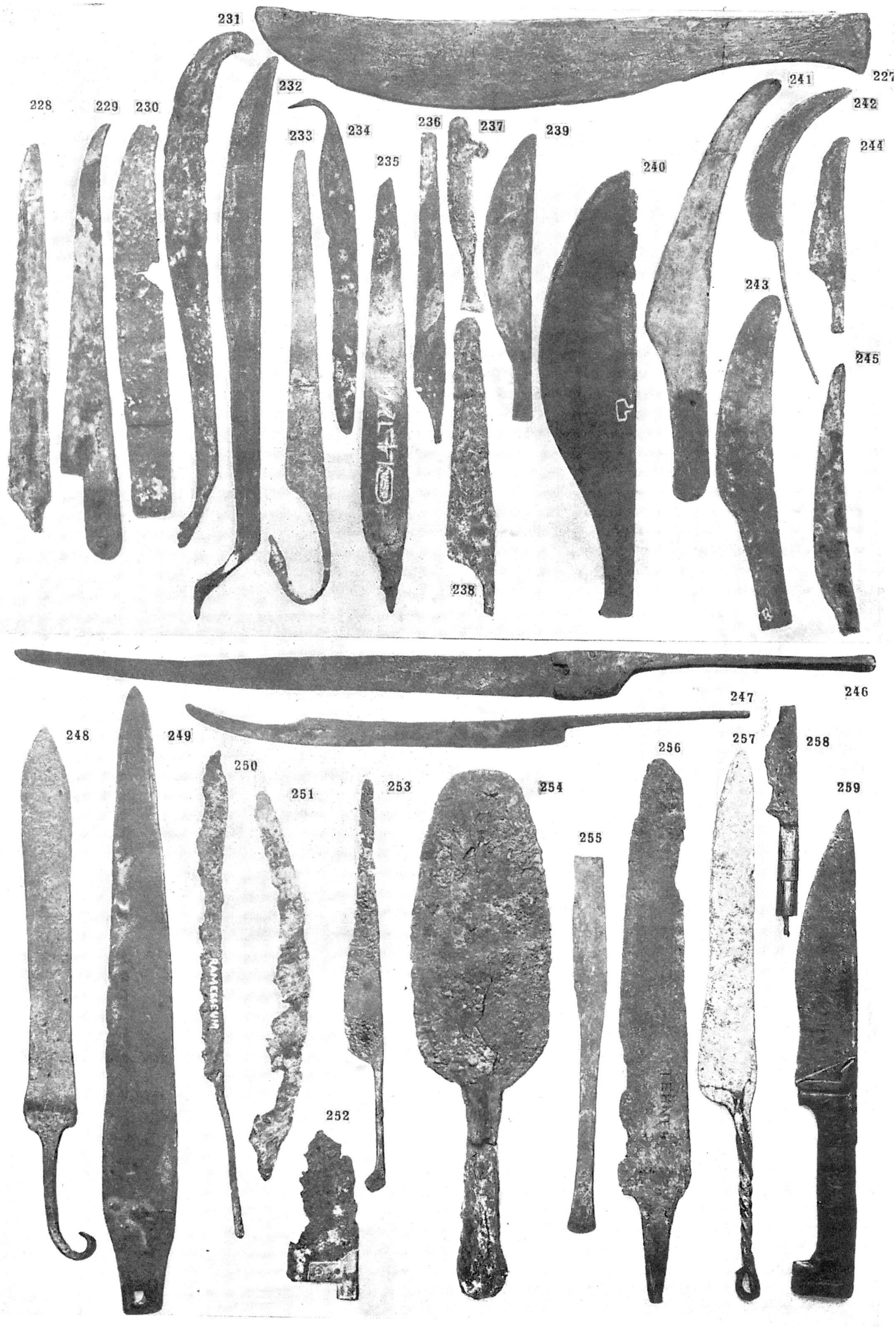
227
228
229
230
231
232
233
234
235
236
237
238
239
240
241
242
243
244
245
246
247
248
249
250
251
252
253
254
255
256
257
258
259

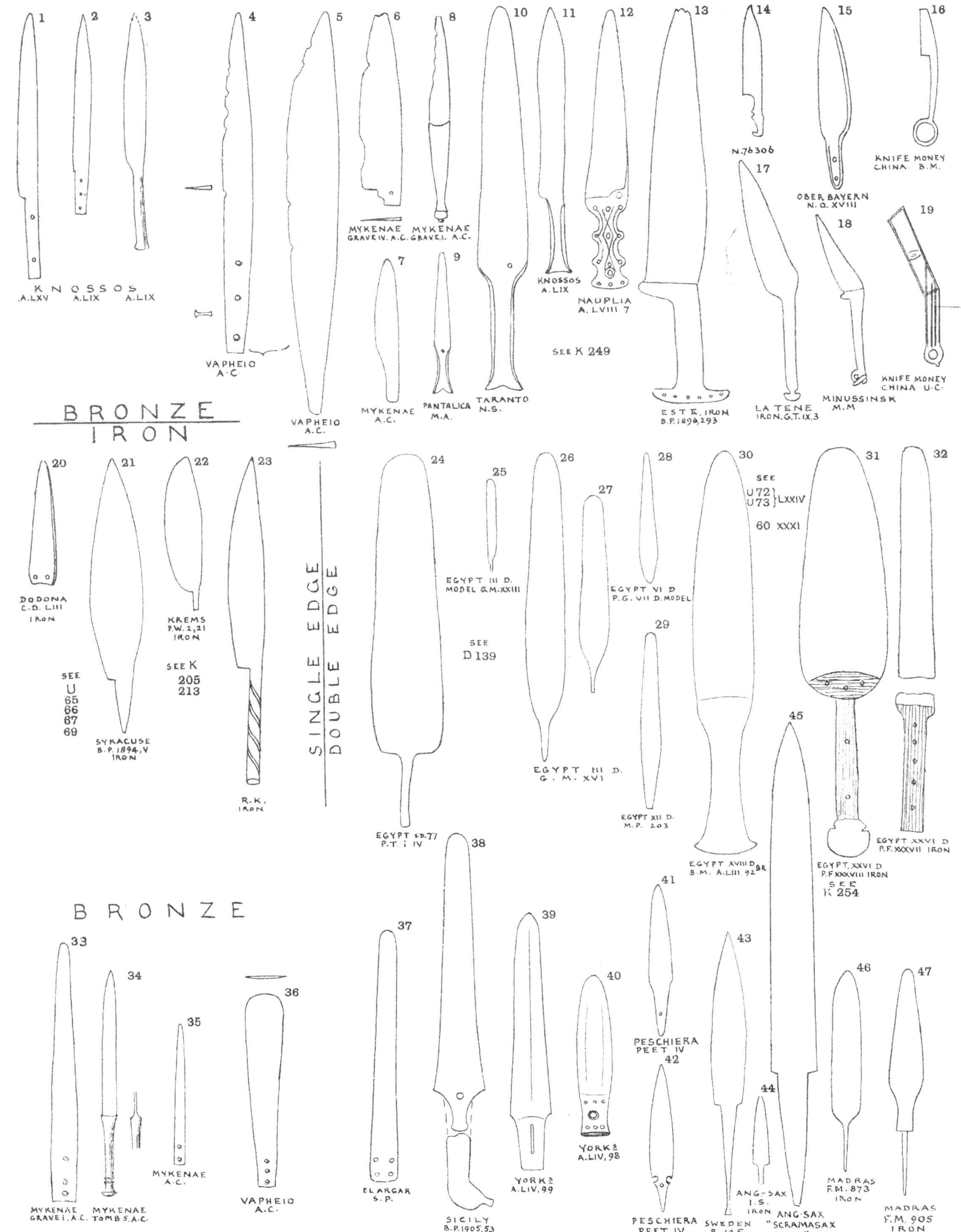

1 2 3 KNOSSOS A.LXV A.LIX A.LIX
4 VAPHEIO A.C.
5 VAPHEIO A.C.
6 MYKENAE GRAVE IV. A.C.
8 MYKENAE GRAVE I. A.C.
7 MYKENAE A.C.
9 PANTALICA M.A.
10 TARANTO N.S.
11 KNOSSOS A.LIX
12 NAUPLIA A.LVIII 7
SEE K 249
13 ESTE. IRON B.P. 1898, 293
14 N.76306
15 OBER BAYERN N.O. XVIII
16 KNIFE MONEY CHINA. B.M.
17 LA TENE IRON. G.T. IX, 3
18 MINUSSINSK M.M
19 KNIFE MONEY CHINA U.C.
BRONZE
IRON
20 DODONA C.D. LIII IRON
21 SYRACUSE B.P. 1894, V IRON
SEE U 65 66 67 69
22 KREMS P.W. 2, 21 IRON
SEE K 205 213
23 R.K. IRON
SINGLE EDGE
DOUBLE EDGE
24 EGYPT S.D. 77 P.T. i IV
25 EGYPT III D. MODEL G.M. XXIII
SEE D 139
26 EGYPT XII D. G. M. XVI
27 EGYPT VI D P.G. VII D. MODEL
28
29 EGYPT XII D. M.P. 203
30 SEE U72 U73 } LXXIV 60 XXXI
EGYPT XVIII D BR B.M. A.LIII, 92
31 EGYPT. XXVI D P.F. XXXVIII IRON SEE K 254
32 EGYPT XXVI D P.F. XXXVII IRON
BRONZE
33 MYKENAE GRAVE I. A.C.
34 MYKENAE TOMB 5. A.C.
35 MYKENAE A.C.
36 VAPHEIO A.C.
37 EL ARGAR S.P.
38 SICILY B.P. 1905, 53
39 YORKS A.LIV, 99
40 YORKS A.LIV, 98
41 PESCHIERA PEET IV
42 PESCHIERA PEET IV
43 SWEDEN R. 145 IRON
44 ANG-SAX I.S. IRON
45 ANG-SAX "SCRAMASAX TYPE" B.M.
46 MADRAS F.M. 873 IRON
47 MADRAS F.M. 905 IRON

F. P.

K 2 6
U 48 49 52 53 56 58 59 61 62
54
3 4 5 50 51 55 57 60 63 64
68
65 66 67
69
70
71
K 260
X 70
71

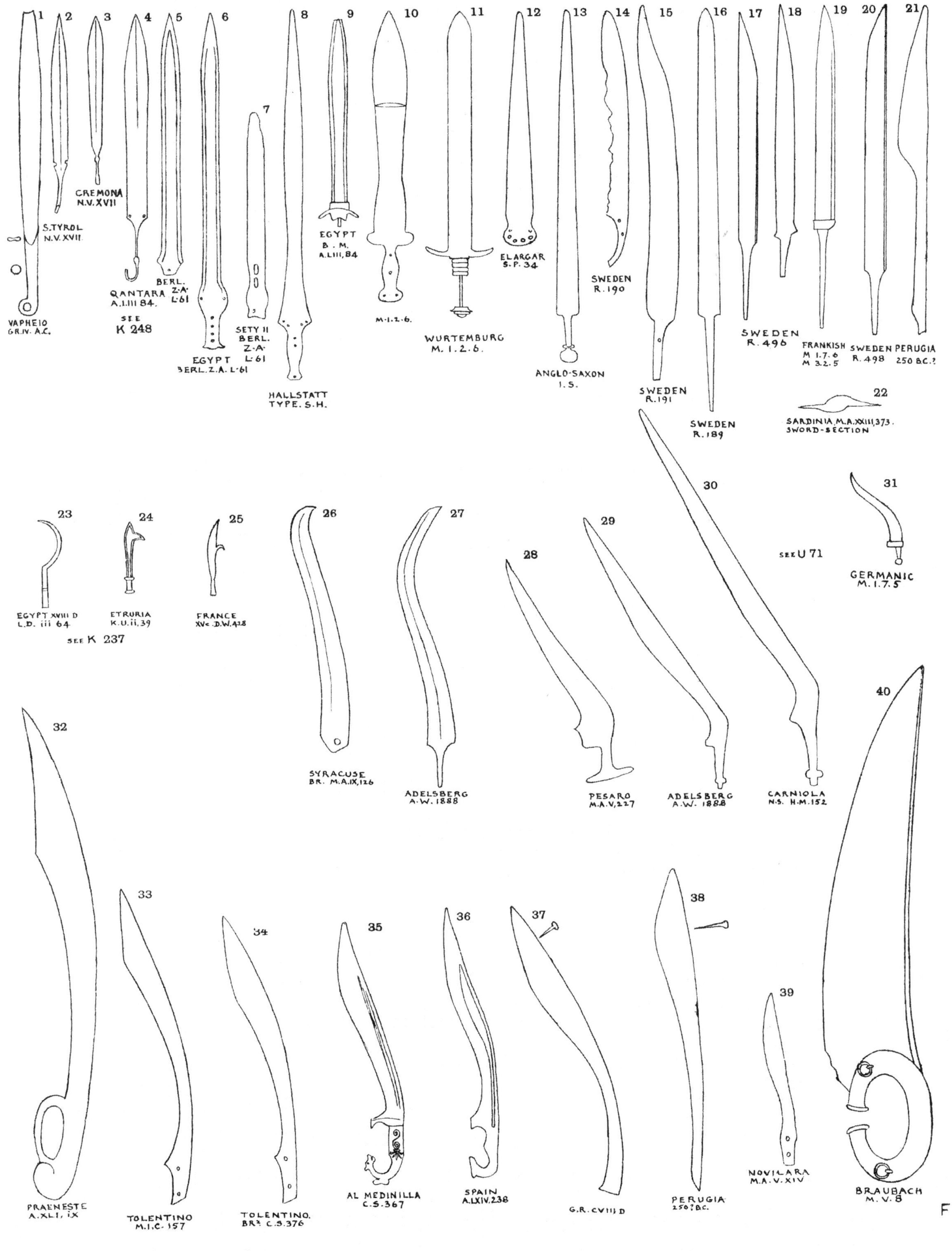
1
2
3
4
5
6
7
8
9
10
11
12
13
14
15
16
17
18
19
20
21
CREMONA N.V.XVII
S.TYROL N.V.XVII
VAPHEIO GR.IV. A.C.
QANTARA A.I.III 84.
SEE K 248
BERL. Z.A. L.61
EGYPT BERL. Z.A. L.61
SETY II BERL. Z.A. L.61
HALLSTATT TYPE. S.H.
EGYPT B. M. A.LIII, 84
M.1.2.6.
WURTEMBURG M. 1.2.6.
EL ARGAR S.P. 34
ANGLO-SAXON I.S.
SWEDEN R.190
SWEDEN R.191
SWEDEN R.189
SWEDEN R.496
FRANKISH M 1.7.6 M 3.2.5
SWEDEN R.498
PERUGIA 250 B.C.?
22
SARDINIA M.A.XXIII,373. SWORD-SECTION
23
24
25
26
27
28
29
30
31
EGYPT XVIII D L.D. iii 64
ETRURIA K.U.ii,39
FRANCE XVc D.W.428
SEE K 237
SEE U 71
GERMANIC M.1.7.5
SYRACUSE BR. M.A.IX,126
ADELSBERG A.W. 1888
PESARO M.A.V,227
ADELSBERG A.W. 1888
CARNIOLA N.S. H.M.152
32
33
34
35
36
37
38
39
40
PRAENESTE A.XLI, ix
TOLENTINO M.I.C. 157
TOLENTINO. BR. C.S.376
AL MEDINILLA C.S.367
SPAIN A.LXIV,238
G.R. CVIII D
PERUGIA 250? B.C.
NOVILARA M.A.V.XIV
BRAUBACH M.V.8

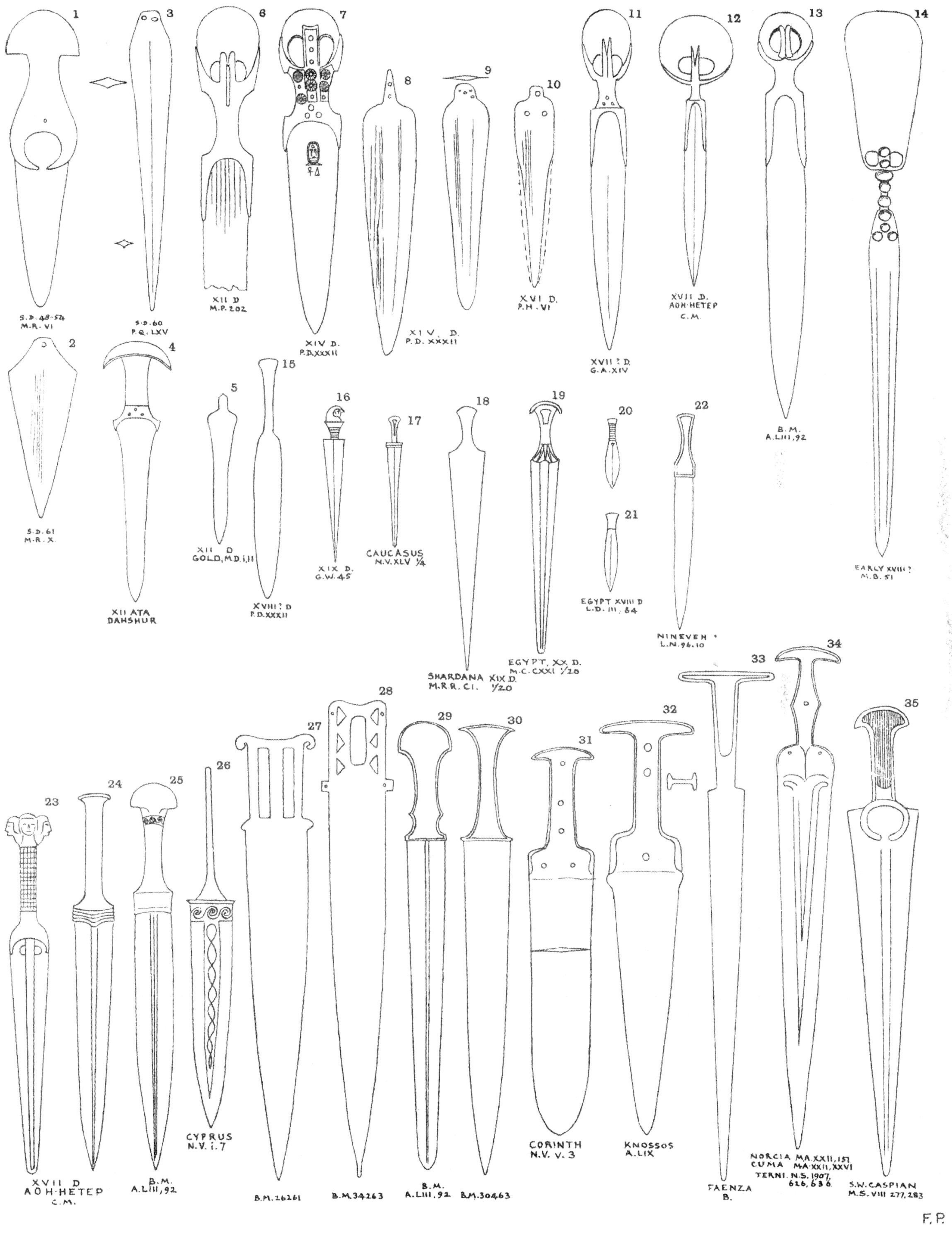
S.D. 48-54 M.R. VI
S.D. 60 P.Q. LXV
XII D M.P. 202
XIV D. P.D. XXXII
XIV D. P.D. XXXII
XVI D. P.H. VI
XVII ? D. G.A. XIV
XVII D. AOH·HETEP C.M.
B.M. A.LIII, 92
S.D. 61 M.R. X.
XII ATA DAHSHUR
XII D GOLD, M.D. i, II
XVIII ? D P.D. XXXII
XIX D. G.W. 45
CAUCASUS N.V. XLV 1/4
SHARDANA XIX D. M.R.R. CI. 1/20
EGYPT, XX D. M.C. CXXI 1/20
EGYPT XVIII D L.D. III, 64
NINEVEH L.N. 96.10
EARLY XVIII ? M.B. 51
XVII D AOH·HETEP C.M.
B.M. A.LIII, 92
CYPRUS N.V. i. 7
B.M. 26261
B.M. 34263
B.M. A.LIII, 92
B.M. 30463
CORINTH N.V. V. 3
KNOSSOS A.LIX
FAENZA B.
NORCIA MA. XXII, 151
CUMA MA. XXII, XXVI
TERNI. N.S. 1907, 626, 636
S.W. CASPIAN M.S. VIII 277, 283
F. P.

36
37
38
39
40
41
42
43
44
45
46
47
48
49
50
51
52
53
54
55
56
57
58
59
60

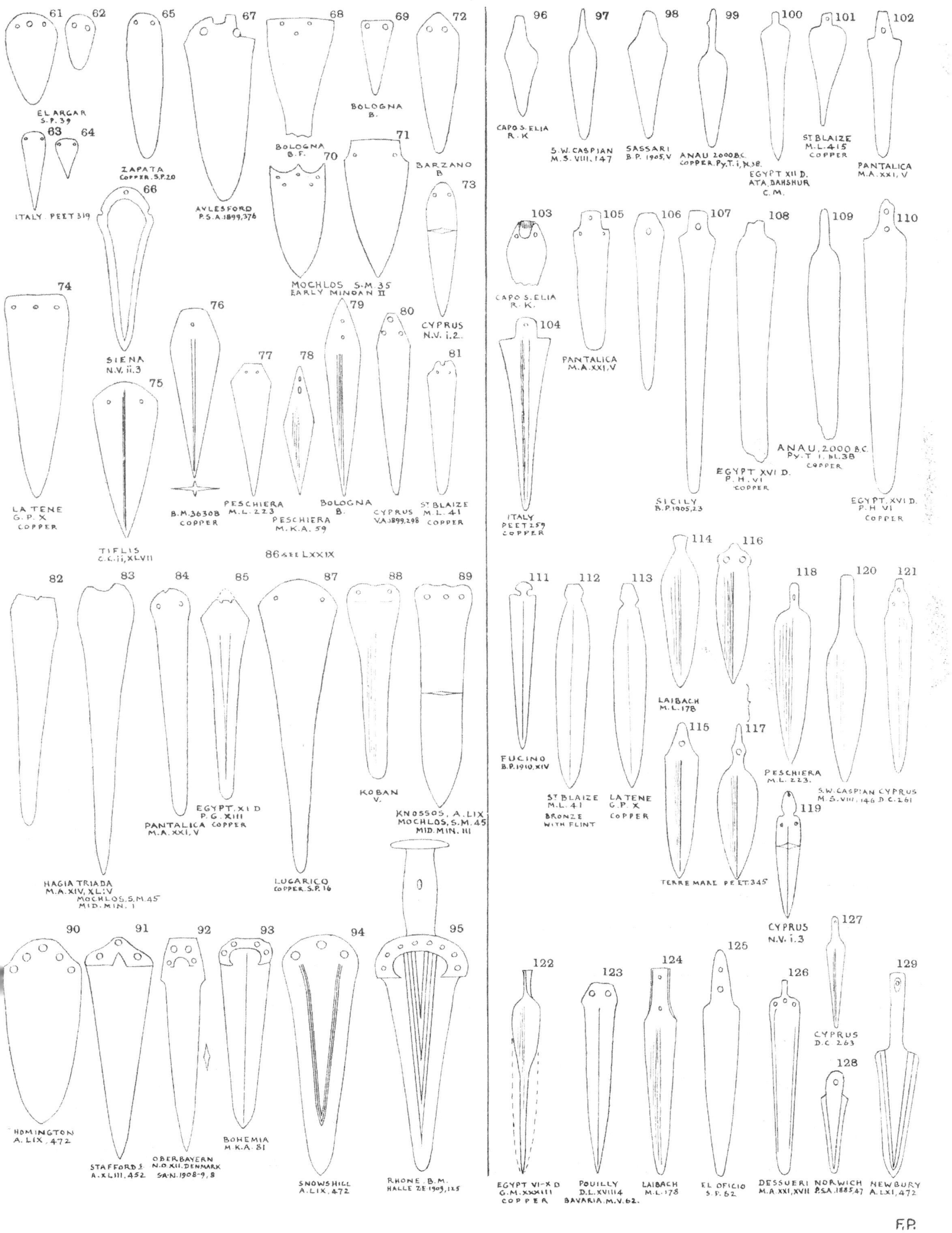
61 62
EL ARGAR S.P. 39
63 64
ITALY. PEET 319
65
ZAPATA COPPER. S.P. 20
66
SIENA N.V. ii. 3
67
AYLESFORD P.S.A. 1899, 376
68
BOLOGNA B.F.
69
BOLOGNA B.
70
71
MOCHLOS S.M. 35 EARLY MINOAN II
72
BARZANO B
73
CYPRUS N.V. i. 2.
74
LA TENE G.P. X COPPER
75
TIFLIS C.C. ii, XLVII
76
B.M. 36308 COPPER
77
PESCHIERA M.L. 223
78
PESCHIERA M.K.A. 59
79
BOLOGNA B.
80
CYPRUS V.A. 1899, 298
81
ST BLAIZE M.L. 41 COPPER
86 SEE LXXIX
82
83
HAGIA TRIADA M.A. XIV, XL:V MOCHLOS. S.M. 45 MID. MIN. I
84
PANTALICA M.A. XXI, V
85
EGYPT. XI D P.G. XIII COPPER
87
LUGARICO COPPER. S.P. 16
88
KOBAN V.
89
KNOSSOS, A. LIX MOCHLOS, S.M. 45 MID. MIN. III
90
HOMINGTON A. LIX, 472
91
STAFFORDS. A. XLIII, 452
92
OBERBAYERN N.O. XII. DENMARK SA-N. 1908-9, 8
93
BOHEMIA M.K.A. 81
94
SNOWSHILL A. LIX, 472
95
RHONE. B.M. HALLE ZE 1909, 125
96
CAPO S. ELIA R.K.
97
S.W. CASPIAN M.S. VIII, 147
98
SASSARI B.P. 1905, V
99
ANAU 2000 B.C. COPPER. Py. T. i, pl. 38.
100
EGYPT XII D. ATA. DAHSHUR C.M.
101
ST BLAIZE M.L. 415 COPPER
102
PANTALICA M.A. XXI, V
103
CAPO S. ELIA R.K.
104
ITALY PEET 259 COPPER
105
PANTALICA M.A. XXI, V
106
107
SICILY B.P. 1905, 23
108
EGYPT XVI D. P.H. VI COPPER
109
ANAU. 2000 B.C. Py. T. i, pl. 38 COPPER
110
EGYPT. XVI D. P.H. VI COPPER
111
FUCINO B.P. 1910, XIV
112
ST BLAIZE M.L. 41 BRONZE WITH FLINT
113
LA TENE G.P. X COPPER
114
LAIBACH M.L. 178
115
116
117
TERRE MARE PEET 345
118
PESCHIERA M.L. 223.
119
CYPRUS N.V. i. 3
120
S.W. CASPIAN M.S. VIII, 146
121
CYPRUS D.C. 261
122
EGYPT VI-X D G.M. XXXIII COPPER
123
POUILLY D.L. XVIII 4 BAVARIA. M.V. 62.
124
LAIBACH M.L. 178
125
EL OFICIO S.P. 62
126
DESSUERI M.A. XXI, XVII
127
CYPRUS D.C. 263
128
NORWICH P.S.A. 1885 47
129
NEWBURY A. LXI, 472
F.P.

1:4 D. DAGGER, BRONZE. XXXVI.

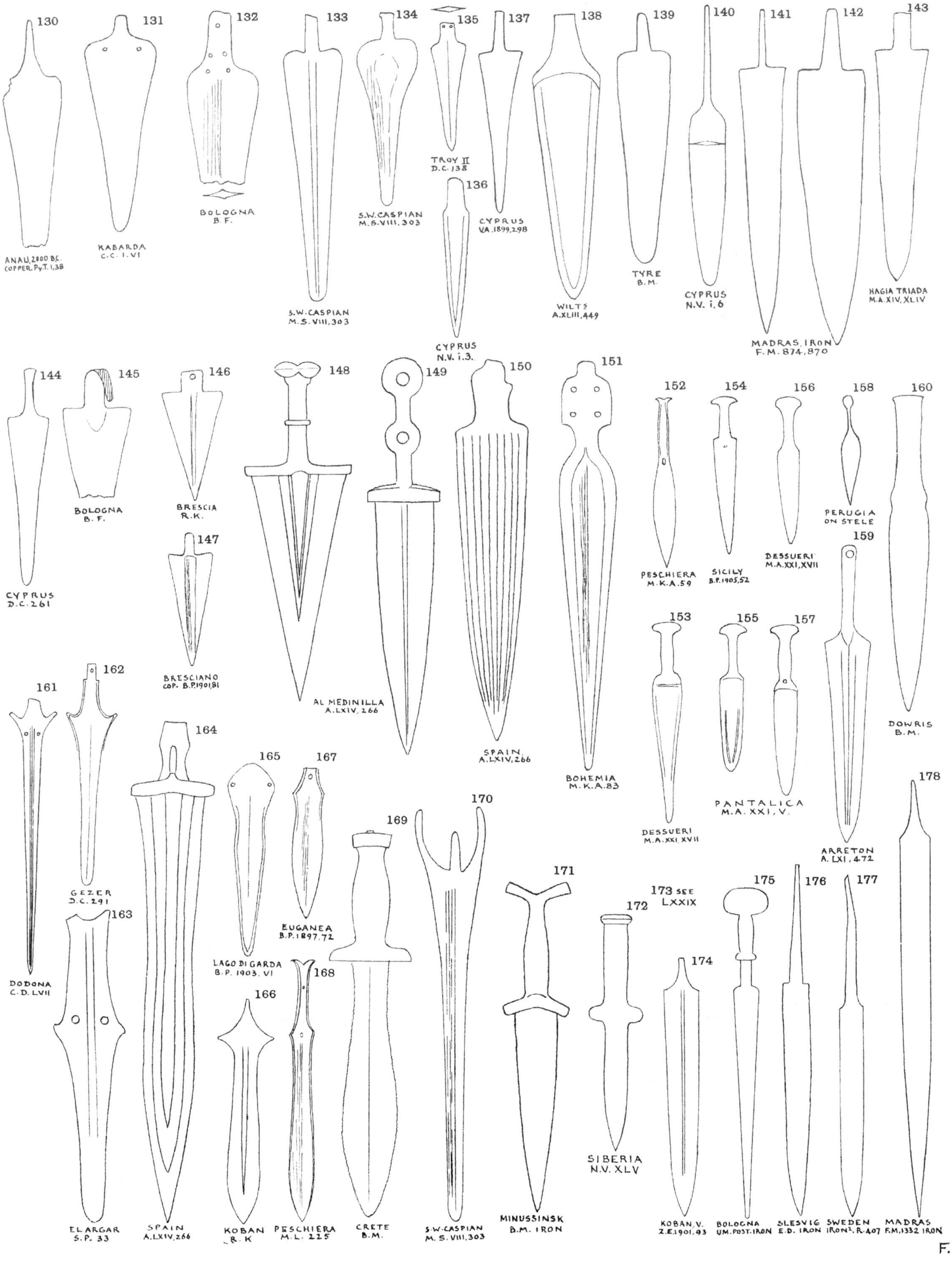

F. P

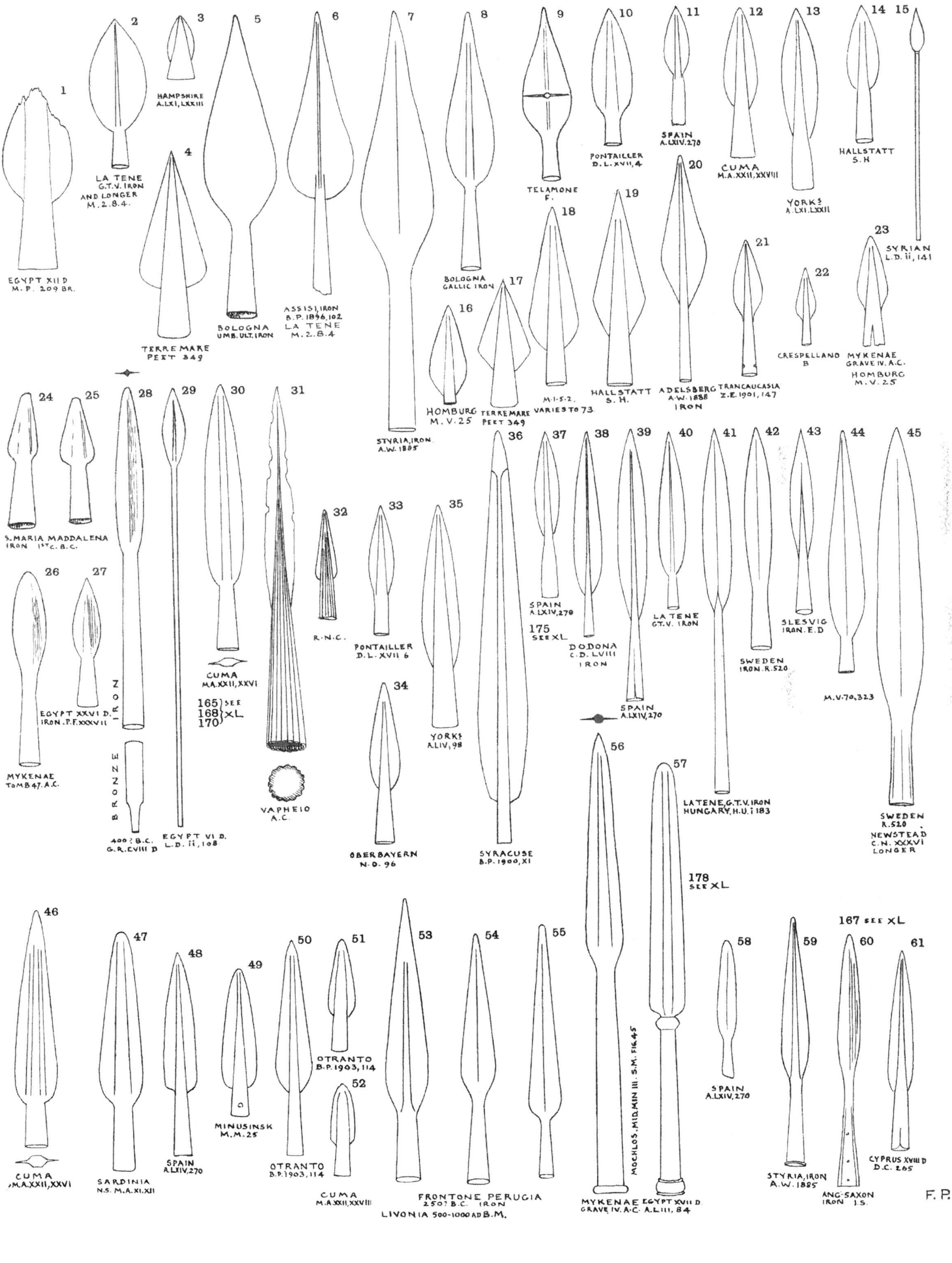
1
EGYPT XII D
M. P. 209 BR.
2
LA TENE
G.T.V. IRON
AND LONGER
M. 2. 8. 4.
3
HAMPSHIRE
A.LXI, LXXIII
4
TERREMARE
PEET 349
5
BOLOGNA
UMB. ULT. IRON
6
ASSISI, IRON
B.P. 1896, 102
LA TENE
M. 2. 8. 4
7
STYRIA, IRON
A.W. 1885
8
BOLOGNA
GALLIC IRON
9
TELAMONE
F.
10
PONTAILLER
D. L. XVII, 4
11
SPAIN
A. LXIV, 270
12
CUMA
M.A. XXII, XXVIII
13
YORKS
A. LXI. LXXIII
14
HALLSTATT
S. H
15
SYRIAN
L. D. ii, 141
16
HOMBURG
M. V. 25
17
TERREMARE
PEET 349
18
M. I. 5. 2.
VARIES TO 73
19
HALLSTATT
S. H.
20
ADELSBERG
A.W. 1888
IRON
21
TRANCAUCASIA
Z. E. 1901, 147
22
CRESPELLANO
B
23
MYKENAE
GRAVE IV. A.C.
HOMBURG
M. V. 25
24
25
S. MARIA MADDALENA
IRON 1ST C. B.C.
26
MYKENAE
TOMB 47. A.C.
27
EGYPT XXVI D.
IRON. P.F. XXXVII
28
IRON
BRONZE
400? B.C.
G.R. CVIII D
29
EGYPT VI D.
L. D. ii, 108
30
CUMA
M.A. XXII, XXVI
165 } SEE
168 } XL
170
31
VAPHEIO
A.C.
32
R. N. C.
33
PONTAILLER
D. L. XVII 6
34
OBERBAYERN
N. O. 96
35
YORKS
A. LIV, 98
36
SYRACUSE
B.P. 1900, XI
37
SPAIN
A. LXIV, 270
175
SEE XL
38
DODONA
C. D. LVIII
IRON
39
SPAIN
A. LXIV, 270
40
LA TENE
G.T.V. IRON
41
LATENE, G.T.V. IRON
HUNGARY, H.U. i 183
42
SWEDEN
IRON. R. 520
43
SLESVIG
IRON. E. D
44
M.V. 70, 323
45
SWEDEN
R. 520
NEWSTEAD
C. N. XXXVI
LONGER
46
CUMA
M.A. XXII, XXVI
47
SARDINIA
N.S. M.A. XI, XII
48
SPAIN
A. LXIV, 270
49
MINUSINSK
M. M. 25
50
OTRANTO
B.P. 1903, 114
51
OTRANTO
B.P. 1903, 114
52
CUMA
M.A. XXII, XXVIII
53
54
55
FRONTONE PERUGIA
250? B.C. IRON
LIVONIA 500-1000 AD B.M.
56
MOCHLOS, MID. MIN III. S.M. FIG. 45
MYKENAE
GRAVE IV. A.C.
57
178
SEE XL
EGYPT XVII D
A. L. III, 84
58
SPAIN
A. LXIV, 270
59
STYRIA, IRON
A.W. 1885
167 SEE XL
60
ANG-SAXON
IRON J.S.
61
CYPRUS XVIII D
D. C. 265
F. P.

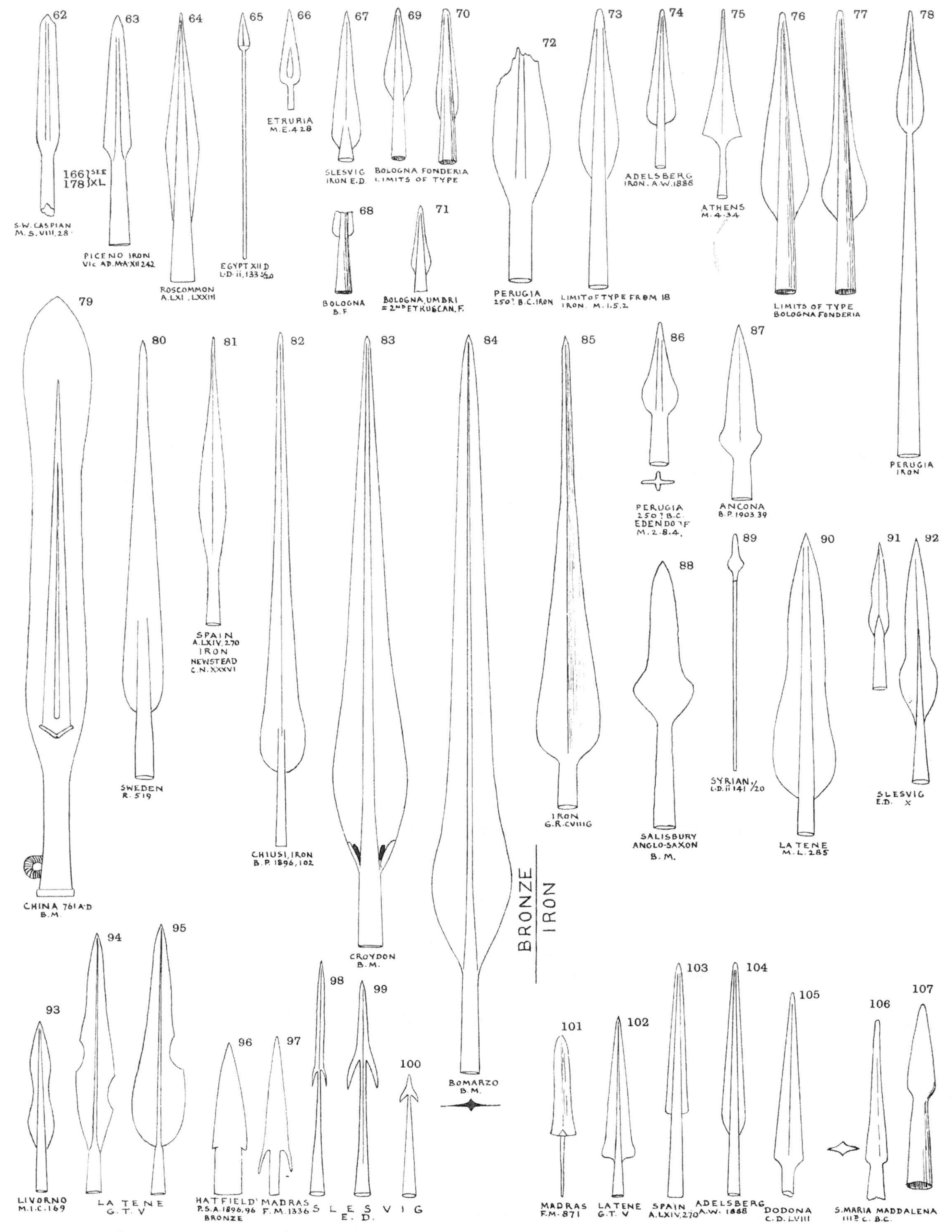
62
S.W. CASPIAN
M. S. VIII, 28
63
166 } SEE
178 } XL.
PICENO IRON
VIc AD. M.A. XII 242
64
ROSCOMMON
A. LXI, LXXIII
65
EGYPT XII D
L.D. ii, 133 1/20
66
ETRURIA
M.E. 428
67
SLESVIG
IRON E.D.
69
70
BOLOGNA FONDERIA
LIMITS OF TYPE
68
BOLOGNA
B.F.
71
BOLOGNA, UMBRI
= 2ND ETRUSCAN. F.
72
PERUGIA
250? B.C. IRON
73
LIMIT OF TYPE FROM 18
IRON. M. 1.5.2
74
ADELSBERG
IRON. A.W. 1888
75
ATHENS
M. 4.34
76
77
LIMITS OF TYPE
BOLOGNA FONDERIA
78
PERUGIA
IRON
79
CHINA 761 A.D.
B.M.
80
SWEDEN
R. 519
81
SPAIN
A. LXIV, 270
IRON
NEWSTEAD
C.N. XXXVI
82
CHIUSI, IRON
B.P. 1896, 102
83
CROYDON
B.M.
84
BOMARZO
B.M.
BRONZE
IRON
85
IRON
G.R. CVIII G
86
PERUGIA
250? B.C.
EDENDORF
M. 2.8.4.
87
ANCONA
B.P. 1903, 39
88
SALISBURY
ANGLO-SAXON
B. M.
89
SYRIAN,
L.D. ii 141 1/20
90
LA TENE
M. L. 285
91
92
SLESVIG
E.D. X
93
LIVORNO
M.I.C. 169
94
95
LA TENE
G. T. V
96
HATFIELD
P.S.A. 1896, 96
BRONZE
97
MADRAS
F. M. 1336
98
99
100
S L E S V I G
E. D.
101
MADRAS
F.M. 871
102
LA TENE
G.T. V
103
SPAIN
A. LXIV, 270
104
ADELSBERG
A.W. 1888
105
DODONA
C.D. LVIII
106
107
S. MARIA MADDALENA
IIIRD C. B.C.
F.P.

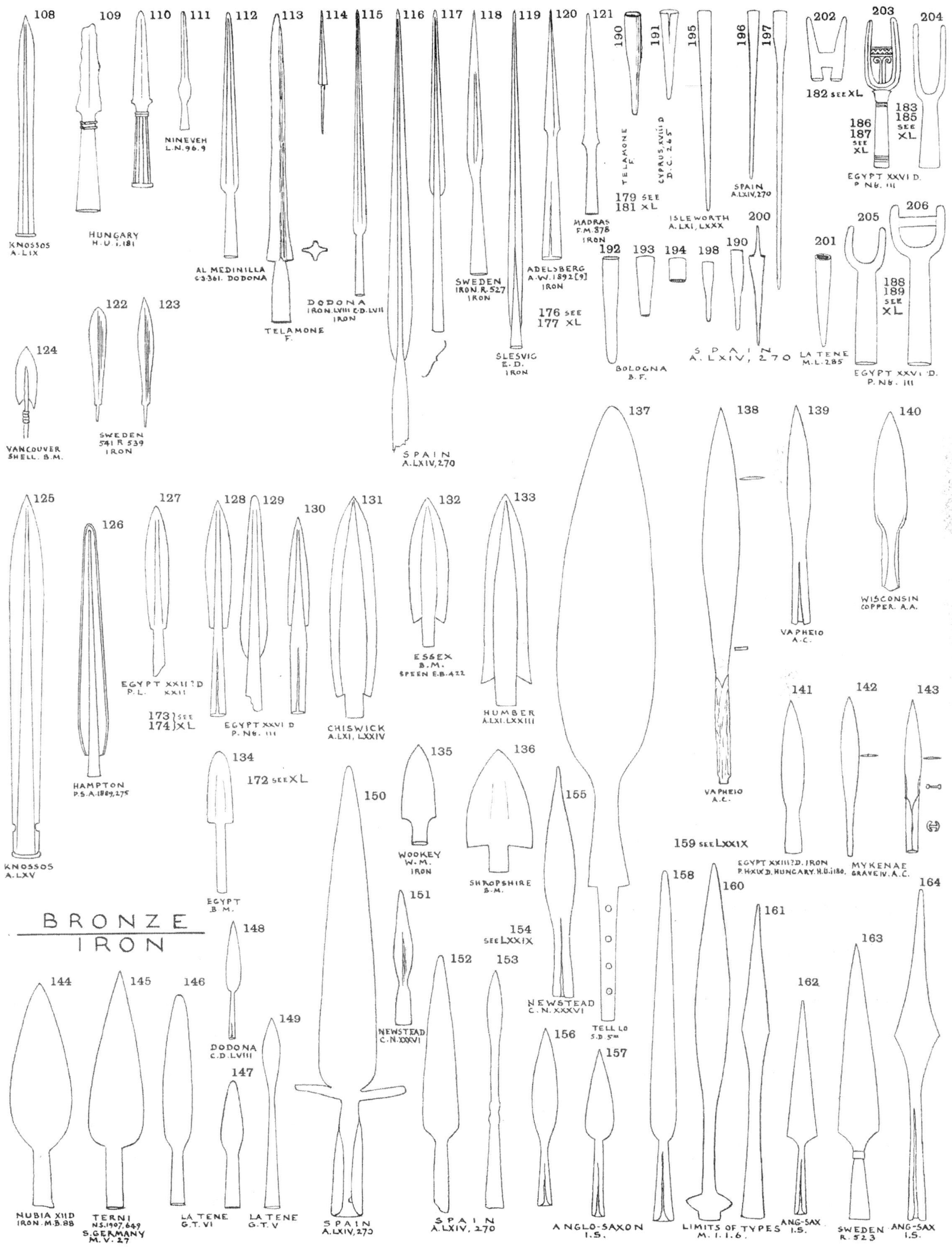
108 KNOSSOS A.LIX
109 HUNGARY H.U.i.181
110
111 NINEVEH L.N.96.9
112 AL MEDINILLA C.S.361. DODONA
113 TELAMONE F.
114
115 DODONA IRON.LVIII C.D.LVII IRON
116 SPAIN A.LXIV,270
117
118 SWEDEN IRON.R.527 IRON
119 SLESVIG E.D. IRON
120 ADELSBERG A.W.1892[9] IRON
121 MADRAS F.M.878 IRON
190 TELAMONE F.
191 CYPRUS.XVIII D D.C.265
195 ISLEWORTH A.LXI, LXXX
196 197 SPAIN A.LXIV,270
202 182 SEE XL
203 204 183 185 SEE XL 186 187 SEE XL EGYPT XXVI D. P.N6.III
179 SEE 181 XL
176 SEE 177 XL
192 BOLOGNA B.F.
193 194 198 190 200 SPAIN A.LXIV, 270
201 LA TENE M.L.285
205 206 188 189 SEE XL EGYPT XXVI D. P.N6.III
122 123 SWEDEN 541 R 539 IRON
124 VANCOUVER SHELL. B.M.
125 KNOSSOS A.LXV
126 HAMPTON P.S.A.1889,275
127 EGYPT XXII?D P.L. XXII
173 174 SEE XL
128 129 130 EGYPT XXVI D P.N6.III
131 CHISWICK A.LXI, LXXIV
132 ESSEX B.M. SPEEN E.B.422
133 HUMBER A.LXI.LXXIII
137 TELL LO S.D.5th
138 VAPHEIO A.C.
139 VAPHEIO A.C.
140 WISCONSIN COPPER. A.A.
141 142 143 EGYPT XXIII?D. IRON P.H.XIX D. HUNGARY.H.U.i.180. MYKENAE GRAVE IV. A.C.
159 SEE LXXIX
134 EGYPT B.M.
172 SEE XL
135 WOOKEY W.M. IRON
136 SHROPSHIRE B.M.
150 SPAIN A.LXIV,270
151 NEWSTEAD C.N.XXXVI
154 SEE LXXIX
155 NEWSTEAD C.N.XXXVI
BRONZE
IRON
144 NUBIA XIID IRON.M.B.88
145 TERNI N.S.1907,649 S.GERMANY M.V.27
146 LA TENE G.T.VI
147 LA TENE G.T.V
148 DODONA C.D.LVIII
149
152 153 SPAIN A.LXIV, 270
156 157 ANGLO-SAXON I.S.
158 160 LIMITS OF TYPES M.I.1.6.
161
162 ANG-SAX I.S.
163 SWEDEN R.523
164 ANG-SAX I.S.
F.P.

1 : 2. H. SPEAR HEAD AND BUTT. XL.

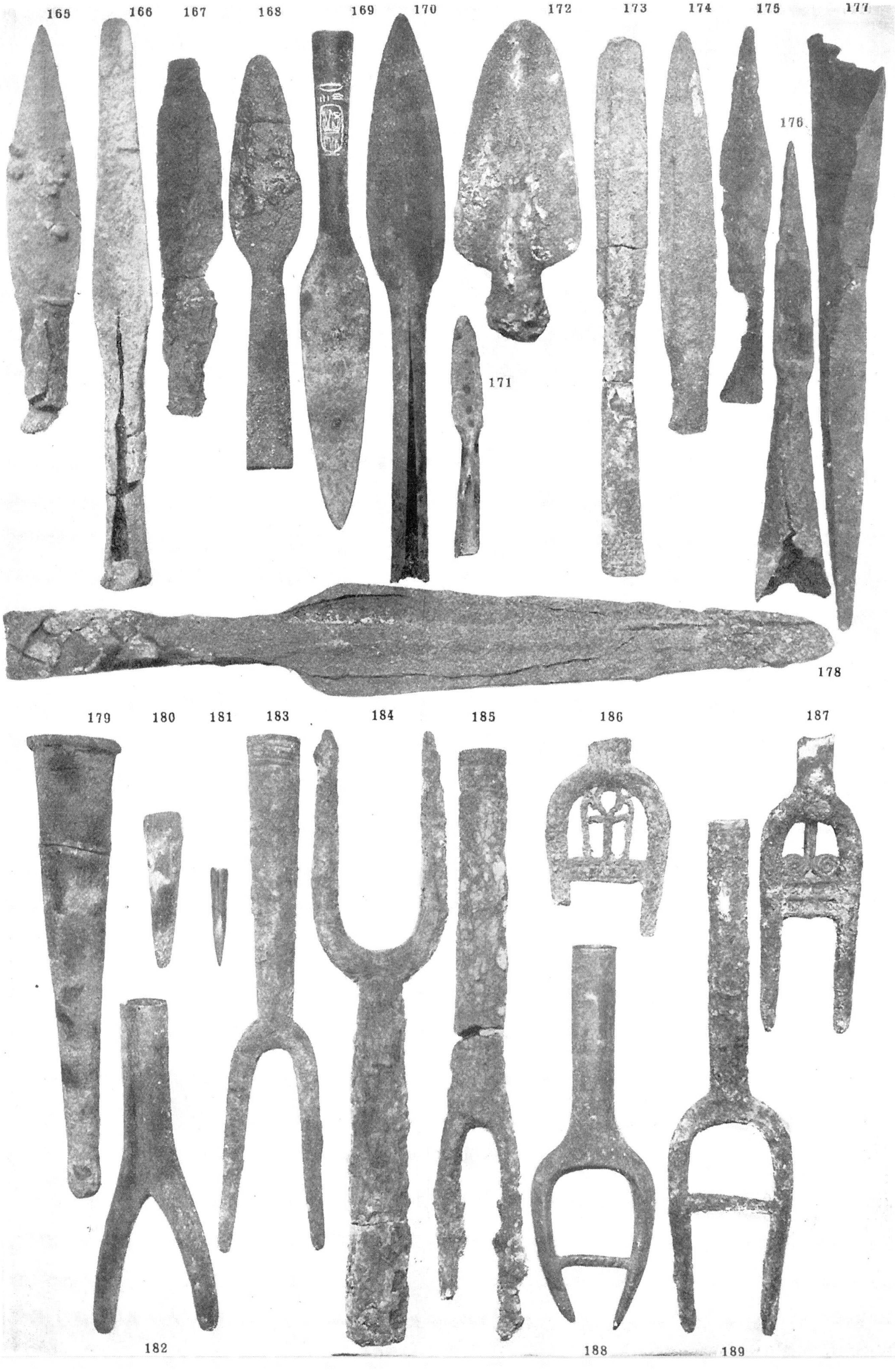

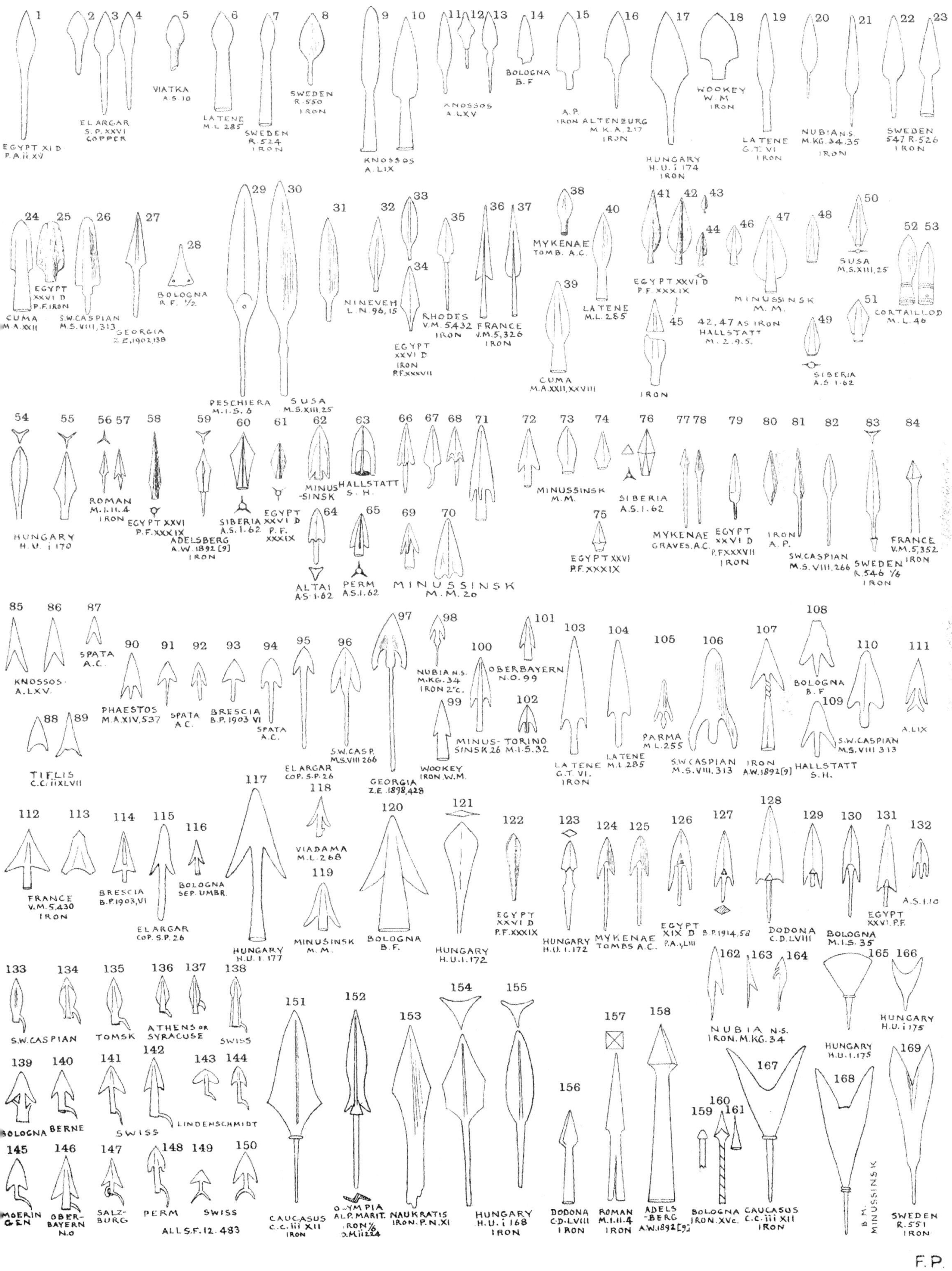
1 EGYPT XI D P.A.ii.XV
2 3 4 EL ARGAR S.P.XXVI COPPER
5 VIATKA A.S.10
6 LA TENE M.L.285
7 SWEDEN R.524 IRON
8 SWEDEN R.550 IRON
9 10 KNOSSOS A.LIX
11 12 13 KNOSSOS A.LXV
14 BOLOGNA B.F
15 A.P. IRON
16 ALTENBURG M.K.A.2.17 IRON
17 HUNGARY H.U.i.174 IRON
18 WOOKEY W.M. IRON
19 LA TENE G.T.VI IRON
20 NUBIA N.S. M.KG.34.35 IRON
21
22 23 SWEDEN 547 R.526 IRON
24 CUMA M.A.XXII
25 EGYPT XXVI D P.F.IRON
26 S.W.CASPIAN M.S.VIII,313
27 GEORGIA Z.E.1902,138
28 BOLOGNA B.F. 1/2
29 PESCHIERA M.I.S.6
30 SUSA M.S.XIII.25
31 32 NINEVEH L.N.96,15
33 34 EGYPT XXVI D IRON P.F.XXXVII
35 RHODES V.M.5432 IRON
36 37 FRANCE V.M.5,326 IRON
38 MYKENAE TOMB. A.C.
39 CUMA M.A.XXII,XXVIII
40 LA TENE M.L.285
41 42 43 44 EGYPT XXVI D P.F.XXXIX
45 IRON
46 47 MINUSSINSK M.M.
42,47 AS IRON HALLSTATT M.2.9.5.
48
49 SIBERIA A.S.1.62
50 SUSA M.S.XIII,25
51
52 53 CORTAILLOD M.L.46
54 55 HUNGARY H.U.i.170
56 57 ROMAN M.I.II.4 IRON
58 EGYPT XXVI P.F.XXXIX
59 ADELSBERG A.W.1892 [9] IRON
60 SIBERIA A.S.1.62
61 EGYPT XXVI D P.F. XXXIX
62 MINUS-SINSK
63 HALLSTATT S.H.
64 ALTAI A.S.1.62
65 PERM A.S.1.62
66 67 68 71
69 70 MINUSSINSK M.M.20
72 73 74 MINUSSINSK M.M.
75 EGYPT XXVI P.F.XXXIX
76 SIBERIA A.S.1.62
77 78 MYKENAE GRAVES.A.C.
79 EGYPT XXVI D P.F.XXXVII IRON
80 81 IRON A.P.
82 SW.CASPIAN M.S.VIII,266
83 SWEDEN R.546 1/6 IRON
84 FRANCE V.M.5,352 IRON
85 86 KNOSSOS A.LXV
87 SPATA A.C.
88 89 TIFLIS C.C.iiXLVII
90 PHAESTOS M.A.XIV.537
91 SPATA A.C.
92 93 BRESCIA B.P.1903 VI
94 SPATA A.C.
95 EL ARGAR COP.S.P.26
96 S.W.CASP. M.S.VIII 266
97 GEORGIA Z.E.1898,428
98 NUBIA N.S. M.KG.34 IRON 2nd C.
99 WOOKEY IRON W.M.
100 MINUS-SINSK 26
101 OBERBAYERN N.O.99
102 TORINO M.I.S.32
103 LA TENE G.T.VI. IRON
104 LATENE M.L.285
105 PARMA M.L.255
106 S.W.CASPIAN M.S.VIII,313
107 IRON A.W.1892[9]
108 BOLOGNA B.F
109 HALLSTATT S.H.
110 S.W.CASPIAN M.S.VIII 313
111 A.LIX
112 113 FRANCE V.M.5.430 IRON
114 BRESCIA B.P.1903,VI
115 EL ARGAR COP.S.P.26
116 BOLOGNA SEP. UMBR.
117 HUNGARY H.U.I.177
118 VIADAMA M.L.268
119 MINUSINSK M.M.
120 BOLOGNA B.F.
121 HUNGARY H.U.I.172
122 EGYPT XXVI D P.F.XXXIX
123 HUNGARY H.U.I.172
124 125 MYKENAE TOMBS A.C.
126 EGYPT XIX D P.A.i,LIII
127 B.P.1914.56
128 DODONA C.D.LVIII
129 130 BOLOGNA M.I.S.35
131 EGYPT XXVI.P.F.
132 A.S.I.10
133 134 S.W.CASPIAN
135 TOMSK
136 137 ATHENS OR SYRACUSE
138 SWISS
139 BOLOGNA
140 BERNE
141 142 SWISS
143 144 LINDENSCHMIDT
145 MOERINGEN
146 OBER-BAYERN N.O
147 SALZ-BURG
148 PERM
149 SWISS
150
ALL S.F.12.483
151 CAUCASUS C.C.iii XII IRON
152 OLYMPIA ALP.MARIT. IRON 1/6 D.M.ii224
153 NAUKRATIS IRON.P.N.XI
154 155 HUNGARY H.U.i 168 IRON
156 DODONA C.D.LVIII IRON
157 ROMAN M.I.II.4 IRON
158 ADELS-BERG A.W.1892[9]
159 160 161 BOLOGNA IRON.XVc.
162 163 164 NUBIA N.S. IRON. M.KG.34
165 HUNGARY H.U.I.175
166 HUNGARY H.U.i 175
167 CAUCASUS C.C.iii XII IRON
168 B.M. MINUSSINSK
169 SWEDEN R.551 IRON

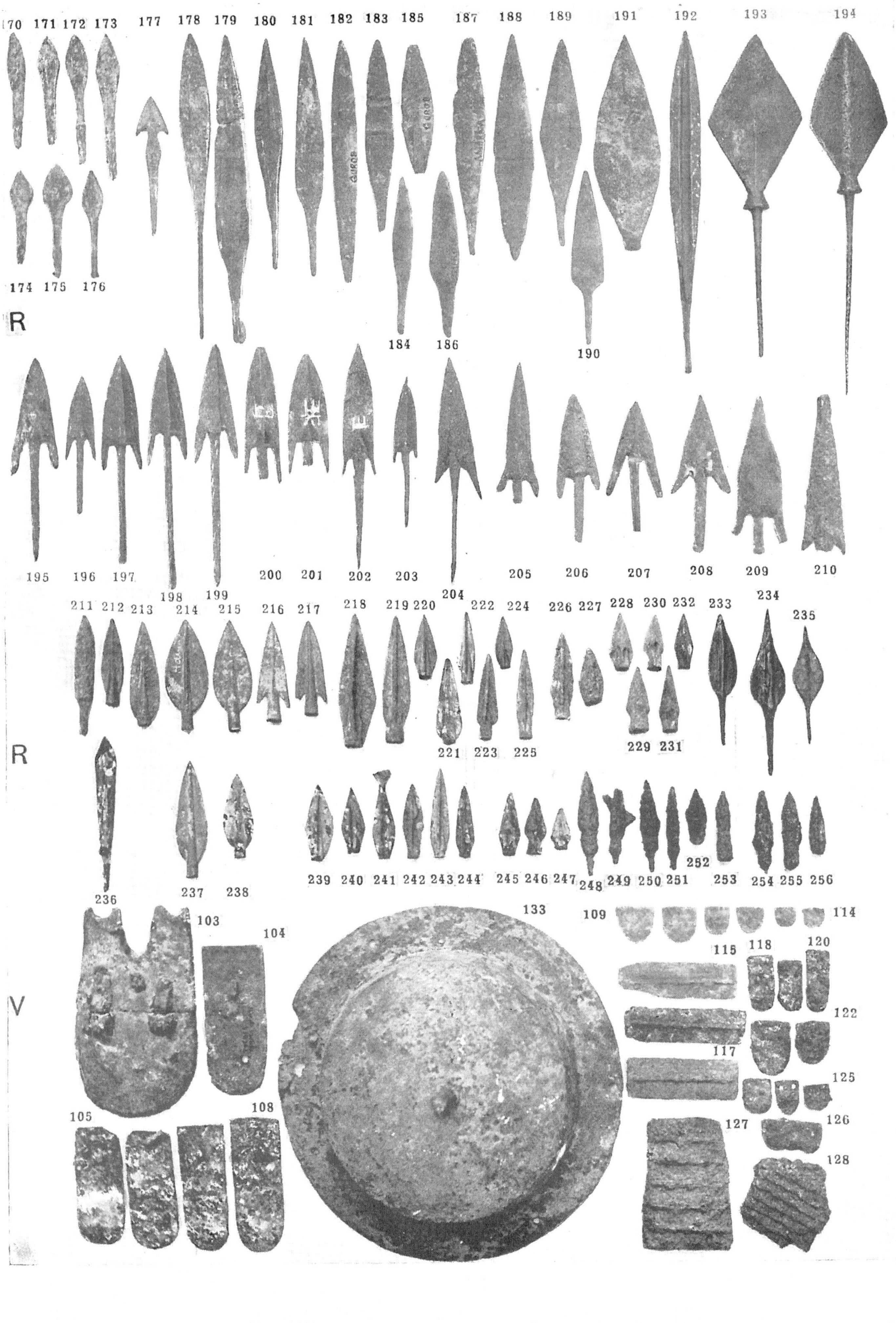
170 171 172 173 177 178 179 180 181 182 183 185 187 188 189 191 192 193 194
174 175 176
R
184 186 190
195 196 197 198 199 200 201 202 203 204 205 206 207 208 209 210
211 212 213 214 215 216 217 218 219 220 222 224 226 227 228 230 232 233 234 235
R
221 223 225 229 231
236 237 238 239 240 241 242 243 244 245 246 247 248 249 250 251 252 253 254 255 256
103 104 133 109 114 115 118 120
V
122 117 125 105 108 127 126 128

R. BOW AND ARROW. V. THROW-STICK, HARPOON, ARMOUR, FISH-HOOK. M. BORING, PLANING. XLIII.

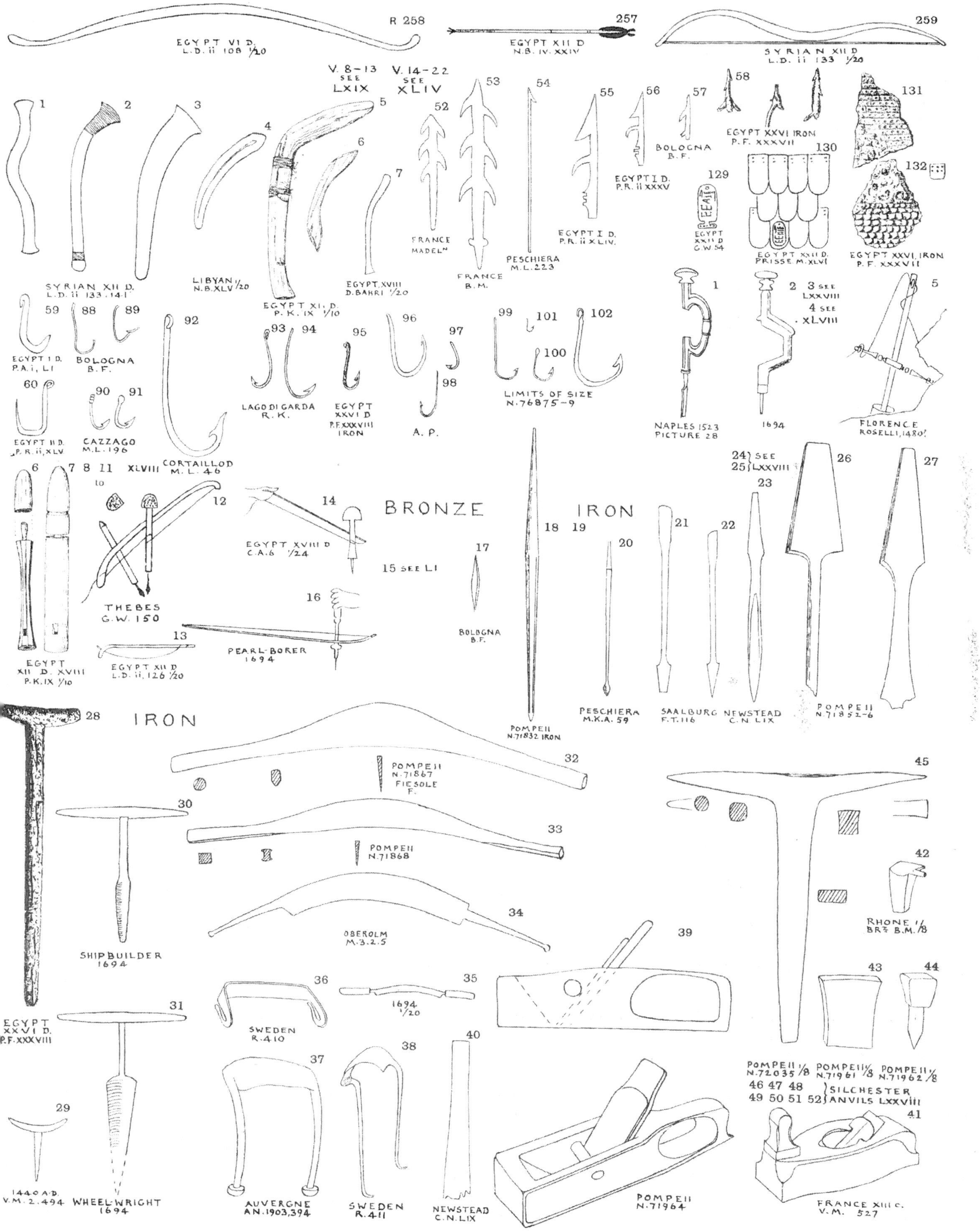

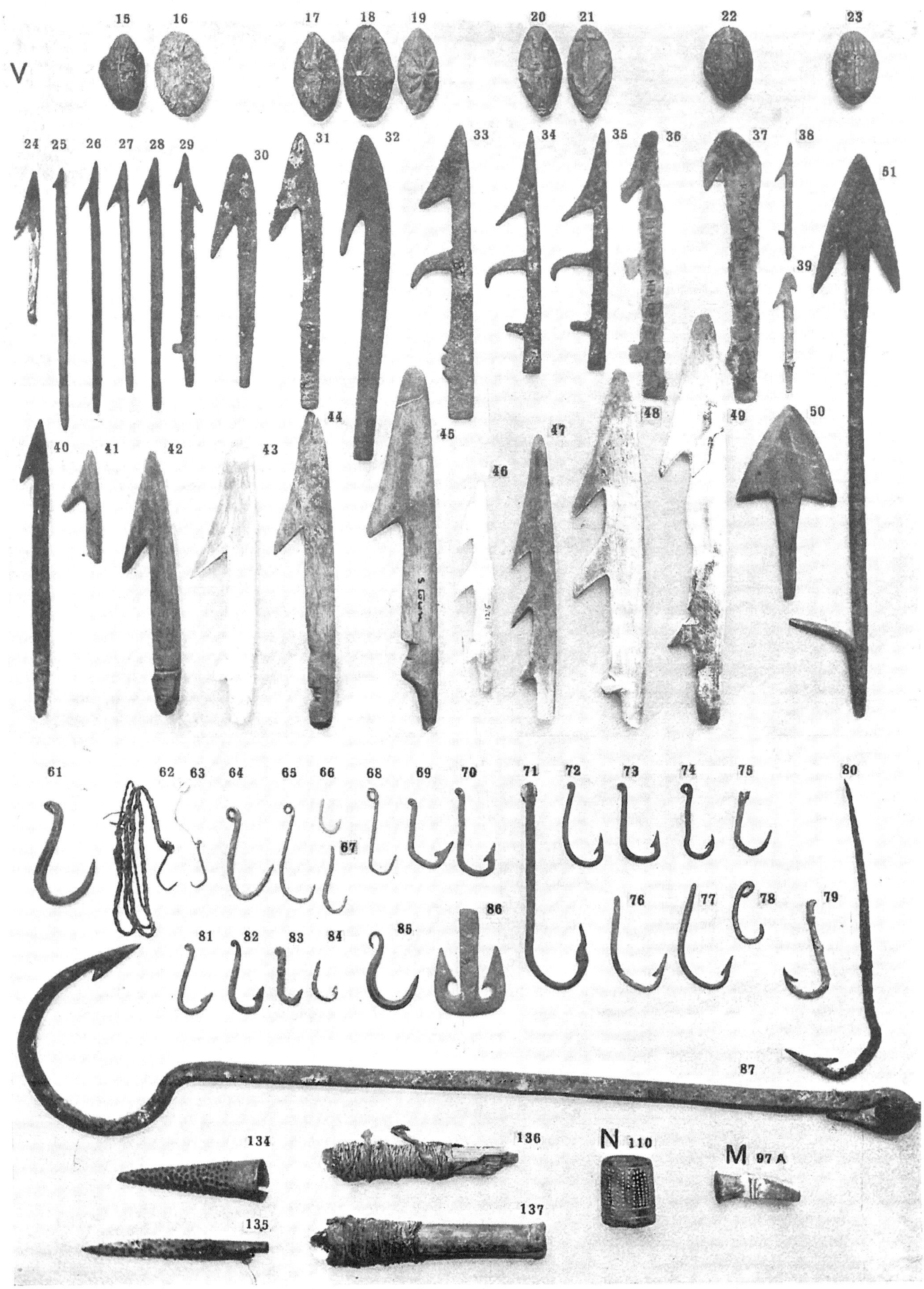
V
15
16
17
18
19
20
21
22
23
24
25
26
27
28
29
30
31
32
33
34
35
36
37
38
39
51
40
41
42
43
44
45
46
47
48
49
50
61
62
63
64
65
66
67
68
69
70
71
72
73
74
75
80
76
77
78
79
81
82
83
84
85
86
87
134
136
N 110
M 97 A
135
137

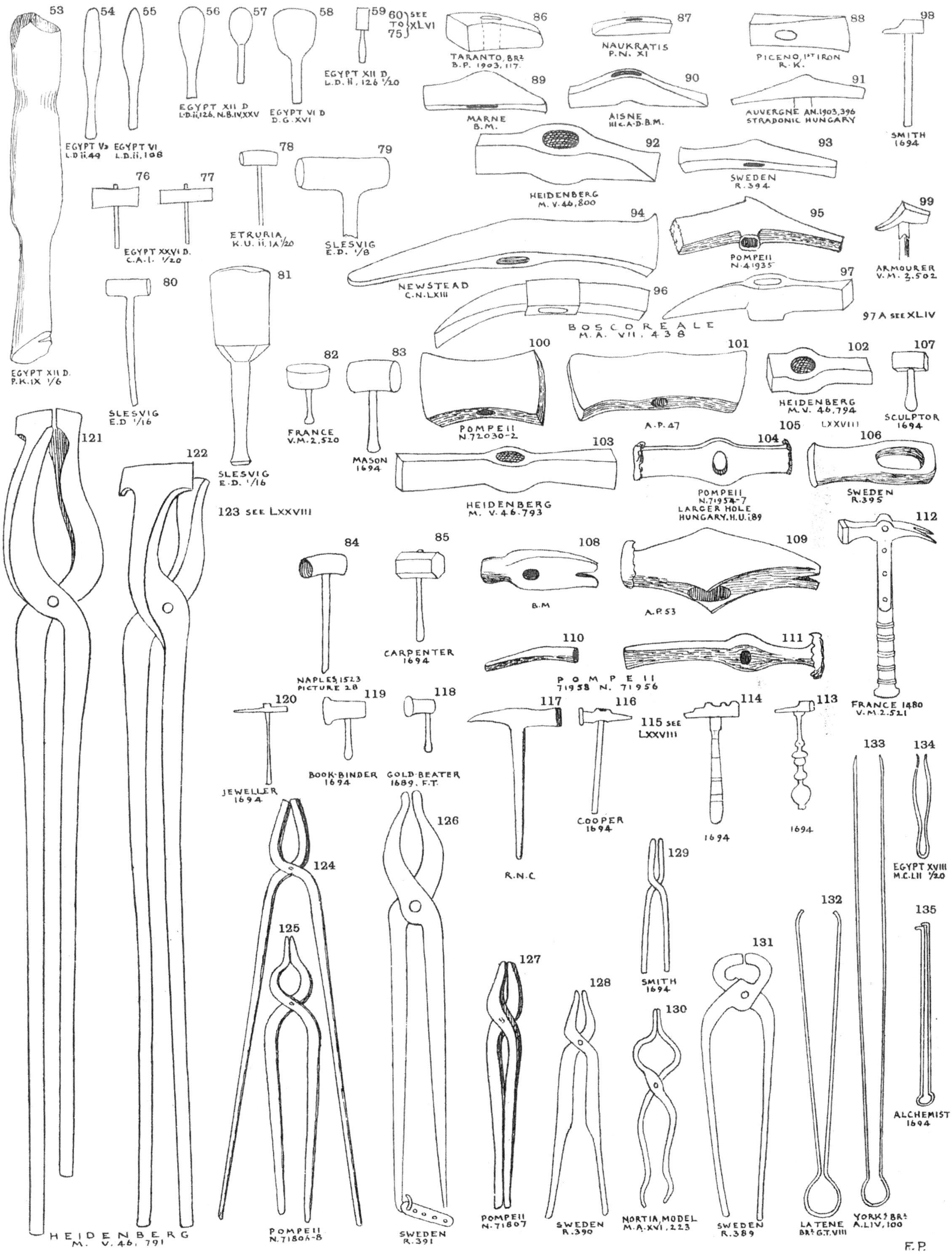
53 EGYPT XII D. P.K.IX 1/6
54 EGYPT V3 L.D.ii.49
55 EGYPT VI L.D.ii.108
56 57 EGYPT XII D L.D.ii.126. N.B.IV.XXV
58 EGYPT VI D D.G.XVI
59 EGYPT XII D. L.D.ii.126 1/20
60 TO 75 SEE XLVI
76 EGYPT XXVI D. C.A.I. 1/20
77
78 ETRURIA K.U.ii.1A 1/20
79 SLESVIG E.D. 1/8
80 SLESVIG E.D 1/16
81 SLESVIG E.D. 1/16
82 FRANCE V.M.2.520
83 MASON 1694
84 NAPLES 1523 PICTURE 28
85 CARPENTER 1694
86 TARANTO, BR.Z B.P. 1903, 117.
87 NAUKRATIS P.N. XI
88 PICENO, 1ST IRON R.K.
89 MARNE B.M.
90 AISNE III c. A.D. B.M.
91 AUVERGNE AN.1903,396 STRADONIC HUNGARY
92 HEIDENBERG M.V.46,800
93 SWEDEN R.394
94 NEWSTEAD C.N.LXIII
95 POMPEII N.41935
96 97 BOSCOREALE M.A. VII, 438
97 A SEE XLIV
98 SMITH 1694
99 ARMOURER V.M.2.502
100 POMPEII N.72030-2
101 A.P.47
102 HEIDENBERG M.V.46,794 LXXVIII
103 HEIDENBERG M. V.46.793
104 105 POMPEII N.71954-7 LARGER HOLE HUNGARY.H.U.189
106 SWEDEN R.395
107 SCULPTOR 1694
108 B.M
109 A.P.53
110 111 POMPEII 71958 N. 71956
112 FRANCE 1480 V.M.2.521
113 1694
114 1694
115 SEE LXXVIII
116 COOPER 1694
117 R.N.C.
118 GOLD-BEATER 1689. F.T.
119 BOOK-BINDER 1694
120 JEWELLER 1694
121 122 HEIDENBERG M. V.46.791
123 SEE LXXVIII
124 125 POMPEII N.71806-8
126 SWEDEN R.391
127 POMPEII N.71807
128 SWEDEN R.390
129 SMITH 1694
130 NORTIA MODEL M.A.XVI.223
131 SWEDEN R.389
132 LA TENE BR.Z G.T.VIII
133 YORKS BR.Z A.LIV.100
134 EGYPT XVIII M.C.LII 1/20
135 ALCHEMIST 1694
F.P.

60
61
62
63
64
65
66
67
68
69
70
71
72
73
74
75

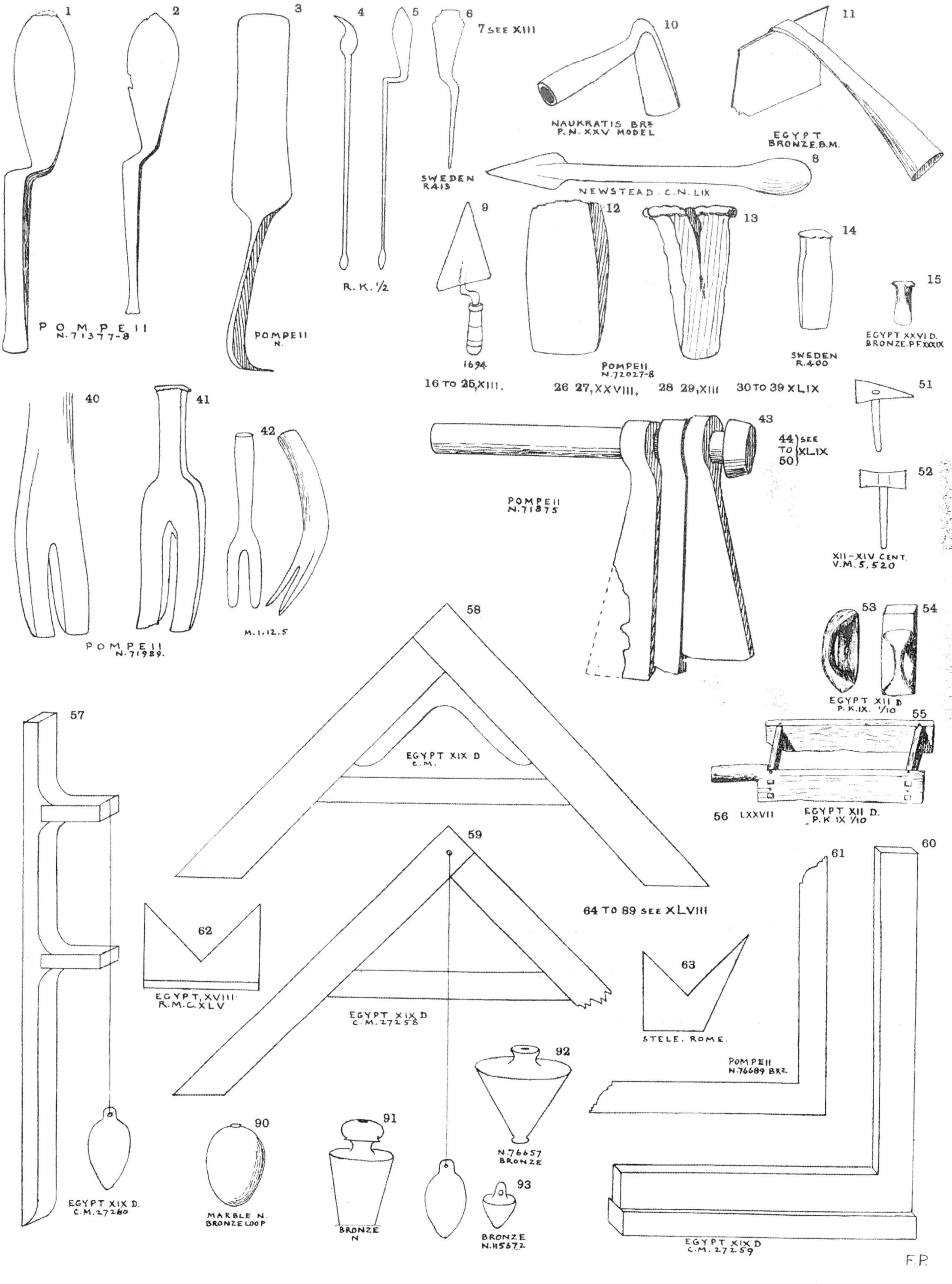
1
2
3
4
5
6
7 SEE XIII
10
11
POMPEII N. 71377-8
POMPEII N.
R. K. 1/2
SWEDEN R413
NAUKRATIS BRZ. P.N. XXV MODEL
EGYPT BRONZE. B.M.
8
NEWSTEAD. C.N. LIX
9
12
13
14
15
1694
POMPEII N. 72027-8
SWEDEN R. 400
EGYPT XXVI D. BRONZE. P.F. XXXIX
16 TO 25, XIII.
26 27, XXVIII.
28 29, XIII
30 TO 39 XLIX
51
40
41
42
43
44 TO 50 SEE XLIX
POMPEII N. 71875
52
XII-XIV CENT. V.M. 5, 520
POMPEII N. 71989.
M. 1. 12. 5
58
53
54
EGYPT XII D P. K. IX. 1/10
57
55
EGYPT XIX D C. M.
56 LXXVII
EGYPT XII D. P. K. IX 1/10
59
61
60
64 TO 89 SEE XLVIII
62
63
EGYPT, XVIII R. M. C. XLV
EGYPT XIX D C. M. 27258
STELE. ROME.
POMPEII N. 76689 BRZ.
92
90
91
N. 76657 BRONZE
93
EGYPT XIX D. C. M. 27260
MARBLE N. BRONZE LOOP
BRONZE N
BRONZE N. 115672
EGYPT XIX D C. M. 27259

F.P.

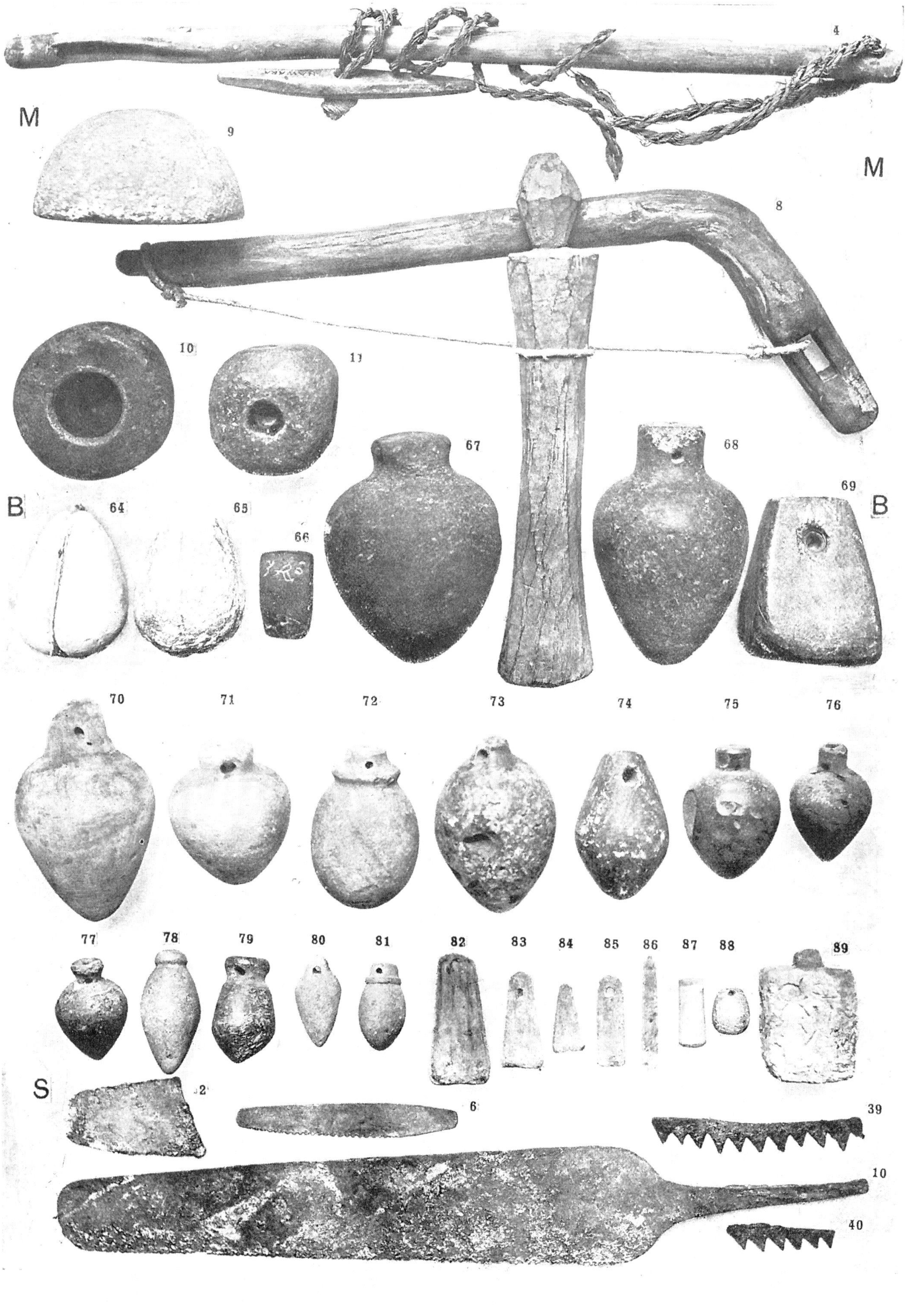
4
M
9
M
8
10
11
67
68
69
B
64
65
66
B
70
71
72
73
74
75
76
77
78
79
80
81
82
83
84
85
86
87
88
89
S
6
39
10
40

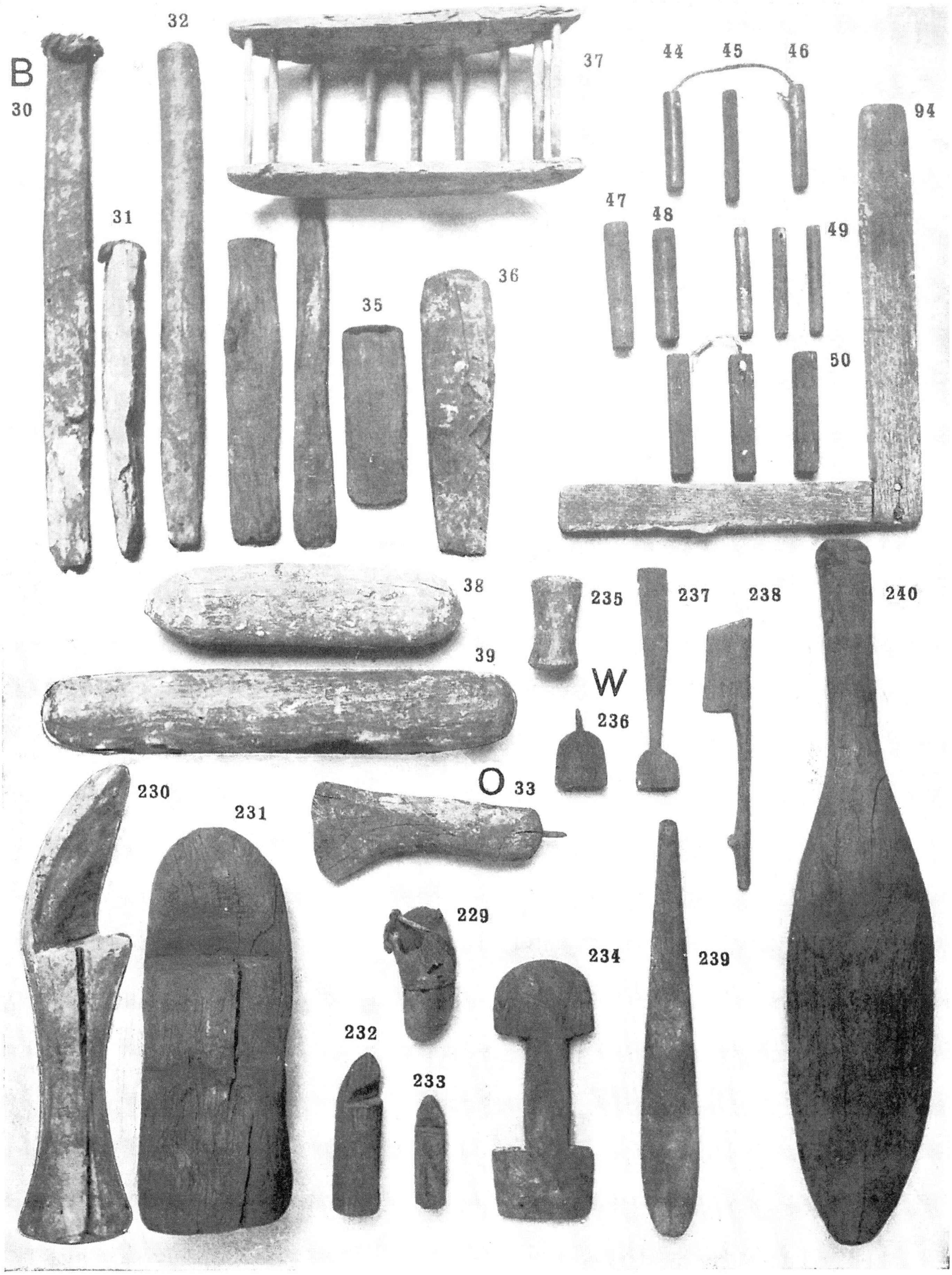
B
30
31
32
35
36
37
44
45
46
47
48
49
50
94
38
39
235
237
238
240
W
236
O 33
230
231
229
234
239
232
233

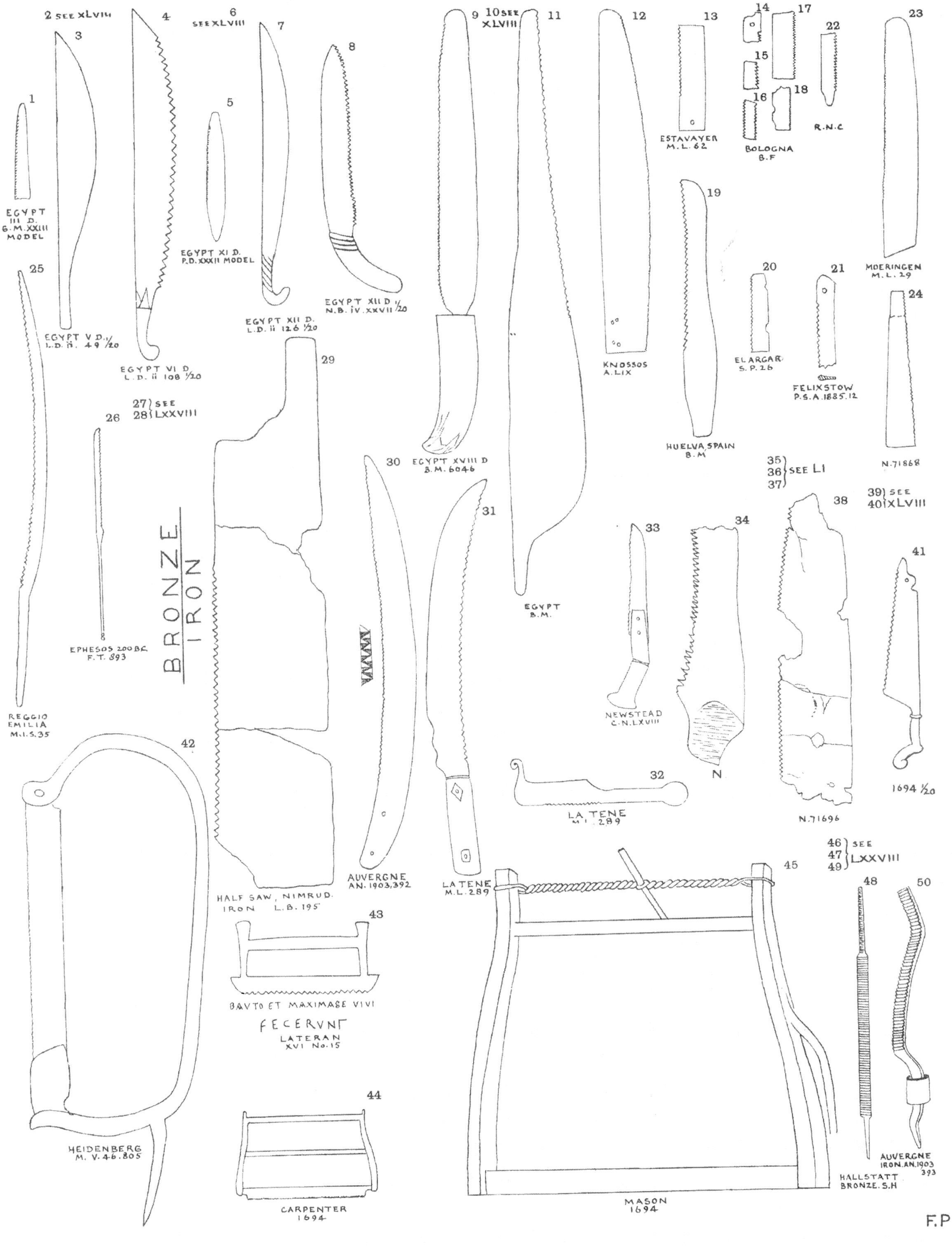
2 SEE XLVIII
3
4
6 SEE XLVIII
7
8
9
10 SEE XLVIII
11
12
13
14
17
22
23
1
5
15
16
18
ESTAVAYER M.L. 62
BOLOGNA B.F
R.N.C
EGYPT III D. G.M.XXIII MODEL
EGYPT XI D. P.D.XXXII MODEL
19
MOERINGEN M.L. 29
25
EGYPT XII D. N.B. iv. XXVII 1/20
20
21
24
EGYPT V D. L.D. ii. 49 1/20
EGYPT XII D. L.D. ii 126 1/20
29
KNOSSOS A.LIX
EL ARGAR S.P. 26
FELIXSTOW P.S.A. 1885. 12
EGYPT VI D. L.D. ii 108 1/20
27 } SEE
28 } LXXVIII
26
EGYPT XVIII D B.M. 6046
HUELVA, SPAIN B.M
N. 71868
30
35 }
36 } SEE LI
37 }
38
39 } SEE
40 } XLVIII
31
33
34
41
BRONZE
IRON
EGYPT B.M.
EPHESOS 200 BC F.T. 893
NEWSTEAD C.N. LXVIII
N
REGGIO EMILIA M.I.S. 35
42
32
LA TENE M.L. 289
1694 1/20
N. 71696
AUVERGNE AN. 1903, 392
LATENE M.L. 289
46 } SEE
47 } LXXVIII
49 }
45
48
50
HALF SAW, NIMRUD. IRON L.B. 195
43
BAVTO ET MAXIMASE VIVI
FECERVNT
LATERAN XVI No. 15
44
HEIDENBERG M. V. 46. 805
CARPENTER 1694
MASON 1694
AUVERGNE IRON. AN. 1903 393
HALLSTATT BRONZE. S.H

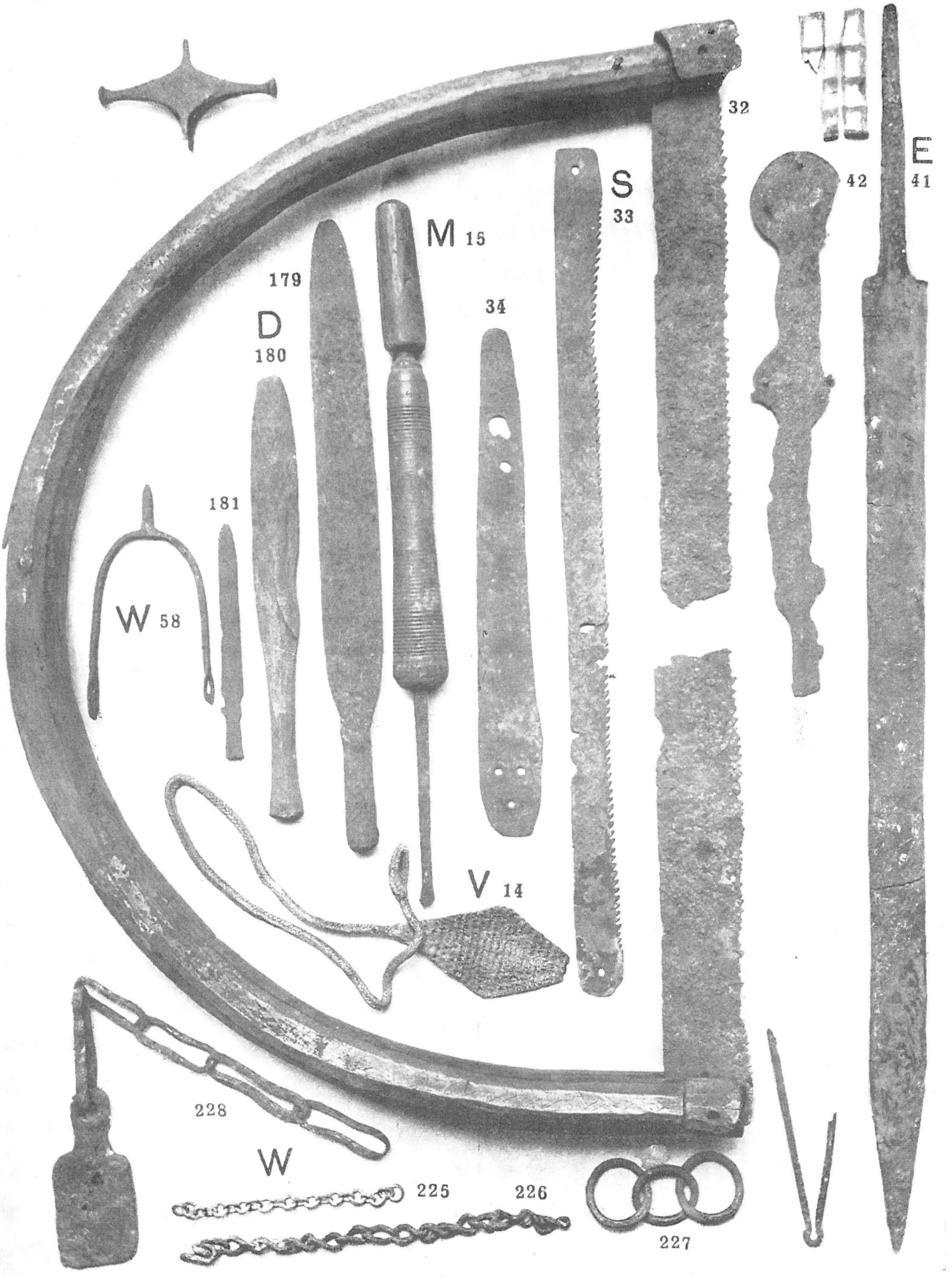

FOR S 32, 33, 34, READ S 35, 36, 37.

51
52
53
54
55
56
57
58
59
60
61
62
63
64
65
66
67
68
69
70
71
72
73

74
75
76
77
78
79
80
82
83
84
85
81
86
87
88
89
90
91
92

1:8 F. SICKLE. LIV.

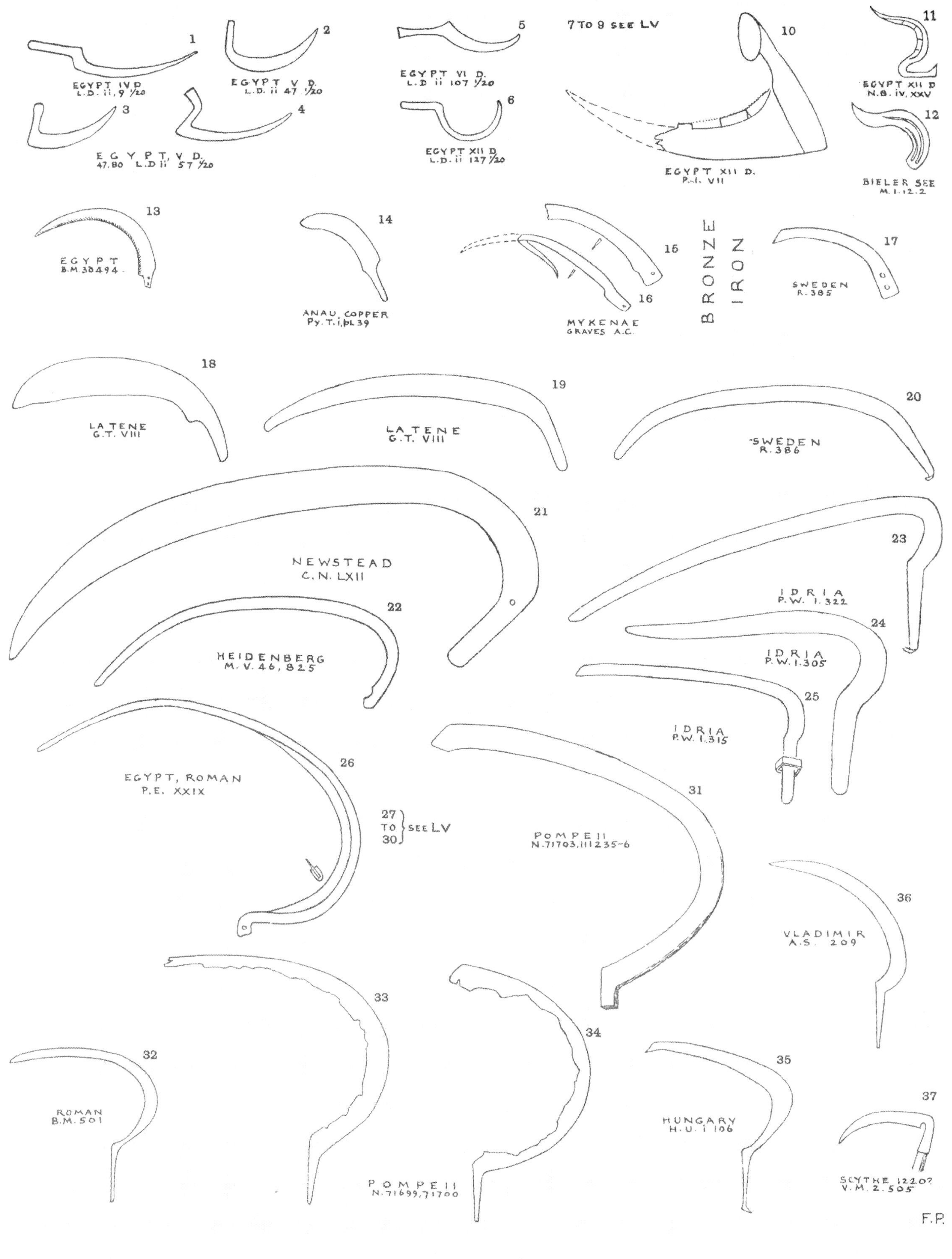

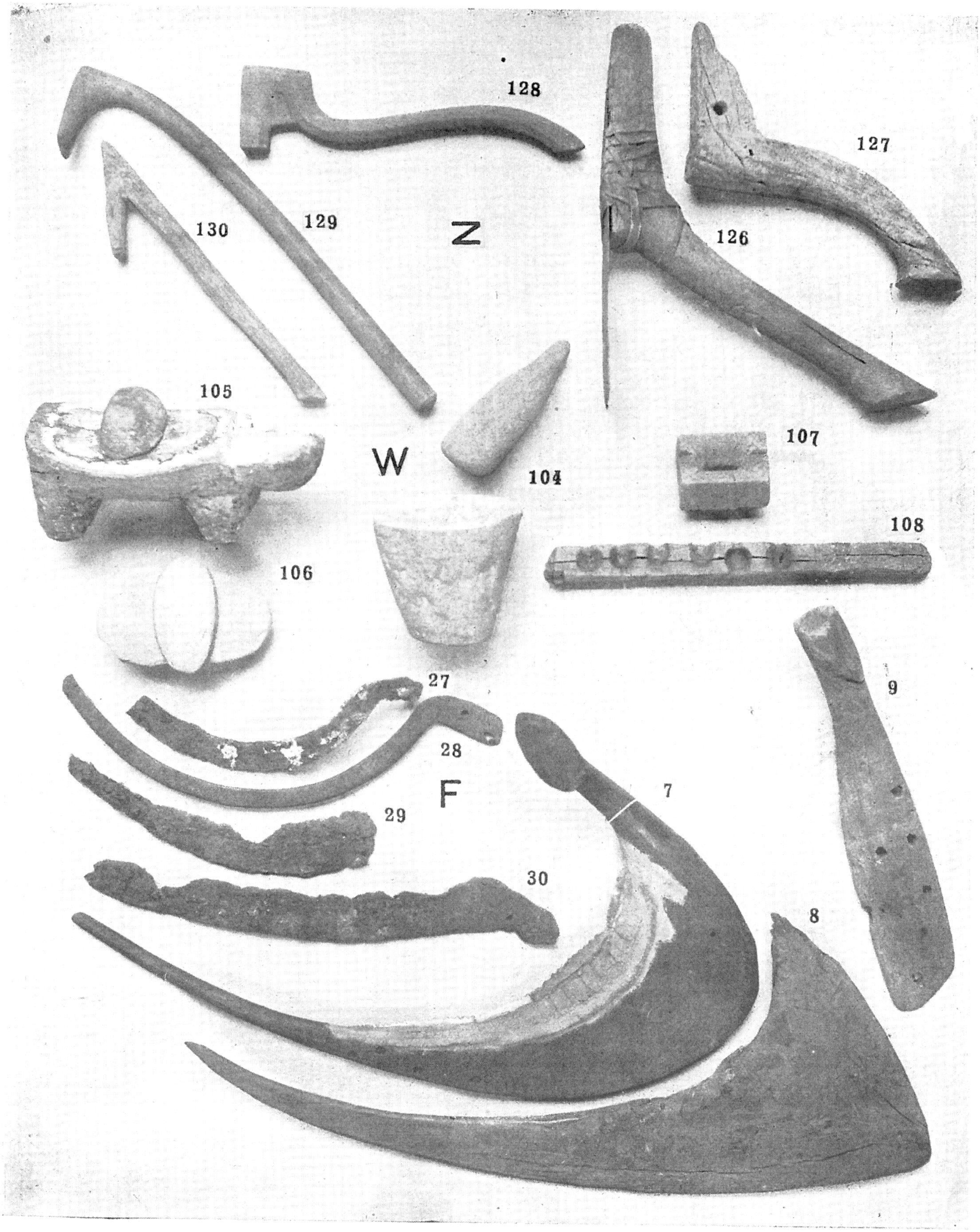
128
127
130
129
Z
126
105
107
W
104
108
106
27
9
28
F
7
29
30
8

P. PRUNING HOOK OR BILL HOOK.

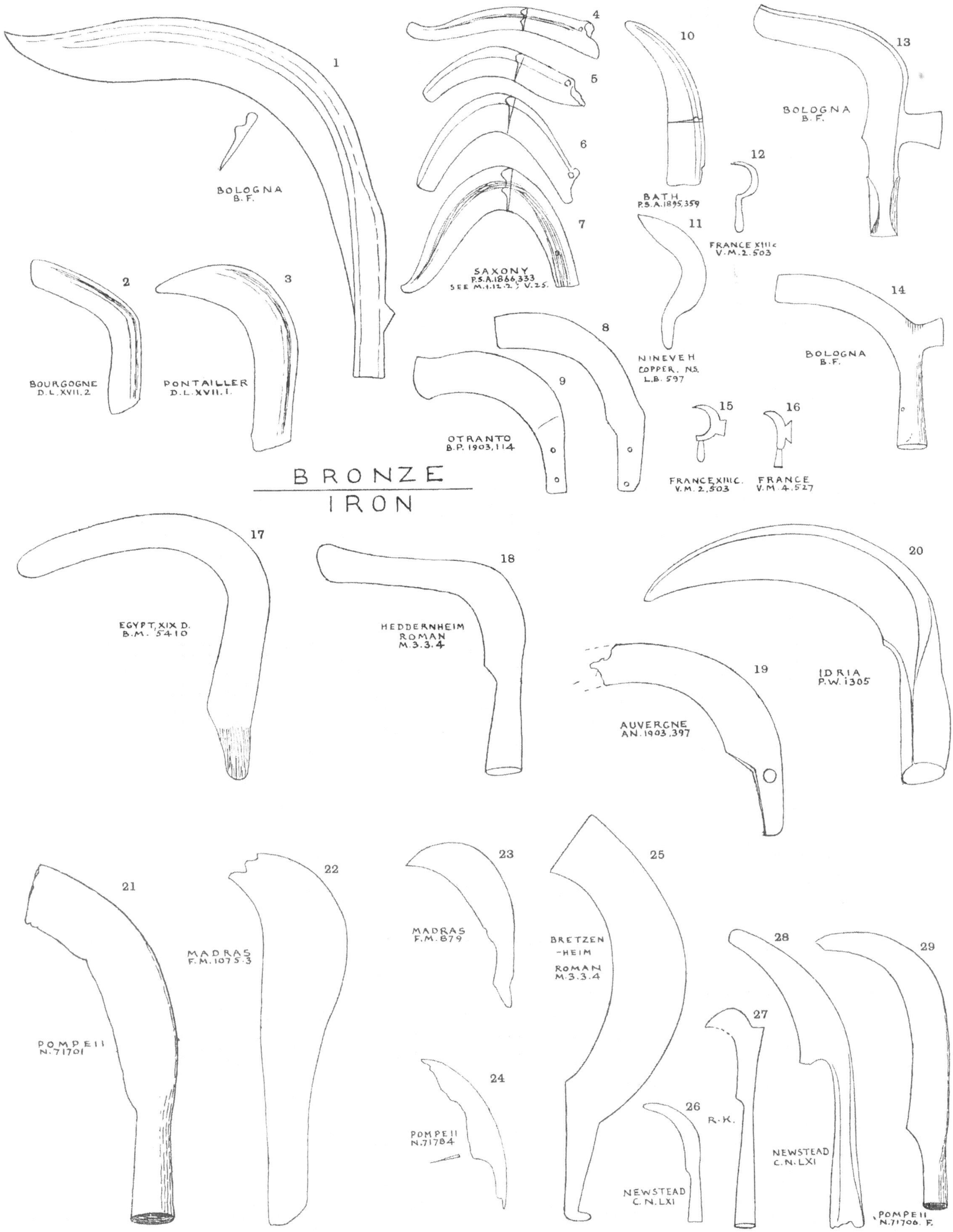

F.

:4 P. PRUNING HOOK OR BILL HOOK, IRON. LVII.

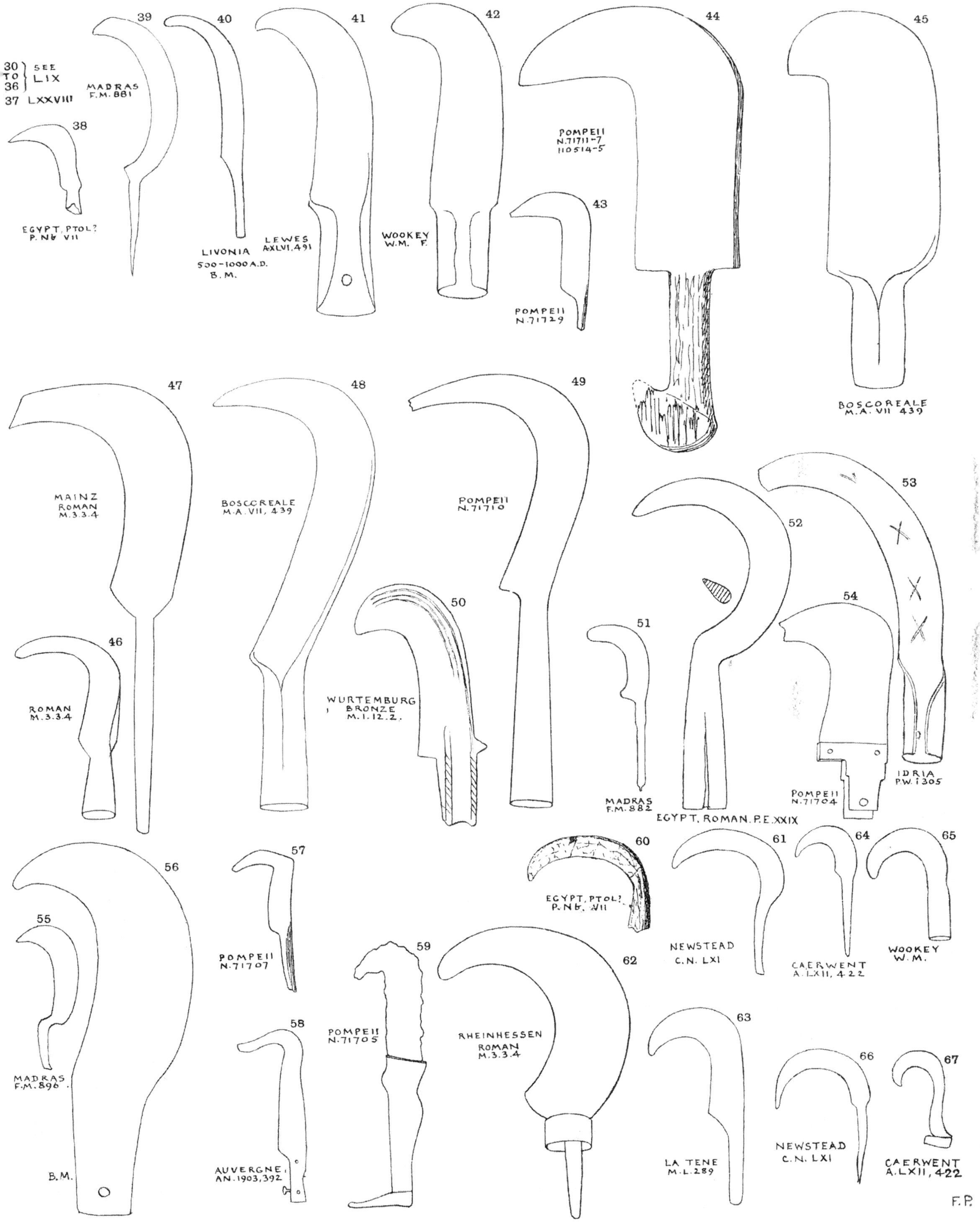

1:4 Q. SHEARS AND SCISSORS, IRON. LVIII.

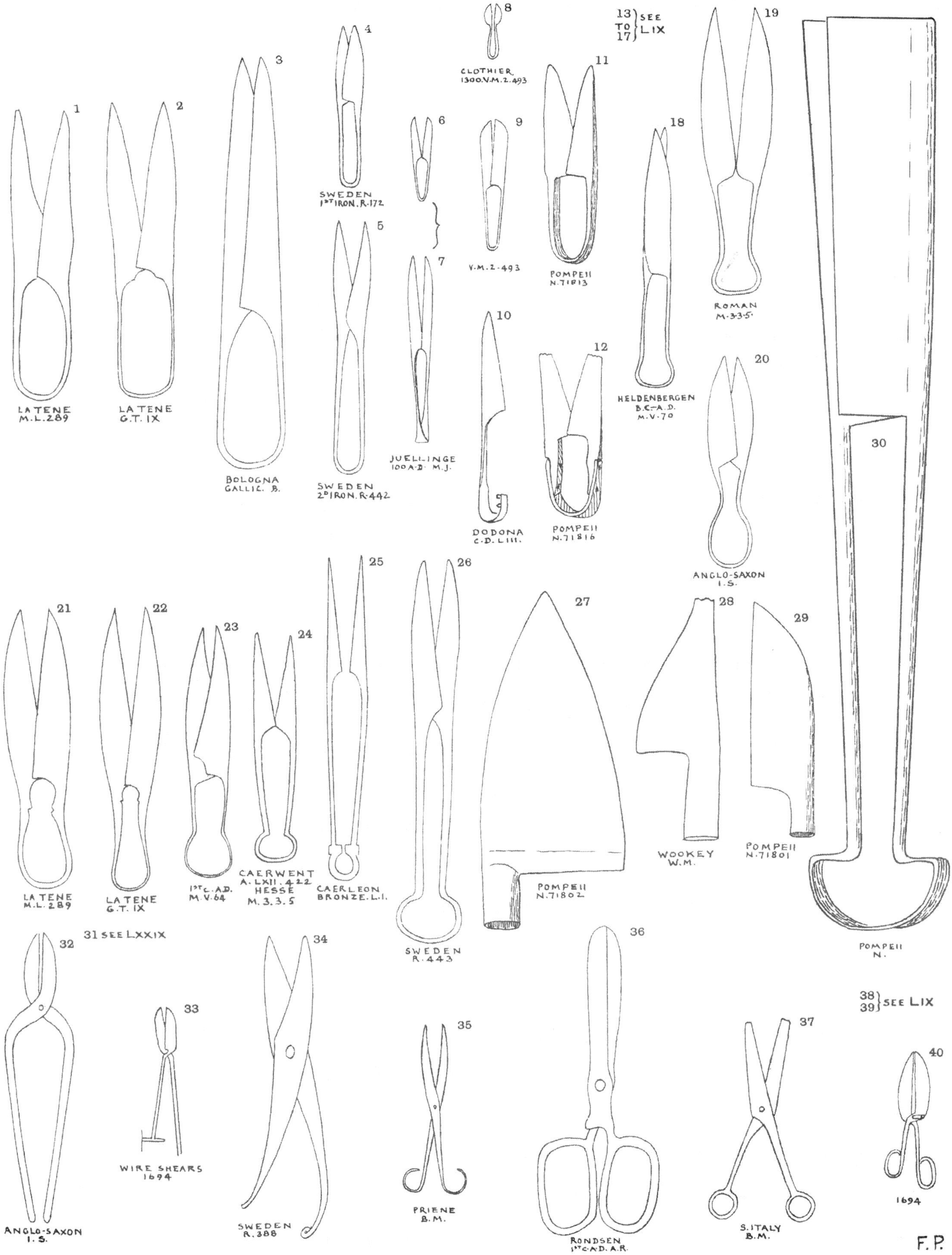

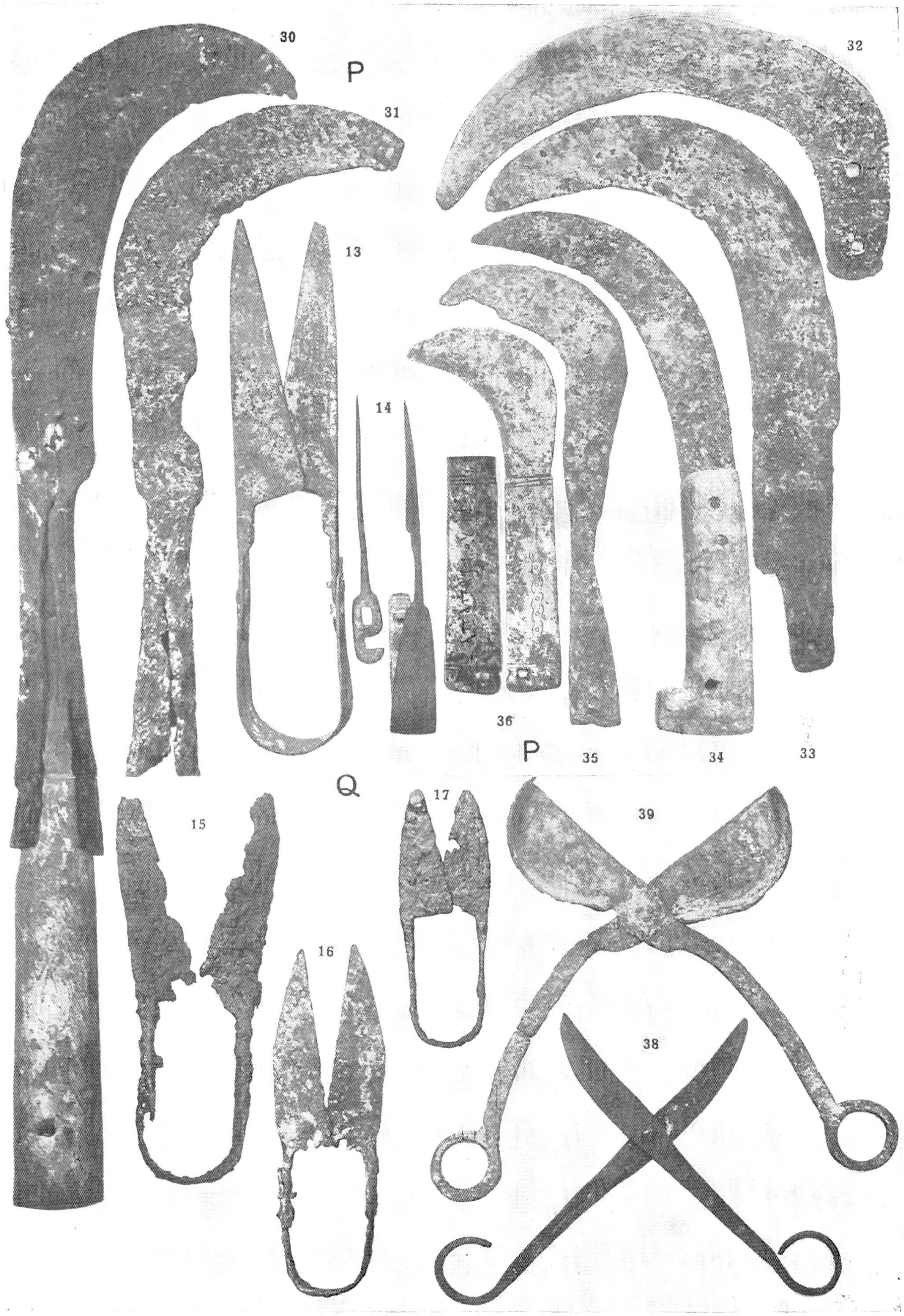
30
P
31
32
13
14
36
P
35
34
33
Q
15
17
39
16
38

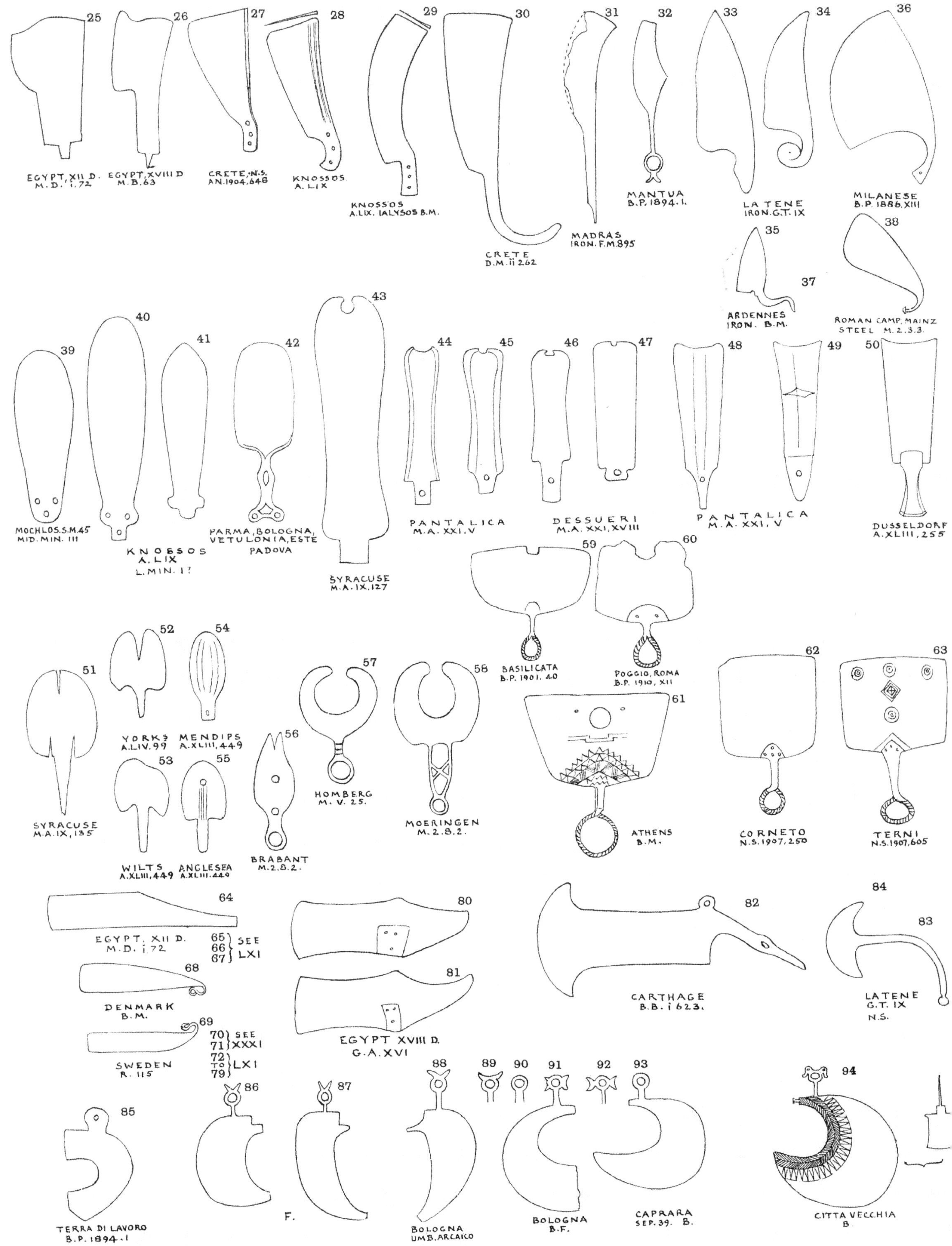

37 SEE LXXIX, 8? SEE LXI

X
1
2
3
4
5
6
7
8
9
10
11
12
13
14
15
16
17
18
19
20
67
66
21
22
23
24
65
72
73
74
75
76
77
78
79
84

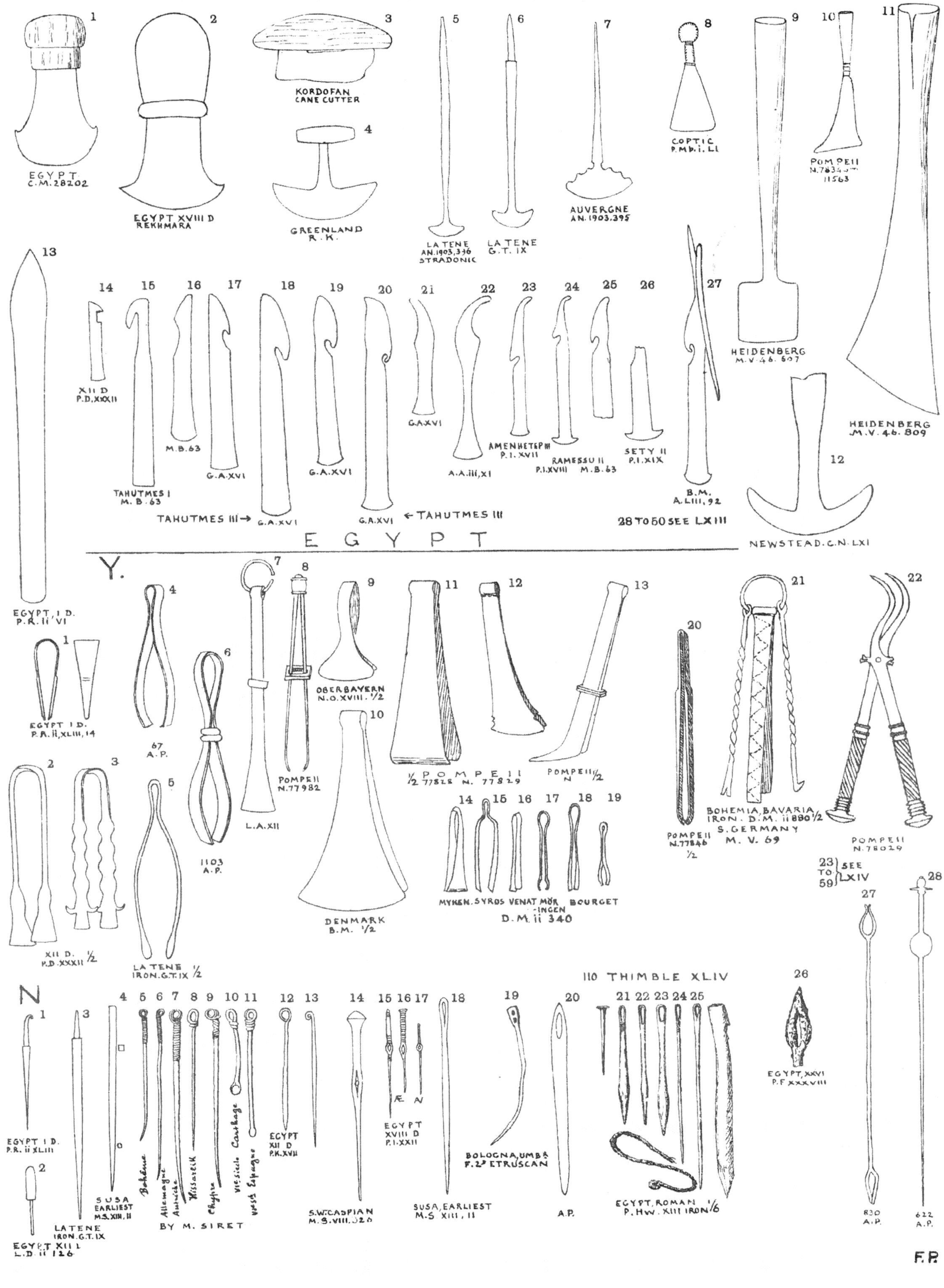

EGYPT C.M. 28202
EGYPT XVIII D REKHMARA
KORDOFAN CANE CUTTER
GREENLAND R.K.
LA TENE AN. 1903,336 STRADONIC
LA TENE G.T. IX
AUVERGNE AN. 1903.395
COPTIC P.M.b.i.LI
POMPEII N.78340 11563
HEIDENBERG M.V.46.507
HEIDENBERG M.V.46.809
NEWSTEAD. C.N. LXI
XII D P.D. XXXII
TAHUTMES I M.B.63
M.B.63
G.A.XVI
TAHUTMES III→
G.A.XVI
←TAHUTMES III
A.A.III, XI
AMENHETEP III P.I.XVII
RAMESSU II P.I.XVIII M.B.63
SETY II P.I.XIX
B.M. A.LIII, 92
28 TO 50 SEE LXIII
EGYPT
EGYPT I D. P.R. II VI
Y.
EGYPT I D. P.R. II, XLIII, 14
XII D. P.D. XXXII ½
67 A.P.
1103 A.P.
LA TENE IRON. G.T. IX ½
L.A. XII
POMPEII N. 77982
OBERBAYERN N.O. XVIII. ½
DENMARK B.M. ½
½ POMPEII 77828 N. 77829
POMPEII N ½
MYKEN. SYROS VENAT MÖR-INGEN BOURGET
D.M. II 340
POMPEII N. 77846 ½
BOHEMIA, BAVARIA IRON. D.M. II 880 ½
S. GERMANY M.V. 69
POMPEII N. 78029
23 TO 59 SEE LXIV
N
EGYPT I D. P.R. II XLIII
EGYPT XII L. L.D. II 126
LATENE IRON. G.T. IX
SUSA EARLIEST M.S. XIII, II
Bohême
Allemagne Autriche
Hissarlik
Chypre
VIe siècle Carthage
Espagne
BY M. SIRET
EGYPT XII D P.K. XVII
S.W. CASPIAN M.S. VIII. 526
Æ N
EGYPT XVIII D P.I. XXII
SUSA, EARLIEST M.S. XIII, II
BOLOGNA, UMB. F. 2ª ETRUSCAN
A.P.
110 THIMBLE XLIV
EGYPT, ROMAN P. Hw. XIII IRON ⅙
EGYPT, XXVI P.F. XXXVIII
830 A.P.
622 A.P.

F.P.

L. CUTTING-OUT KNIFE.

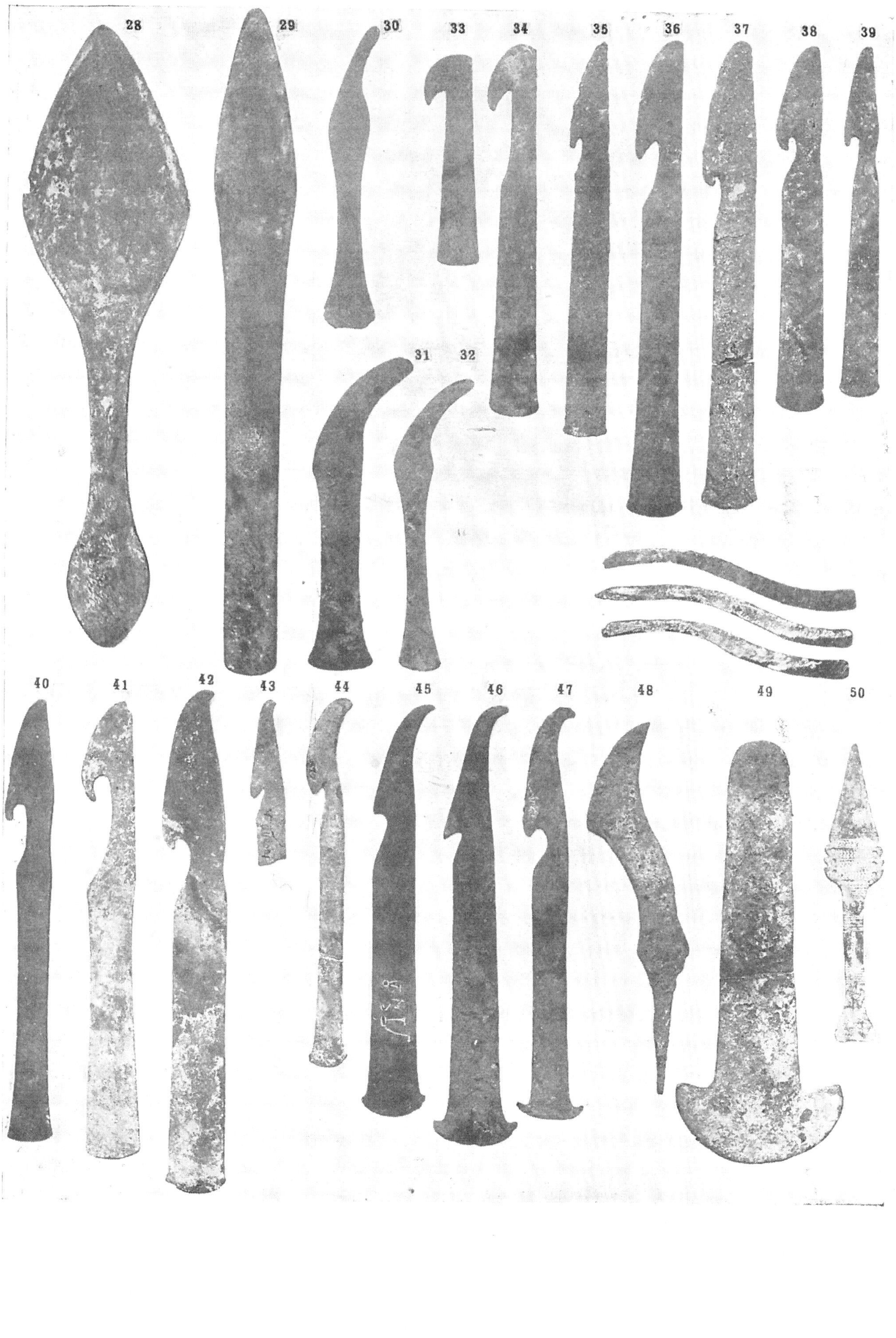

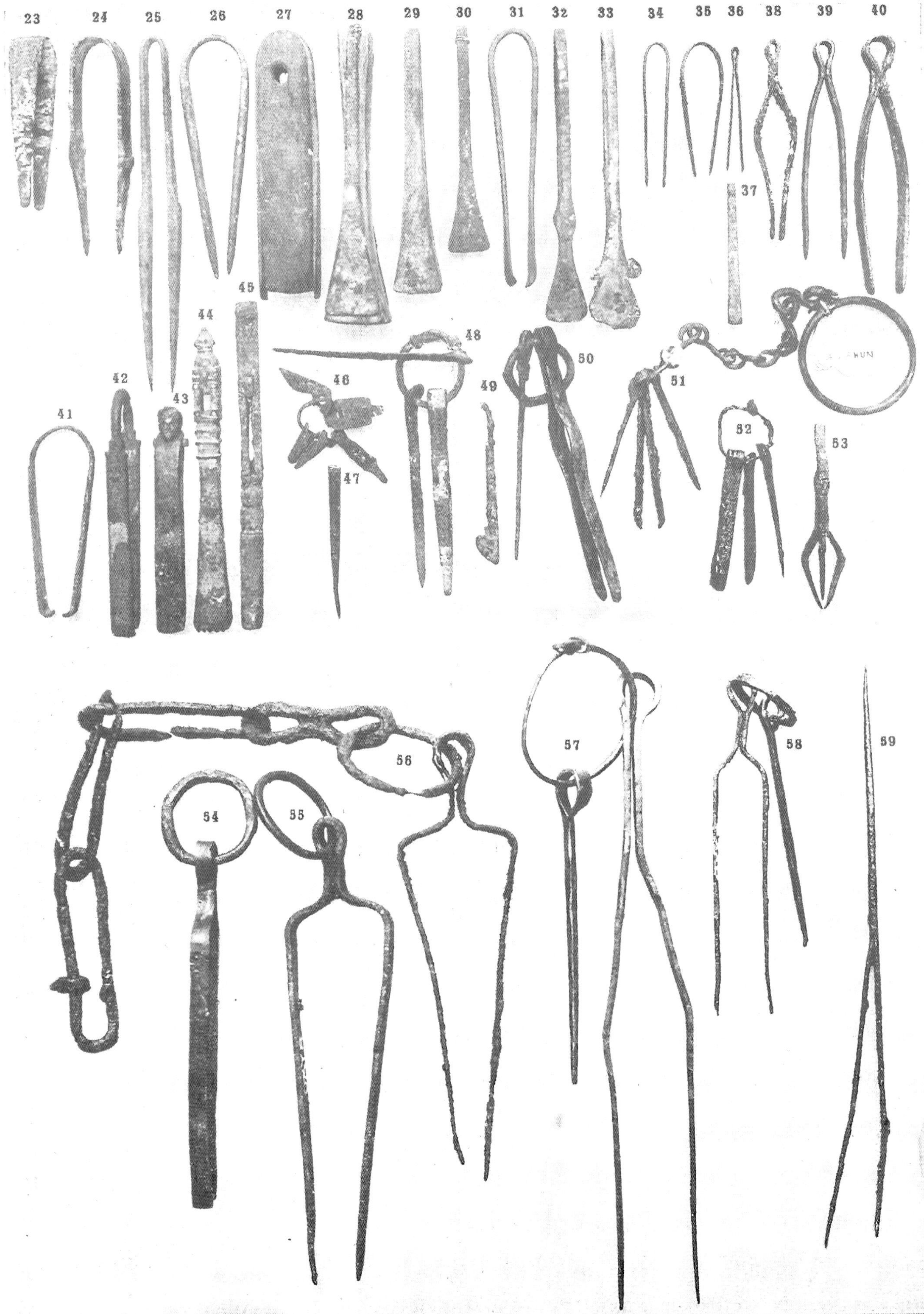
23 24 25 26 27 28 29 30 31 32 33 34 35 36 38 39 40
37
45
44
48
42
46
50
43
49
51
41
52
53
47
57
56
54
55
58
59

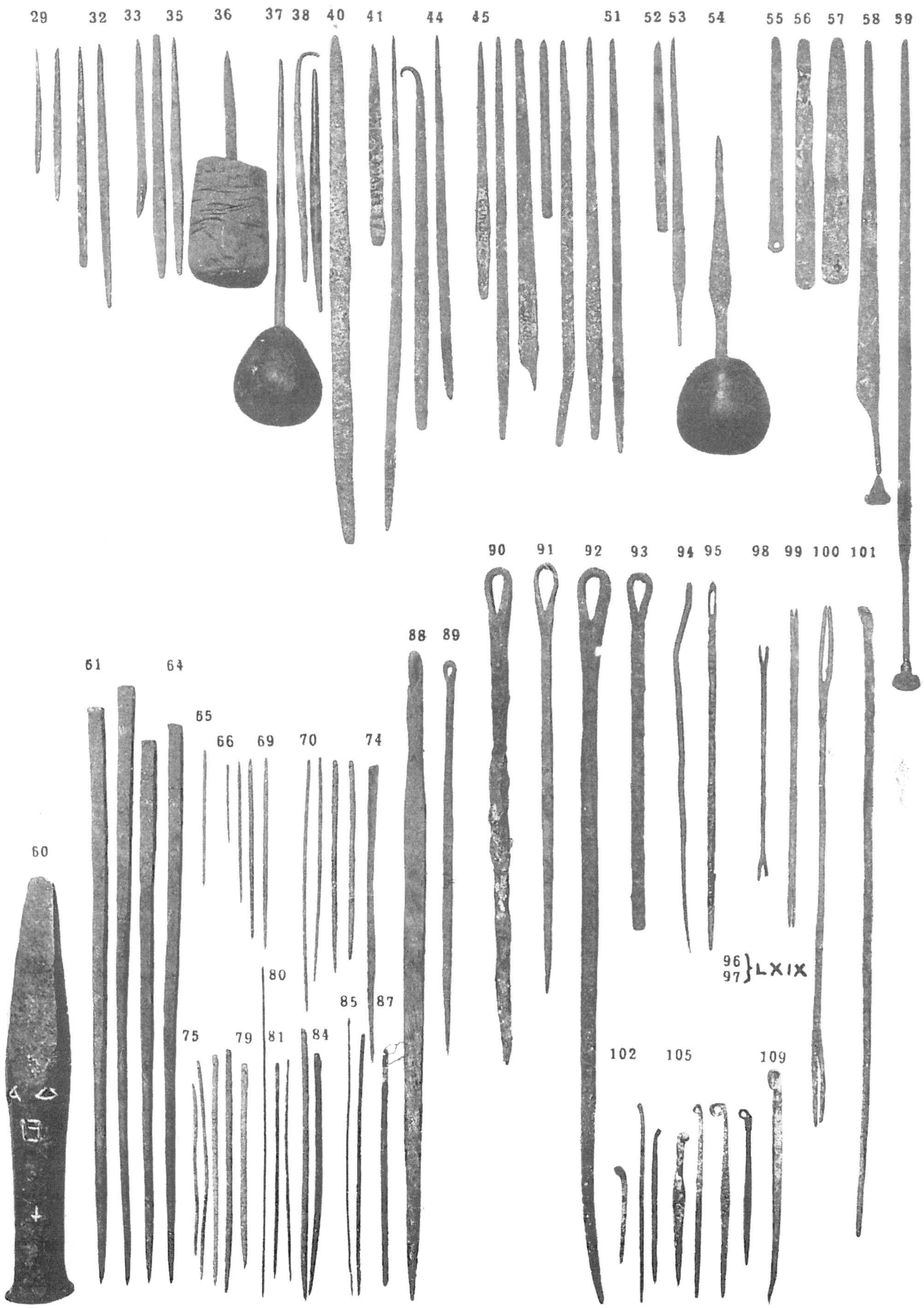
29 32 33 35 36 37 38 40 41 44 45 51 52 53 54 55 56 57 58 59
90 91 92 93 94 95 98 99 100 101
88 89
61 64
65
66 69 70 74
60
80
85 87
75 79 81 84
96
97 } LXIX
102 105 109

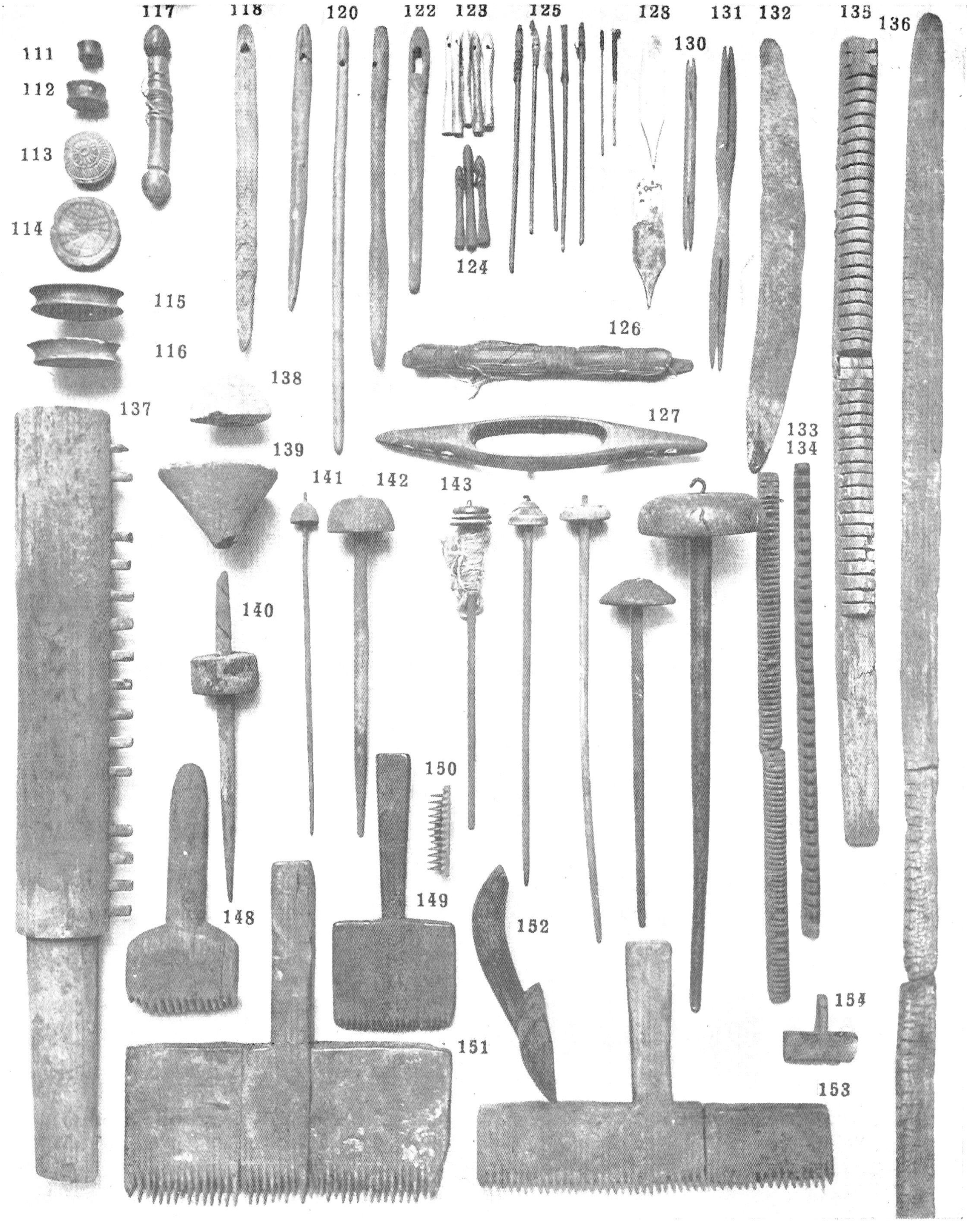
111
112
113
114
115
116
117
118
120
122
123
124
125
126
127
128
130
131
132
133
134
135
136
137
138
139
140
141
142
143
148
149
150
151
152
153
154

1:6 G. AGRICULTURAL TOOLS. LXVII.

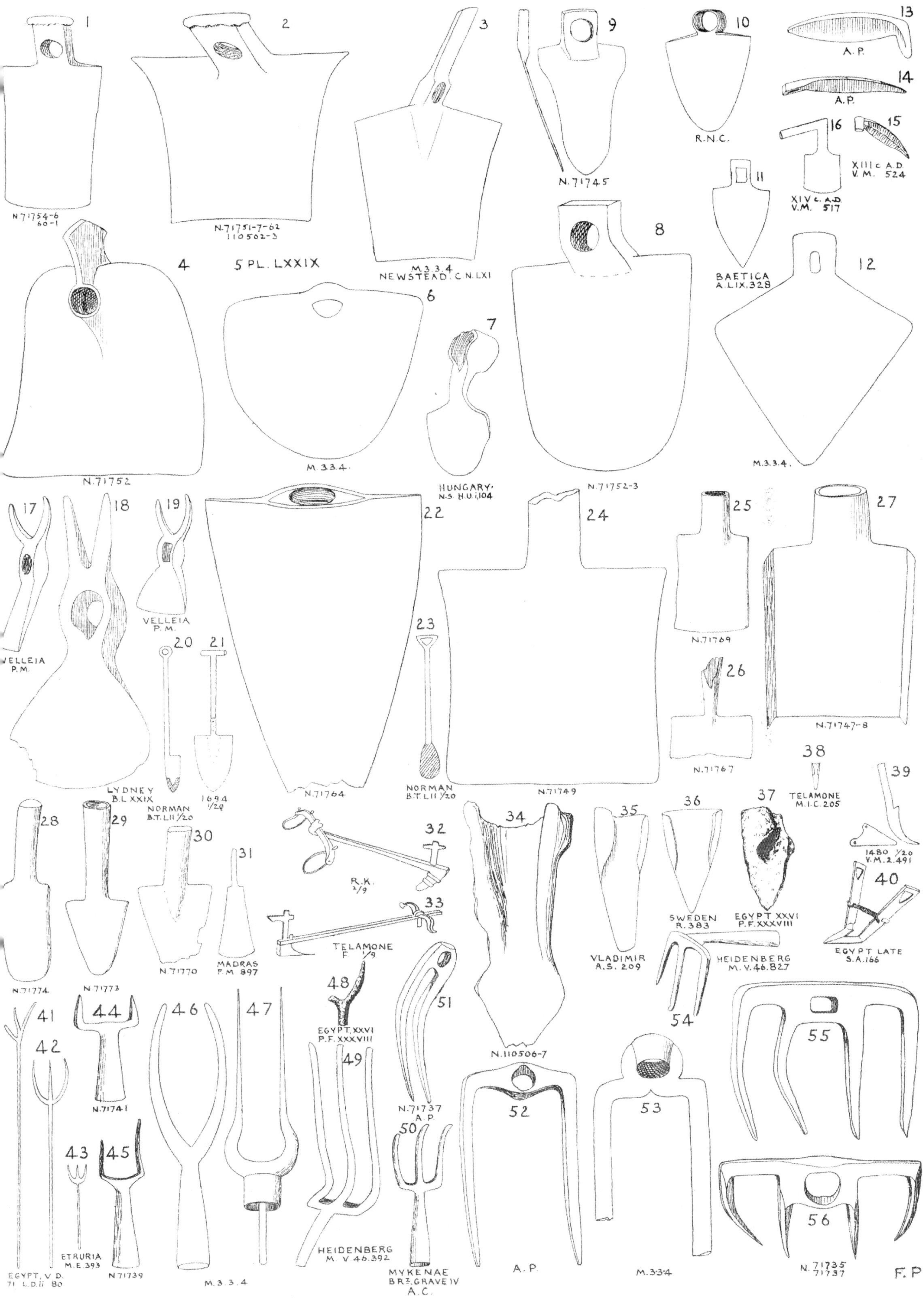

57
59
63
58
60
62
61
64
65
66
67

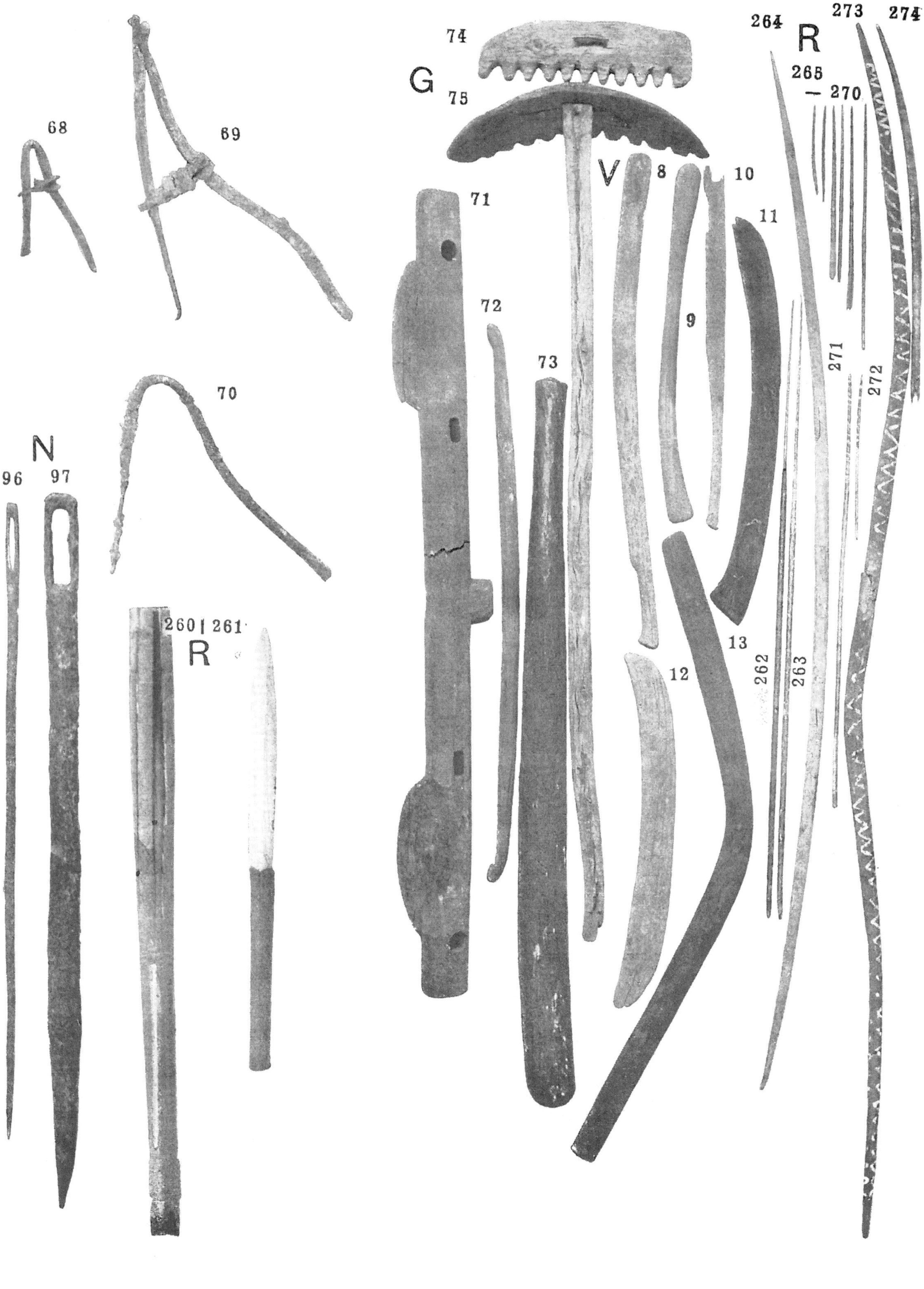
68
69
70
G
74
75
71
72
73
V
8
9
10
11
12
13
N
96
97
R
260 | 261
R
264
265
— 270
271
272
273
274
262
263

1:4 **W. HORSE BIT, BRONZE.** LXX.

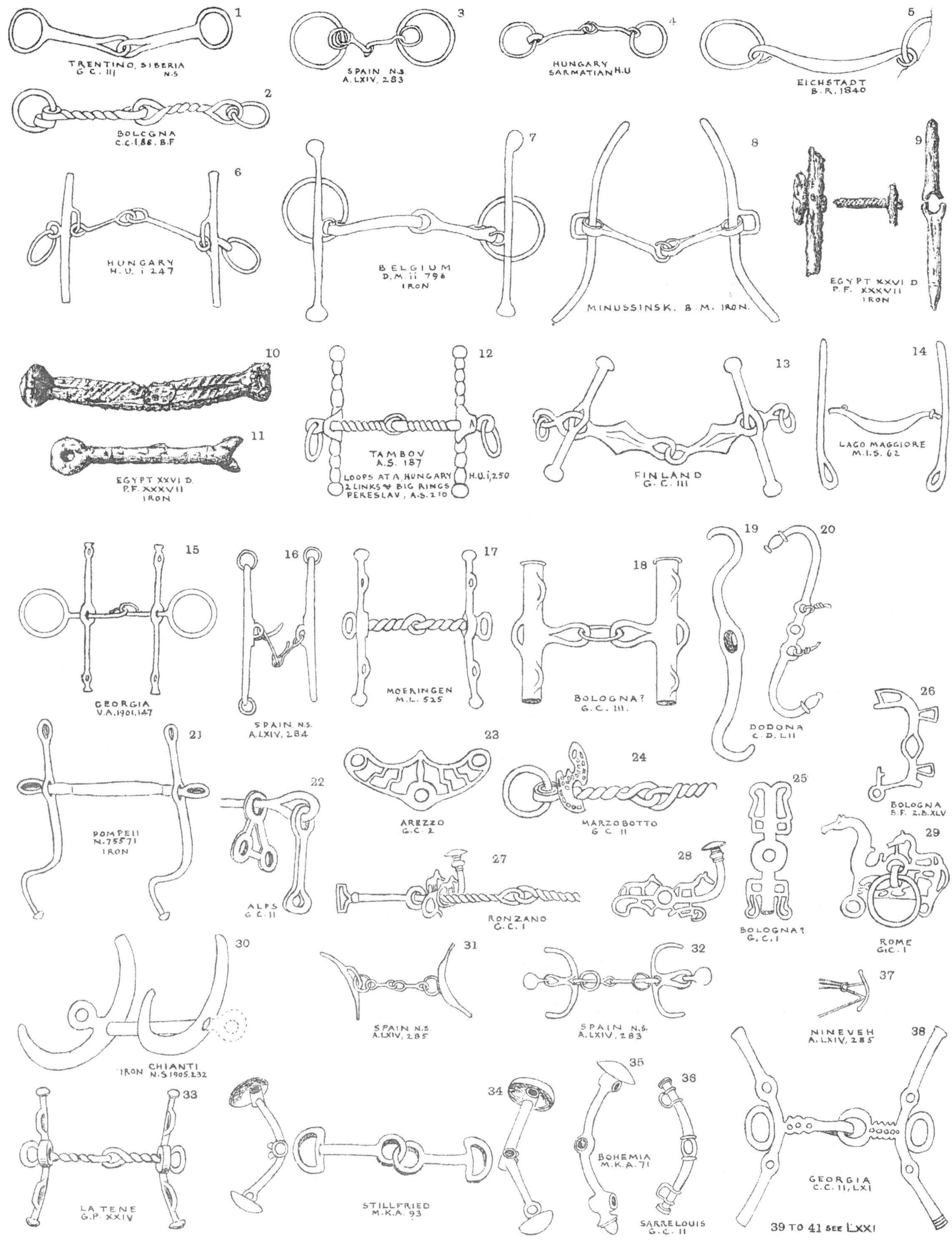

F.

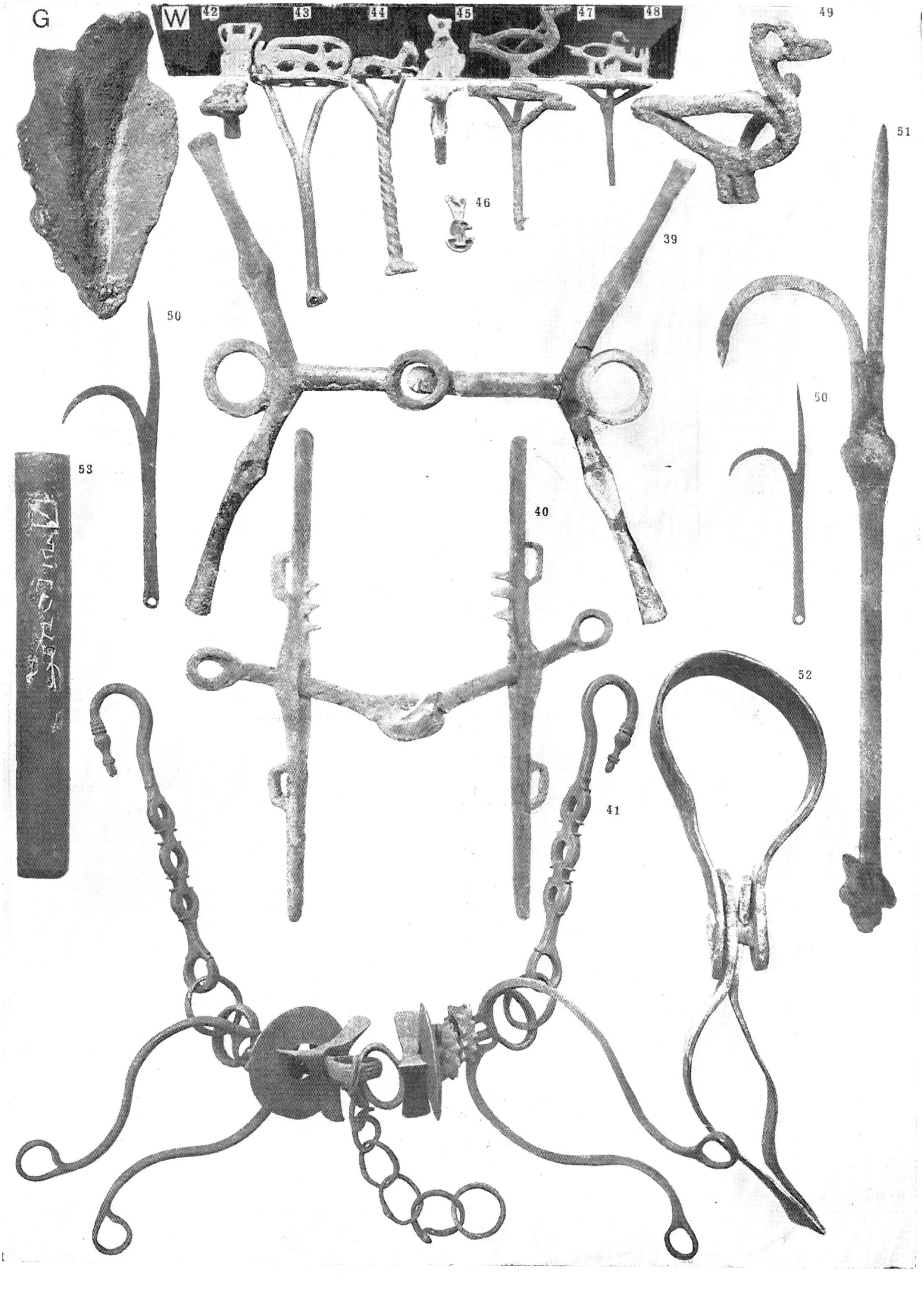
G
W
42
43
44
45
47
48
49
46
51
39
50
50
53
40
52
41

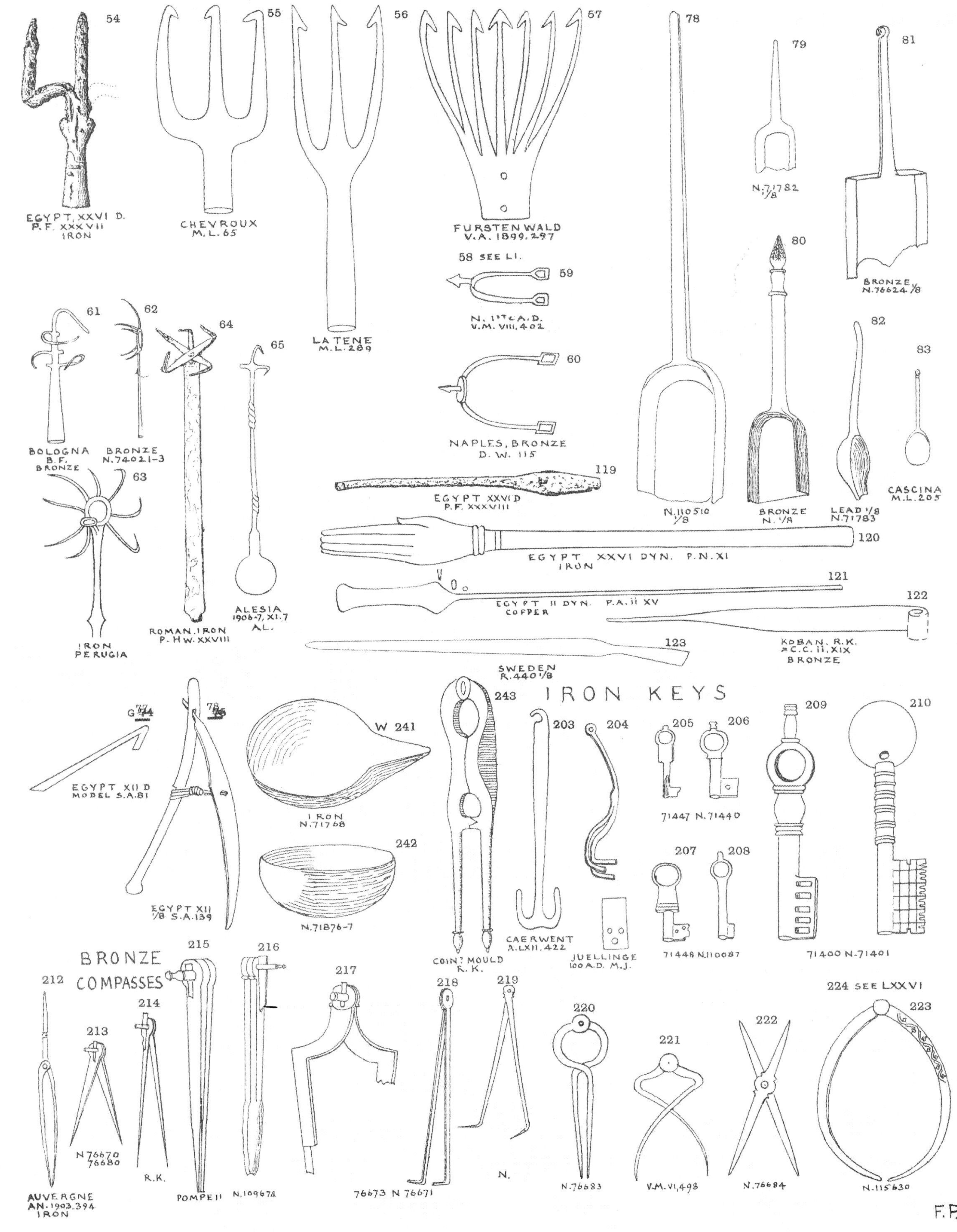
54
EGYPT, XXVI D.
P. F. XXXVII
IRON
55
CHEVROUX
M. L. 65
56
LA TENE
M. L. 289
57
FURSTENWALD
V. A. 1899, 297
58 SEE LI.
59
N. 1st C. A. D.
V. M. VIII, 402
60
NAPLES, BRONZE
D. W. 115
78
N. 110510
1/8
79
N. 71782
1/8
80
BRONZE
N. 1/8
81
BRONZE
N. 76624 1/8
82
LEAD 1/8
N. 71783
83
CASCINA
M. L. 205
61
BOLOGNA
B. F.
BRONZE
62
BRONZE
N. 74021-3
63
IRON
PERUGIA
64
ROMAN, IRON
P. HW. XXVIII
65
ALESIA
1906-7, XI. 7
AL.
119
EGYPT XXVI D
P. F. XXXVIII
120
EGYPT XXVI DYN. P. N. XI
IRON
121
EGYPT II DYN. P. A. ii XV
COPPER
122
KOBAN. R. K.
≈C. C. ii. XIX
BRONZE
123
SWEDEN
R. 440 1/8
IRON KEYS
G 77 74
EGYPT XII D
MODEL S. A. 81
78 75
EGYPT XII
1/8 S. A. 139
W 241
IRON
N. 71768
242
N. 71876-7
243
COIN? MOULD
R. K.
203
CAERWENT
A. LXII, 422
204
JUELLINGE
100 A. D. M. J.
205
206
71447 N. 71440
207
208
71448 N. 110087
209
210
71400 N. 71401
BRONZE
COMPASSES
212
AUVERGNE
AN. 1903, 394
IRON
213
N 76670
76680
214
R. K.
215
POMPEII
216
N. 109674
217
218
76673 N 76671
219
N.
220
N. 76683
221
V. M. VI, 498
222
N. 76684
224 SEE LXXVI
223
N. 115630
F. P.

A
62
W
66
68
67
70
J
59
75
77
69
73
71
74
72
76

A 71
W 87 89
90
91
92
94
96
98
99
100
101
73
U 72
W 84
85
86
88
93
95
97
102
51
W
103
114
117
118
109
191
112
110
111
113
O 119
A
95
171
A
170

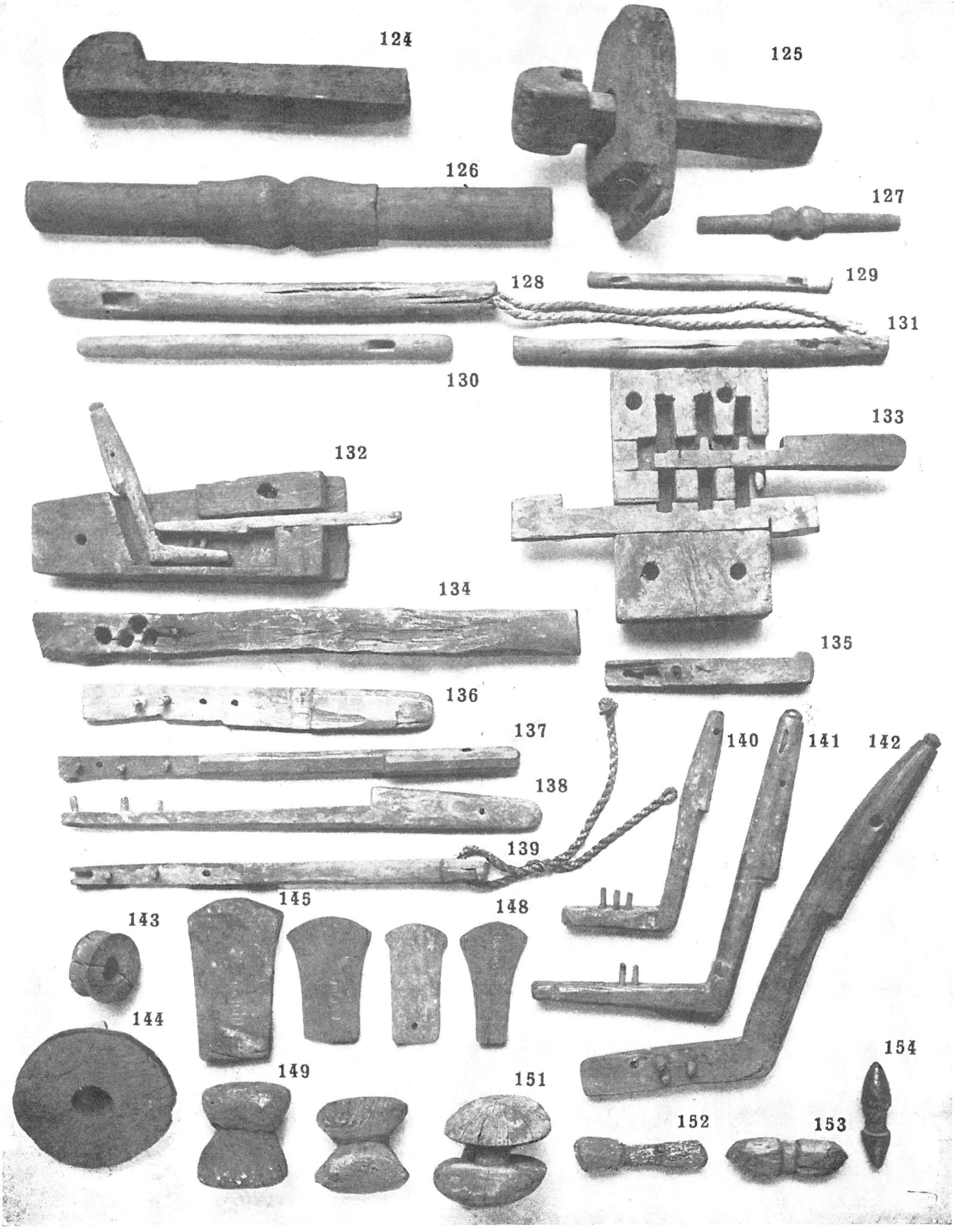
124
125
126
127
128
129
131
130
133
132
134
135
136
137
140
141
142
138
139
145
148
143
144
154
149
151
152
153

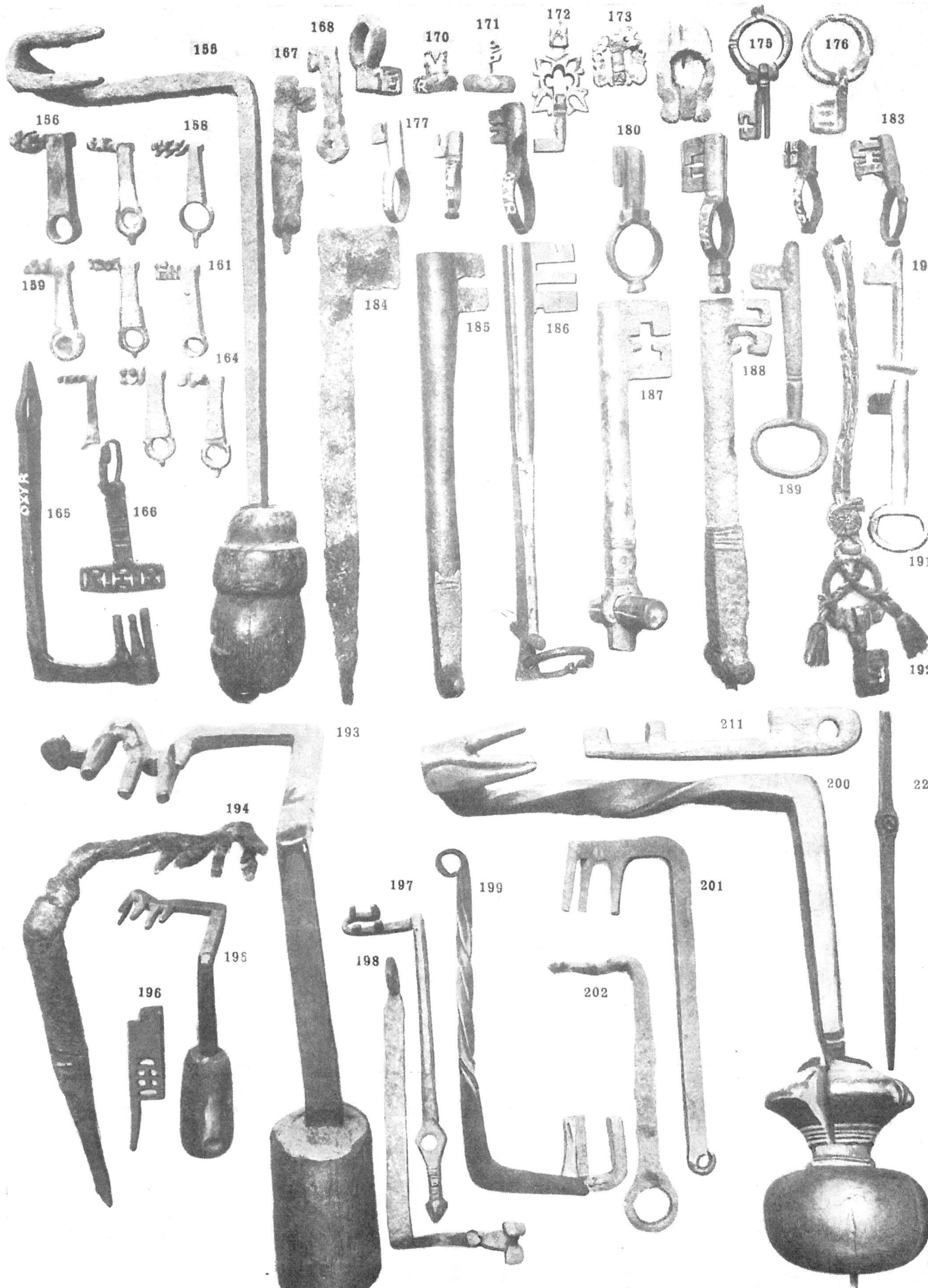
155
167
168
170
171
172
173
175
176
156
158
177
180
183
159
161
164
184
185
186
187
188
190
189
165
166
191
192
193
211
200
224
194
197
199
201
195
198
196
202

B 56
244
249
245
246
247
248
250
251
252
253
254
255
256
257
258
259
260
261
262
263
264
265
266
267

ASSYRIAN GROUP OF IRON TOOLS. THEBES.

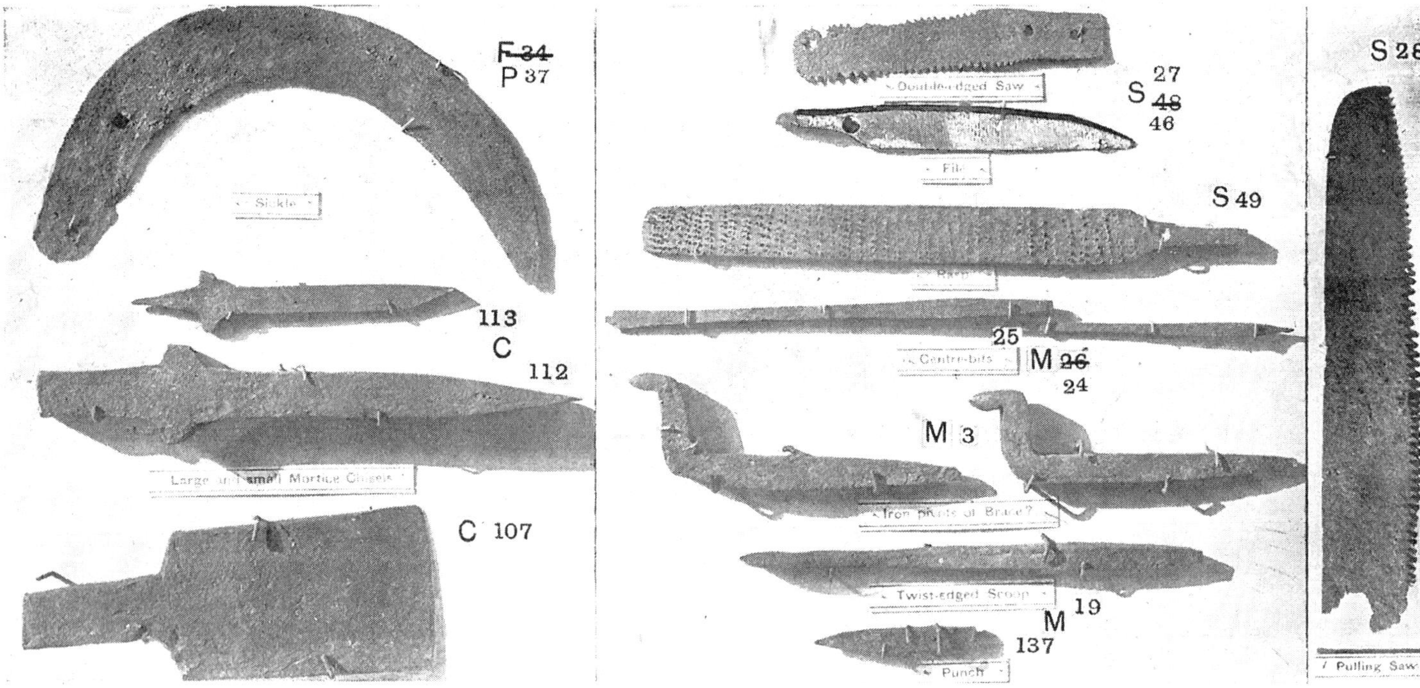

ROMAN GROUP OF IRON TOOLS. SILCHESTER.

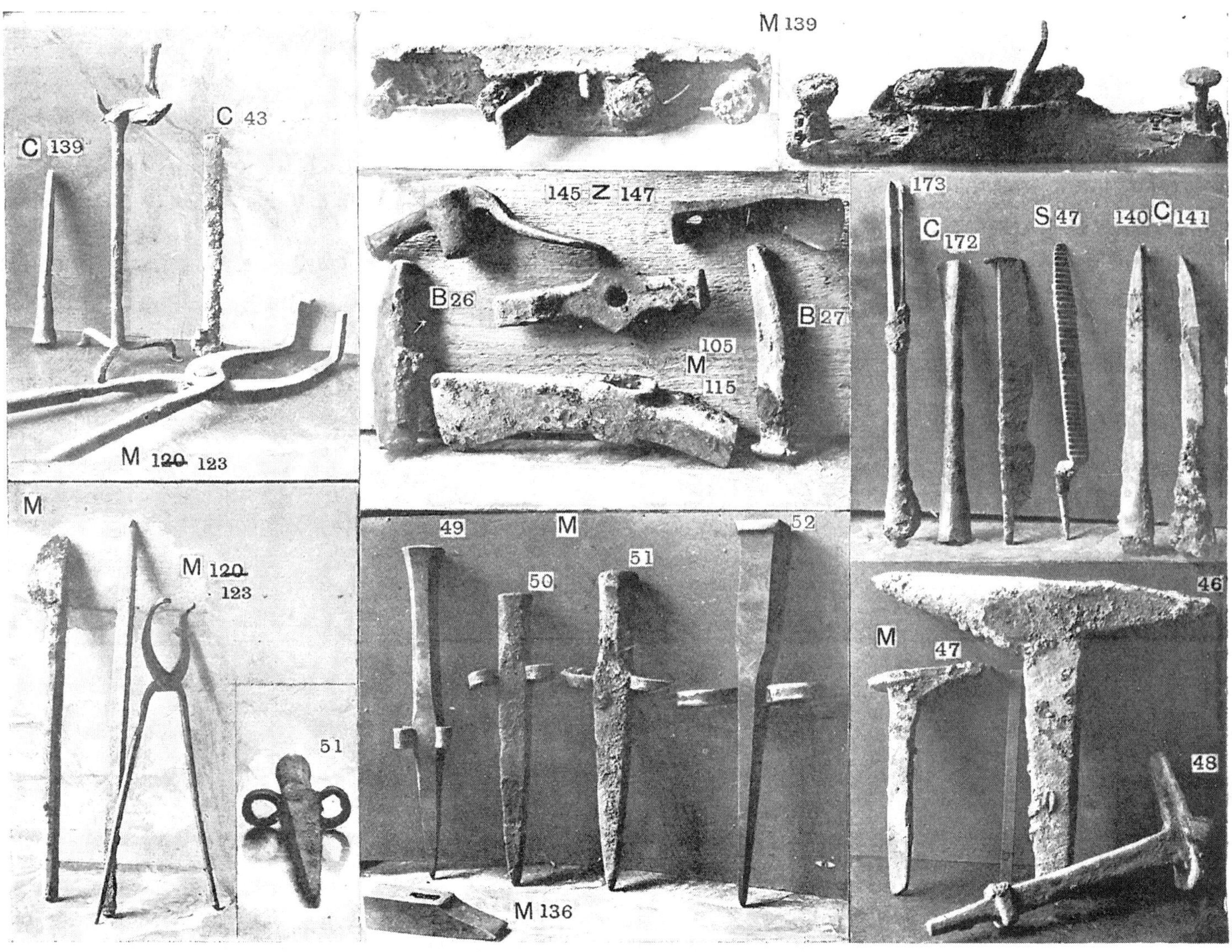

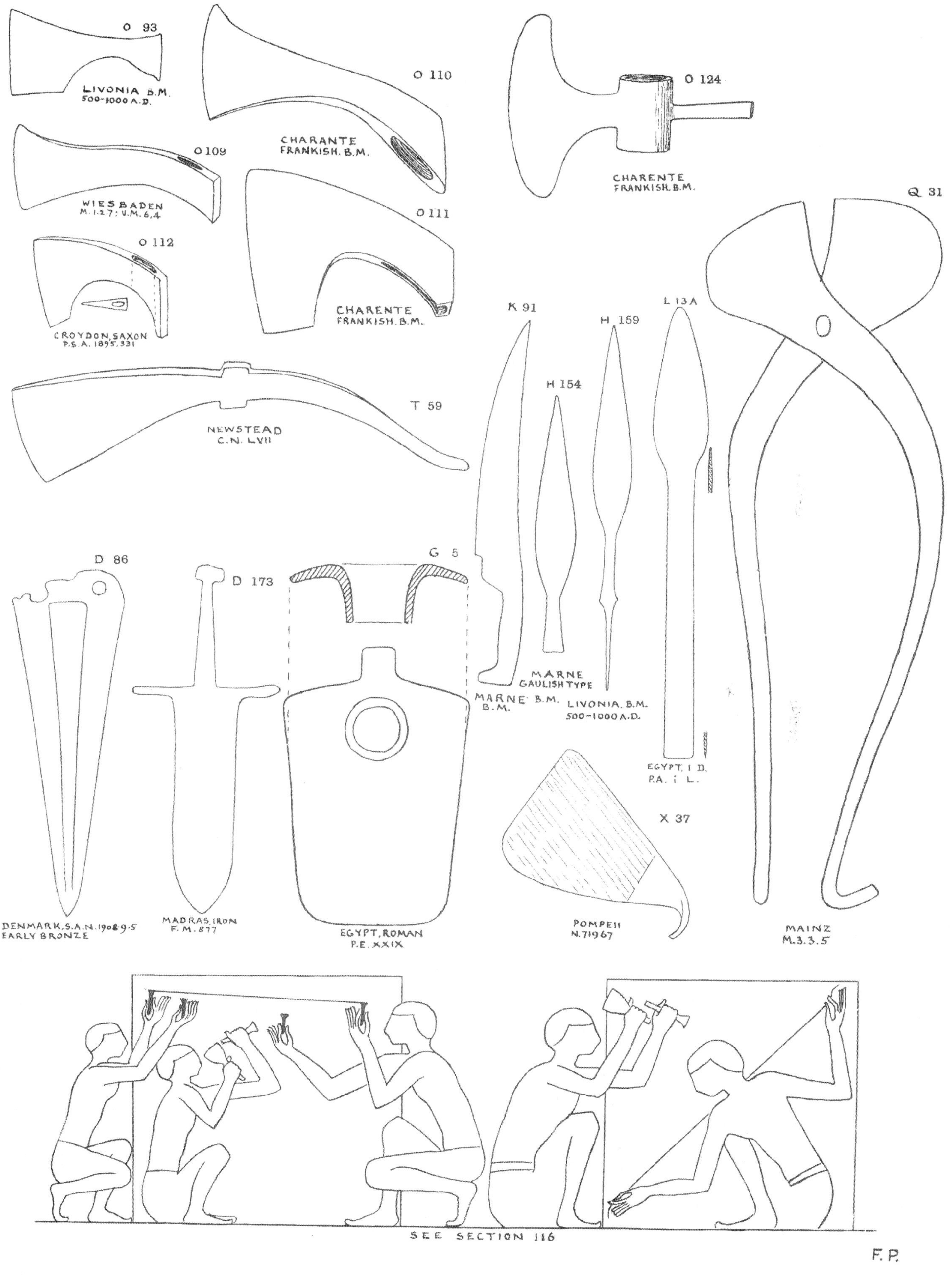
O 93
LIVONIA B.M.
500-1000 A.D.
O 110
CHARANTE
FRANKISH. B.M.
O 124
CHARENTE
FRANKISH. B.M.
O 109
WIESBADEN
M.1.2.7: U.M.6.4
O 111
CHARENTE
FRANKISH. B.M.
O 112
CROYDON, SAXON
P.S.A. 1895.331
Q 31
K 91
H 159
L 13A
H 154
T 59
NEWSTEAD
C.N. LVII
D 86
D 173
G 5
MARNE
GAULISH TYPE
MARNE B.M.
B.M.
LIVONIA. B.M.
500-1000 A.D.
EGYPT. I D.
P.A. i L.
X 37
DENMARK, S.A.N. 1908.9.5
EARLY BRONZE
MADRAS, IRON
F.M. 877
EGYPT, ROMAN
P.E. XXIX
POMPEII
N.71967
MAINZ
M.3.3.5
SEE SECTION 116
F. P.